DIRECTING STAFF EDITION

RESTRICTED
The information given in this document is not to be communicated either directly or indirectly to the Press or to any person not authorised to receive it.

BRITISH ARMY OF THE RHINE

BATTLEFIELD TOUR

OPERATION PLUNDER

OPERATIONS OF 12 BRITISH CORPS CROSSING THE RIVER RHINE, ON 23, 24 and 25 MARCH 1945

The Naval & Military Press Ltd

Published by

The Naval & Military Press Ltd
Unit 5 Riverside, Brambleside
Bellbrook Industrial Estate
Uckfield, East Sussex
TN22 1QQ England

Tel: +44 (0)1825 749494

www.naval-military-press.com
www.nmarchive.com

*In reprinting in facsimile from the original, any imperfections are inevitably reproduced
and the quality may fall short of modern type and cartographic standards.*

BATTLEFIELD TOURS

Headquarters, British Army of the Rhine compiled Battlefield Tours during 1947 covering the following operations in the Campaign in North-West EUROPE (June 1944–May 1945):—

Name of Operation	*Action covered*
GOODWOOD	Operations of 8 Corps East of the River ORNE (NORMANDY) 18–22 July 1944, with particular reference to 11th Armoured Division.
BLUECOAT	Operations of 8 Corps South of CAUMONT (NORMANDY) 30–31 July 1944, with particular reference to 15th (Scottish) Infantry Division.
TOTALIZE	Operations of 2 Canadian Corps astride the road CAEN–FALAISE (NORMANDY) 7–8 August 1944, with particular reference to 51st (Highland) Infantry Division.
NEPTUNE	Assault crossing of the River SEINE by 43rd (Wessex) Infantry Division 25–28 August 1944.
VERITABLE	Operations of 30 Corps between the Rivers MAAS and RHINE 8–10 February 1945, with particular reference to 15th (Scottish) Infantry Division.
PLUNDER	Assault crossing of the River RHINE by 12 Corps 24–25 March 1945, with particular reference to 15th (Scottish) Infantry Division.
VARSITY	Airborne operations of XVIII United States Corps (Airborne) in support of the crossing of the River RHINE 24–25 March 1945, with particular reference to 6th British Airborne Division.

A similar book was written on each of these operations, of which four hundred copies were printed, one hundred of these containing notes for Directing Staff. A further fifty Directing Staff copies and two hundred and fifty Spectator's copies have been distributed to various libraries, original speakers and certain other individuals.

Directorate of Military Training, War Office, or Headquarters, British Army of the Rhine can supply information as to where these books are kept.

FOREWORD

By
Lieutenant General Sir Richard L. McCREERY, KCB, KBE, DSO, MC
General Officer Commanding-in-Chief the British Army of the Rhine

Battlefield Tours of Operations VERITABLE, PLUNDER and VARSITY have been prepared to provide material for the study of operations of a different character and under different conditions from the NORMANDY battles which were the subject of the British Army of the Rhine Battlefield Tour in June 1947.

Operations PLUNDER and VARSITY are complementary to each other and should whenever possible be studied together. Operation VARSITY is of particular interest, as it was the first occasion on which Airborne Forces were dropped within the range of our own supporting arms.

We have again been fortunate in obtaining the personal accounts of Army and Royal Air Force officers who took part in Operations PLUNDER and VARSITY. The personal accounts of operation VERITABLE were obtained by permission of the Staff College CAMBERLEY from their Battlefield Tour held in the Summer of 1947. These personal accounts introduce, as far as this is possible, the atmosphere of war.

When a battlefield is revisited at a later date, in full possession of all the information and with a clear picture of the situation, it is comparatively easy to say what should have been done. In war, the situation is rarely clear, the information is never complete, and actions must be considered in the light of the situation as it was known to the Commanders at the time. The view of the Commander on the spot in each of the various situations is supplied in the personal accounts.

These past operations must be studied with an eye to the future if full benefit is to be derived from them. In studying the problems, constant consideration must be given to the conditions which are likely to be met and the material and equipment which is likely to be available in the next war. It is certain, however, that whatever form land warfare may take in the future, certain fundamental factors which constantly stand out in these operations, such as morale, training, junior leadership and surprise will retain their pre-eminent importance.

R. L. McCreery

Lieutenant General

OBJECT OF THE BOOK

This book describes the operations of 12 British Corps of Second British Army crossing the River RHINE.

It is especially concerned with the part played by 15 (Scottish) Division in these operations on 24 and 25 March, and the Air Operations connected therewith.

It forms the necessary background to a detailed study of the battle carried out on the ground.

CONTENTS

PART I—PLANNING THE OPERATION

		Page
SECTION I	Introduction	1
	A. General Situation	1
	B. 21 Army Group Intention	1
	C. Previous Planning	1
	D. Morale	1
SECTION II	Topography	3
	A. The River RHINE	3
	B. Precautions against Flooding	3
	C. Bridges and Ferries	3
	D. Effect of Weather	3
	E. Artificial Flooding	3
	F. Concentration Areas	4
	G. Approaches	4
	H. Railways and other Roads	4
	J. Other Water Obstacles	4
SECTION III	The Enemy	5
	A. General	5
	B. Enemy Deployment and Order of Battle	5
	C. Enemy Forces opposing 12 Corps	5
	D. Defences	6
	E. Artillery	6
	F. Armour	6
SECTION IV	HQ 12 Corps Preliminary Planning	7
	A. Object of Planning	7
	B. Basic Assumptions	7
	C. The Evolution of a Crossing Technique	8
	D. Operational Planning	8
	E. Concentration	9
SECTION V	The Plan	11
	A. 12 Corps Intention	11
	B. Troops available for 12 Corps	11
	C. Factors affecting the Corps Plan	11
	D. 12 Corps Plan	12
	E. 15 (Scottish) Infantry Division Plan	14
	F. RE Plan	15
	G. Traffic Control	18
SECTION VI	Plans of other Formations	19
	A. XVIII US Corps (Airborne) (Operation VARSITY)	19
	B. Ninth US Army (Operation FLASHPOINT)	19
	C. 30 British Corps (Operation TURNSCREW)	19

SECTION VII	The 12 Corps Fire Plan		21
	A.	Artillery Resources and Grouping	21
	B.	Deployment	21
	C.	The Timed Programme	21
	D.	Targets	23
	E.	Smoke	23
	F.	Counter Battery and Artillery Reconnaissance	23
	G.	Artillery Regrouping after P Hour	23
	H.	Regrouping on 25 March	23
	J.	Safety Precautions and their Effect	24
	K.	Communications	24
SECTION VIII	The Air Plan		27
	A.	Introduction	27
	B.	Preliminary Air Operations	27
	C.	The Main Air Plan	28
	D.	Progress of Air Operations up to D Day	29
	E.	Day-to-day Support from D Day onwards	30
	F.	Air Support Signals Organisation	30
	G.	Forward Control of Aircraft	30
SECTION IX	Preliminary Training		33
SECTION X	The Cover Plan		35

PART II—ACCOUNT OF THE BATTLE

Introductory Note—D Day			39
SECTION I	12 Corps Operations 23/25 March		41
	A.	1 Cdo Bde (Operation WIDGEON)	41
	B.	15 (S) Div (Operation TORCHLIGHT)	41
	C.	4 Armd Bde	47
	D.	157 Inf Bde (52 (L) Inf Div)	48
	E.	RE Operations	48
SECTION II	Operations by other Corps of Second Army 23/25 March		51
	A.	XVIII US Corps (Airborne)	51
	B.	30 British Corps	52
SECTION III	Enemy Operations		53
SECTION IV	Build-up in Operation PLUNDER		55
	A.	Administrative	55
	B.	Tactical	55
SECTION V	Close Air Support		57

PART III—PERSONAL ACCOUNTS OF ACTIONS FOR STUDY

SECTION I	Introductory Lectures	61
SECTION II	Itinerary	65
SECTION III	Personal Accounts, including Problem	67
SECTION IV	Notes for the Guidance of Conducting Officers	91
SECTION V	Planning PLUNDER—a Play	95

AIR PHOTOGRAPH

227 (H) Bde Assault Sector . . . . In end pocket

MAPS

General Map of RHINE, WESEL-REES area . . . . . . In end pocket

PART I
MAPS TO ILLUSTRATE GROUND PLAN

Facing Page

No. 1.	General Situation 23 March	1
No. 2.	Appreciated enemy positions opposite 12 and XVIII Corps	5
No. 3.	Boundaries, axes of advance, and objectives	11
No. 4.	(a) Locations of assaulting troops in Assembly Areas	13
	(b) Gun areas on the West bank of the RHINE	13
No. 5.	15 (S) Div plan	15
No. 6.	Layout of bridges, ferries, bank control, marshalling areas and forward routes	17
No. 7.	Fire Plan (Operation WIDGEON)	25
No. 8.	Fire Plan (Operation TORCHLIGHT)	25

MAPS TO ILLUSTRATE AIR PLAN

No. 9.	RUHR Interdiction Programme	27
No. 10.	PLUNDER Interdiction Programme	27
No. 11.	Heavy and Medium Bomber Programme	29
No. 12.	Air Support to 1 Cdo Bde	29

PART II
MAPS TO ILLUSTRATE OPERATIONS

No. 13.	44 (L) Bde assault 24 March	41
No. 14.	(a) 227 (H) Bde assault and subsequent operations 24/25 March	45
	(b) 46 (H) Bde operations 24/25 March	45
	(c) 44 (L) Bde operations 25 March	45
No. 15.	XVIII US Corps (Airborne) operations 24/25 March	49
No. 16.	30 Corps operations 24/25 March	51

PART III

No. 17.	Battlefield Tour Operation PLUNDER (Itinerary)	65

DIAGRAMS AND TABLES

PART I

Diagram No.

1.	Bank Group layout	17
2.	Air Support Tentacles	31

Table No. — *Page*

1.	Guns by types and numbers	25
2.	Ammunition expenditure	26

APPENDICES

Page

A1.	Order of Battle 12 Corps	111
A2.	RA Order of Battle 12 Corps	113
A3.	RE Order of Battle 12 Corps	115
A4.	RAF and USAAF Order of Battle	117
B.	Organisation and equipment of forces taking part	119

C.	List of reference maps	125
D.	12 Corps Planning Instruction No. 1	127
E.	Glossary of terms used in the assault crossing of the RHINE	131
F.	Some problems in the technique of an opposed crossing of a major river obstacle	135
G.	15 (S) Div Operation Order for Operation TORCHLIGHT	137
H.	7 day training syllabus for an assault brigade group	141

PLATES

Plate No.

1. DD tank
2. AVRE and CENTAUR tankdozer
3. LVT IV (Buffalo)
4. Rocket projector
5. 25-pr SP gun (RAM)
6. Stormboat
7. Class 9 (close-support) Raft
8. Class 50/60 Raft
9. Class 9 FBE Bridge
10. Class 40 (tactical) Bailey pontoon bridge
11. Class 40 (high-level) Bailey pontoon bridge

(following Page 142)

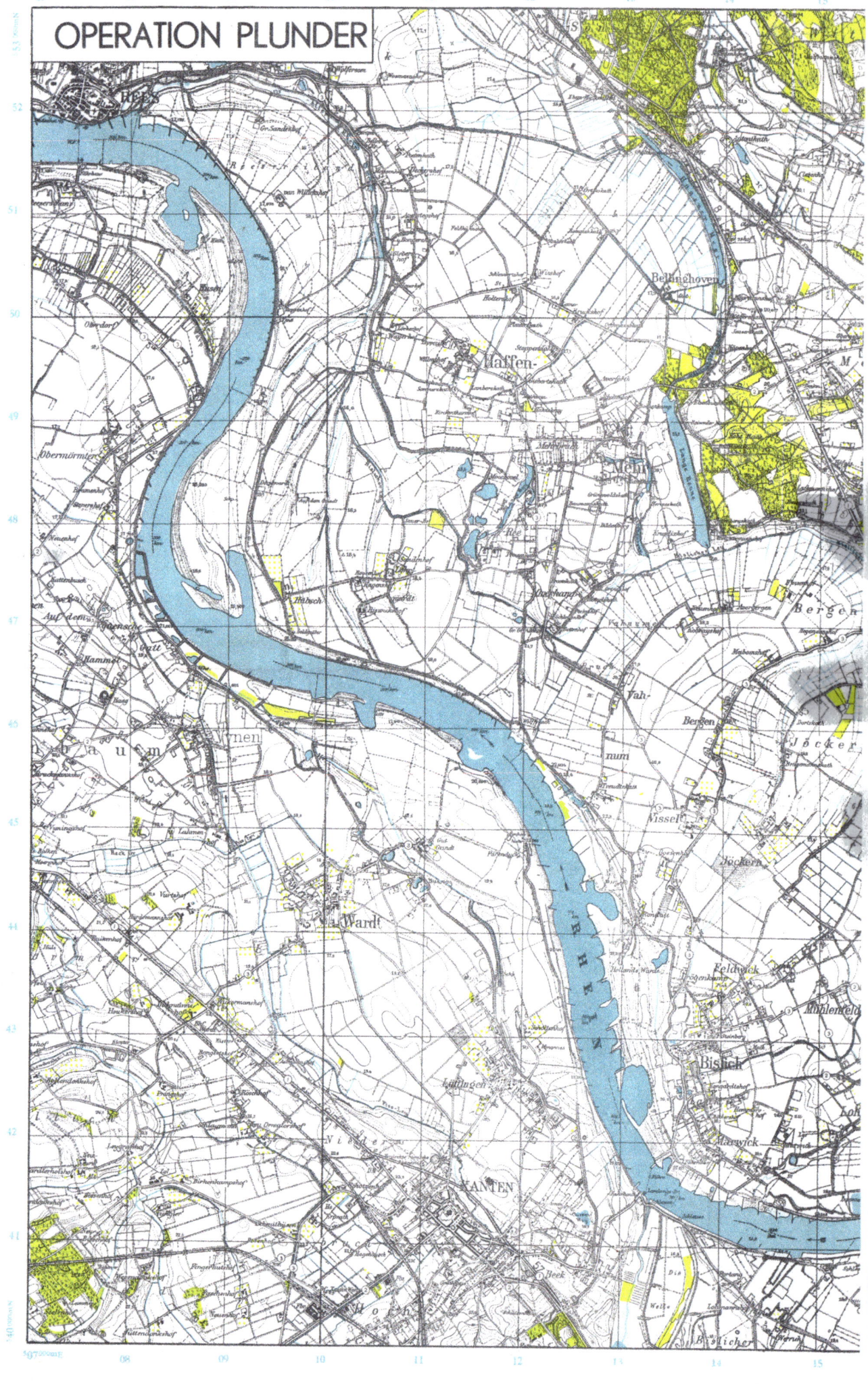

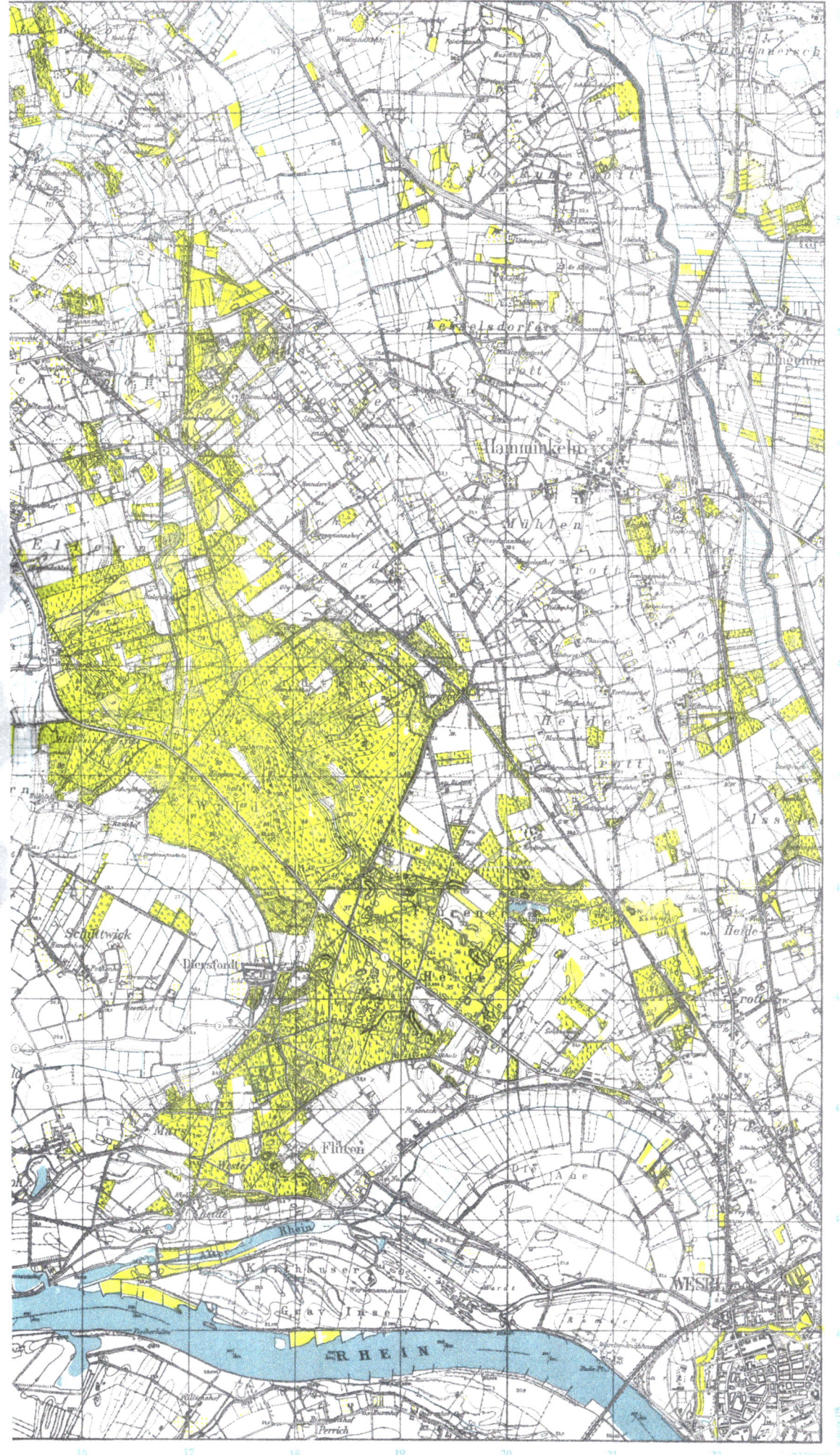

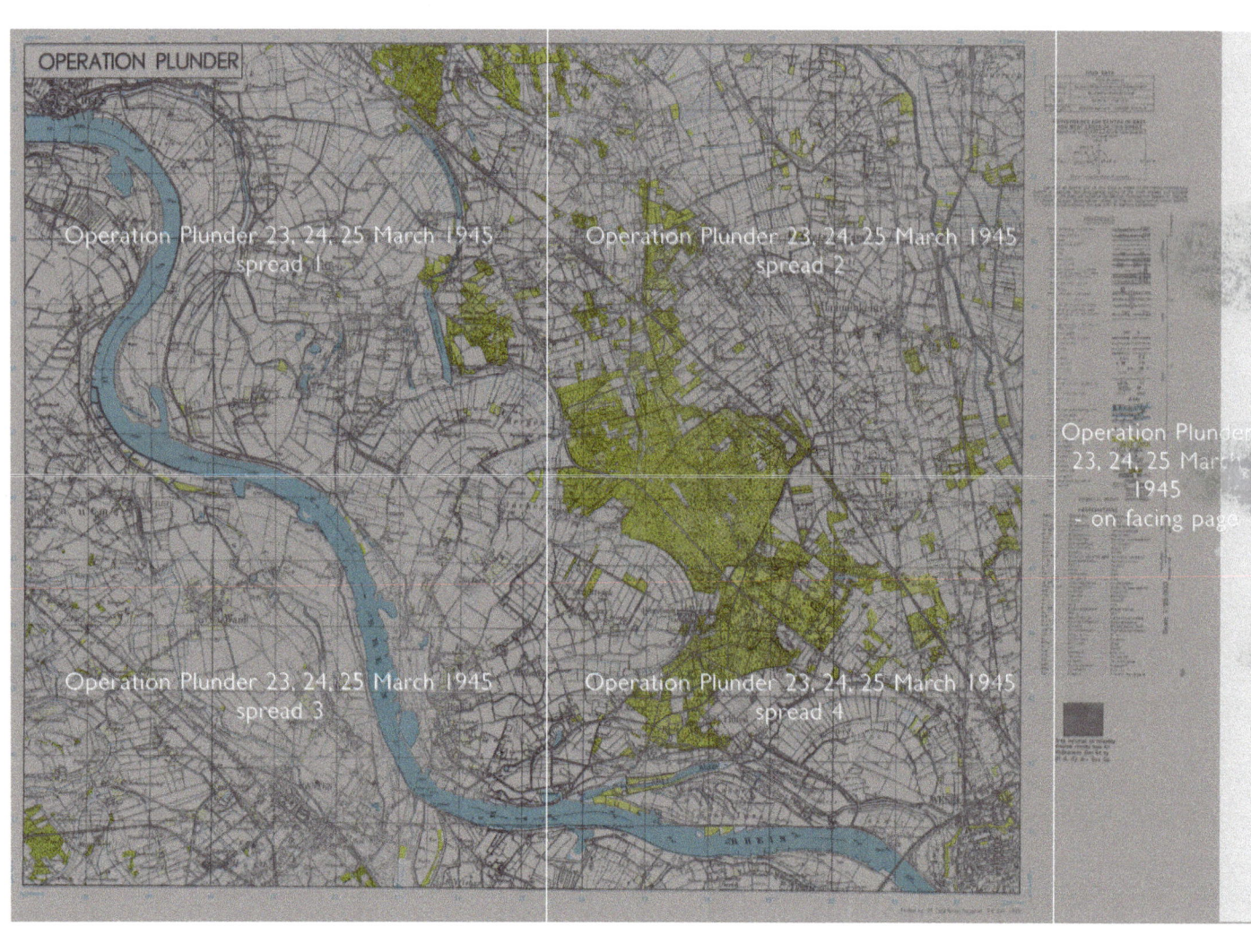

GRID DATA

	Nord de Guerre
Projection	Lambert (Modified) Conical Orthomorphic
Spheroid	Du Plessis (Reconstituted)
Origin	49° 30' N. 7° 44' 14" E.
False co-ords. of origin	600,000 metres E. 300,000 metres N.

CONVERGENCE FOR CENTRE OF EAST AND WEST EDGES OF THIS SHEET

Magnetic N. (June 1944) and Grid N. from True N. for centre of sheet

Annual variation about 8' easterly

The Nord de Guerre grid on this sheet is based on the French Geographical System or graticule. The geographical values of the sheet corners and graticule tick marks on this sheet are based on the German Geographical System or graticule. To convert German Geographical values to French Geographical values subtract 1.3" from German Latitudes and add 3.15" to German Longitudes.

REFERENCE

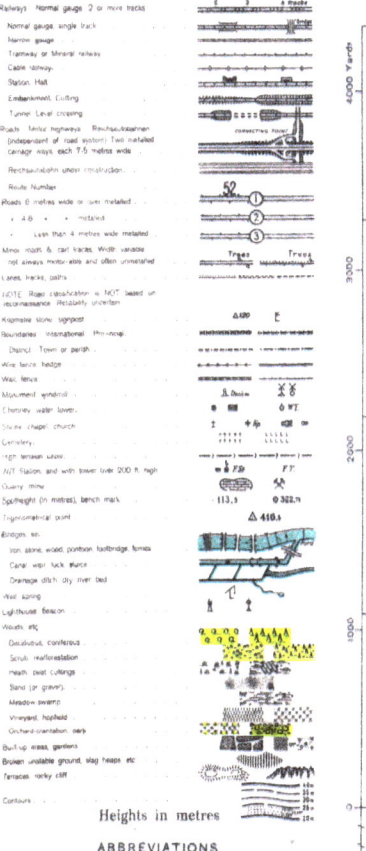

Heights in metres

Scale 1:25,000

ABBREVIATIONS

Abbr.	German.	Meaning
Abl.	Ablage	Depot
Anl. st.	Anlegestelle	Landing stage
Bf. Bnf.	Bahnhof	Railway station
Bl. st.	Blockstation	Signal box
B.W.	Bahnwärter	Railway linesman's hut
Chs.	Chausseehaus	Toll house
Dm.	Dampfmühle	Steam mill
Dom.	Domäne	Estate
Ehr. Fdhf.	Ehrenhfriedhof (Krieger)	Cemetery (military)
E. St.	Eisenbahnstation	Railway station
Fabr.	Fabrik	Factory
H.	Hütte	Hut
Hp.	Haltepunkt	Halt
Hst., H. St.	Haltestelle	Halt
Jg Hb.	Jugendherberge	Youth hostel
Klbf, Kibhf.	Kleinbahnhof	Small railway station
K.O.	Kalkofen	Lime kiln
Kas.	Kaserne	Barracks
K.	Kirche	Church
Kr.	Krug	Inn
El. Wk.	Elektrizitätswerk	Power station
M.	Mühle	Mill
N.D.	Naturdenkmal	Natural monument
N.S.G.	Naturschutzgebiet	Game preserve
O.M.	Ölmühle	Oil extraction mill
Usphs.	Umspannerhaus	Transformer station
Sch.	Scheune	Barn
S.	Schornstein	Chimney
Schp.	Schuppen	Shed
St.	Stall	Stable
S.W.	Sägewerk	Saw mill
T.O.	Teerofen	Tar works
Vw.	Vorwerk	Farm building
Wbh.	Wasserbehälter	Reservoir
Whs.	Wirtshaus	Pub, inn
Zgl.	Ziegelei	Tile kiln, brick yard

Area indicated on reliability diagram revised from Air Photographs Dec '44 by 21 A. Gp Air Svy Gp.

Operation Plunder 23, 24, 25 March 1945 — spread 1

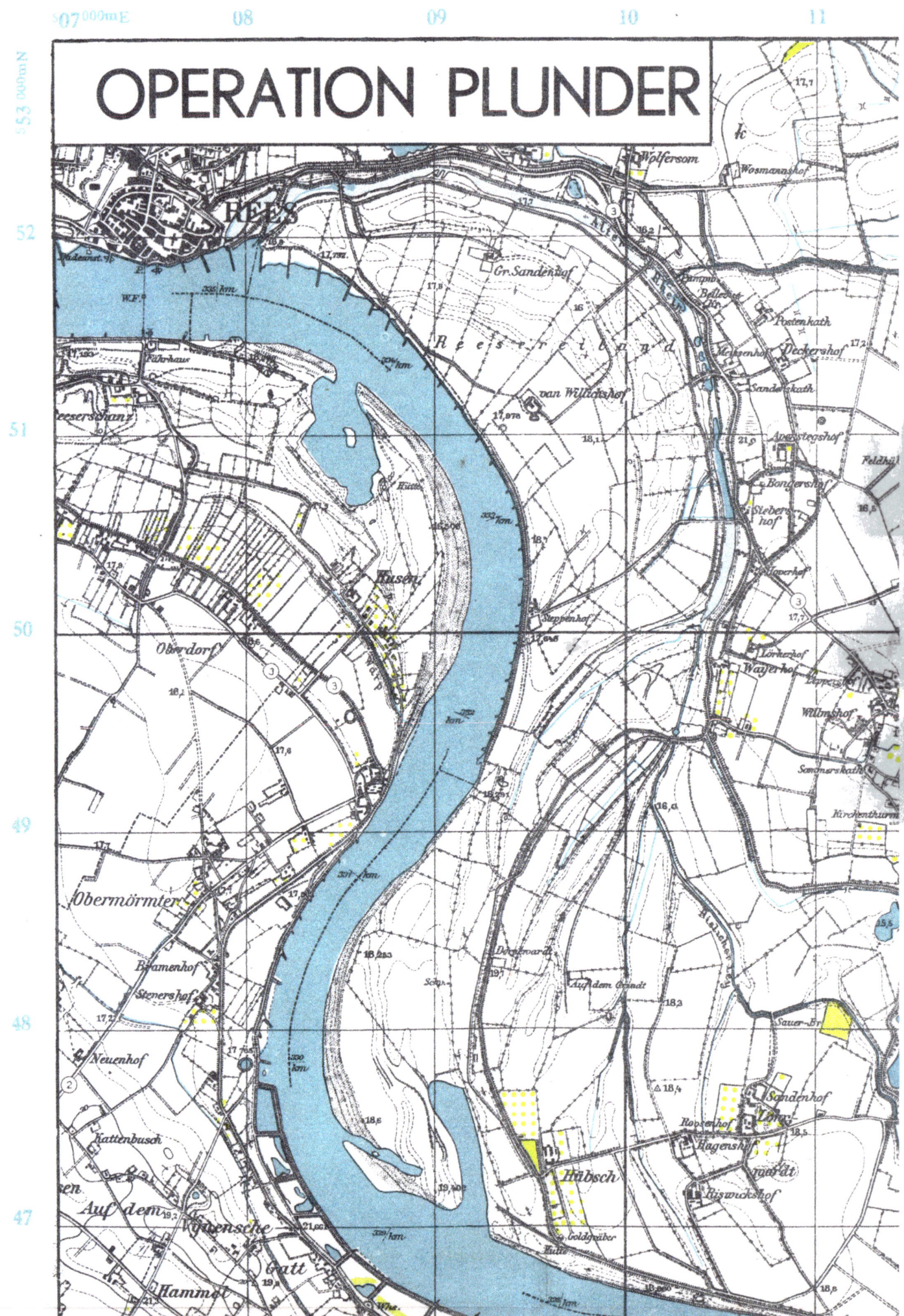

Operation Plunder 23, 24, 25 March 1945 — spread 1

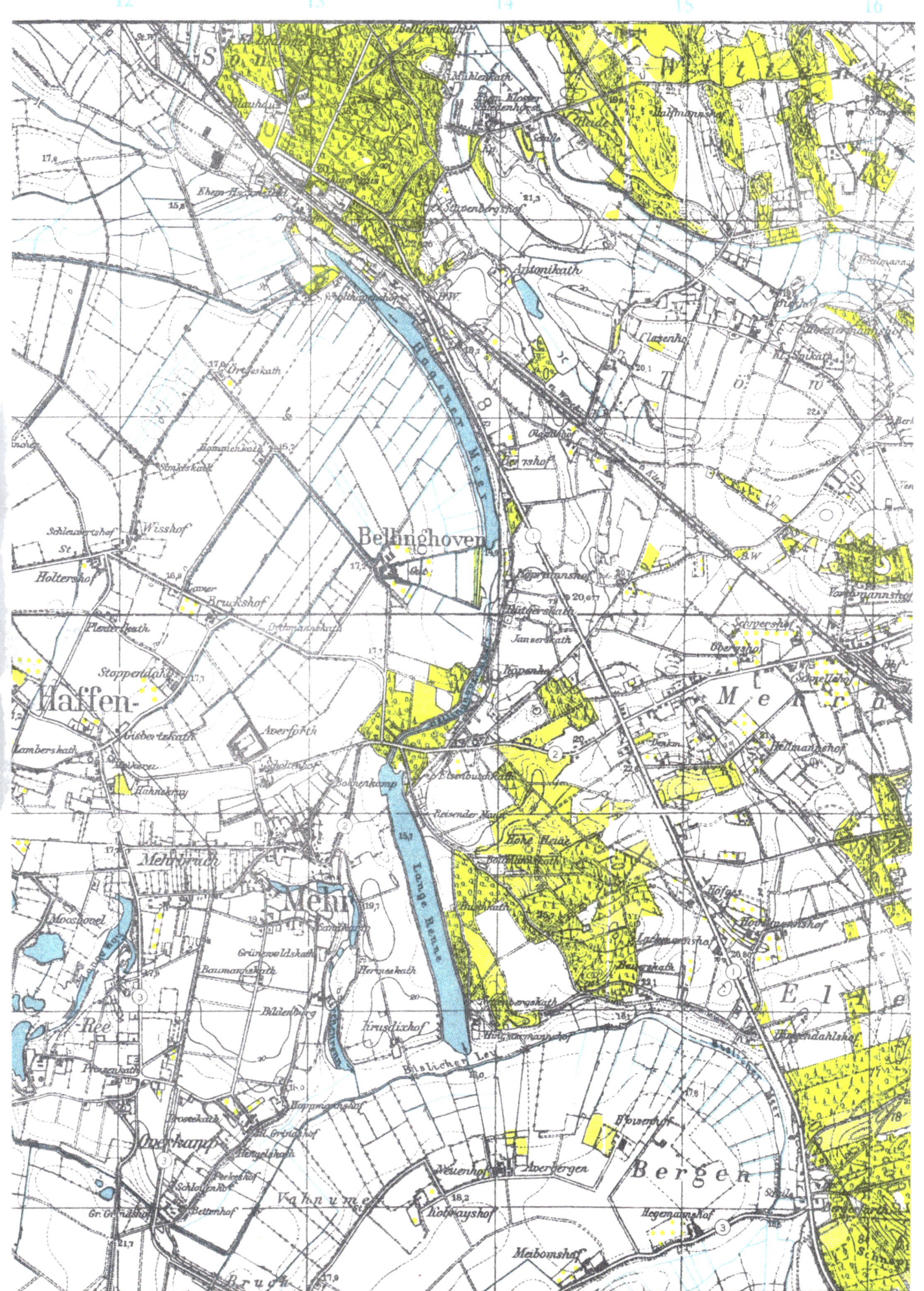

Operation Plunder 23, 24, 25 March 1945 — spread 2

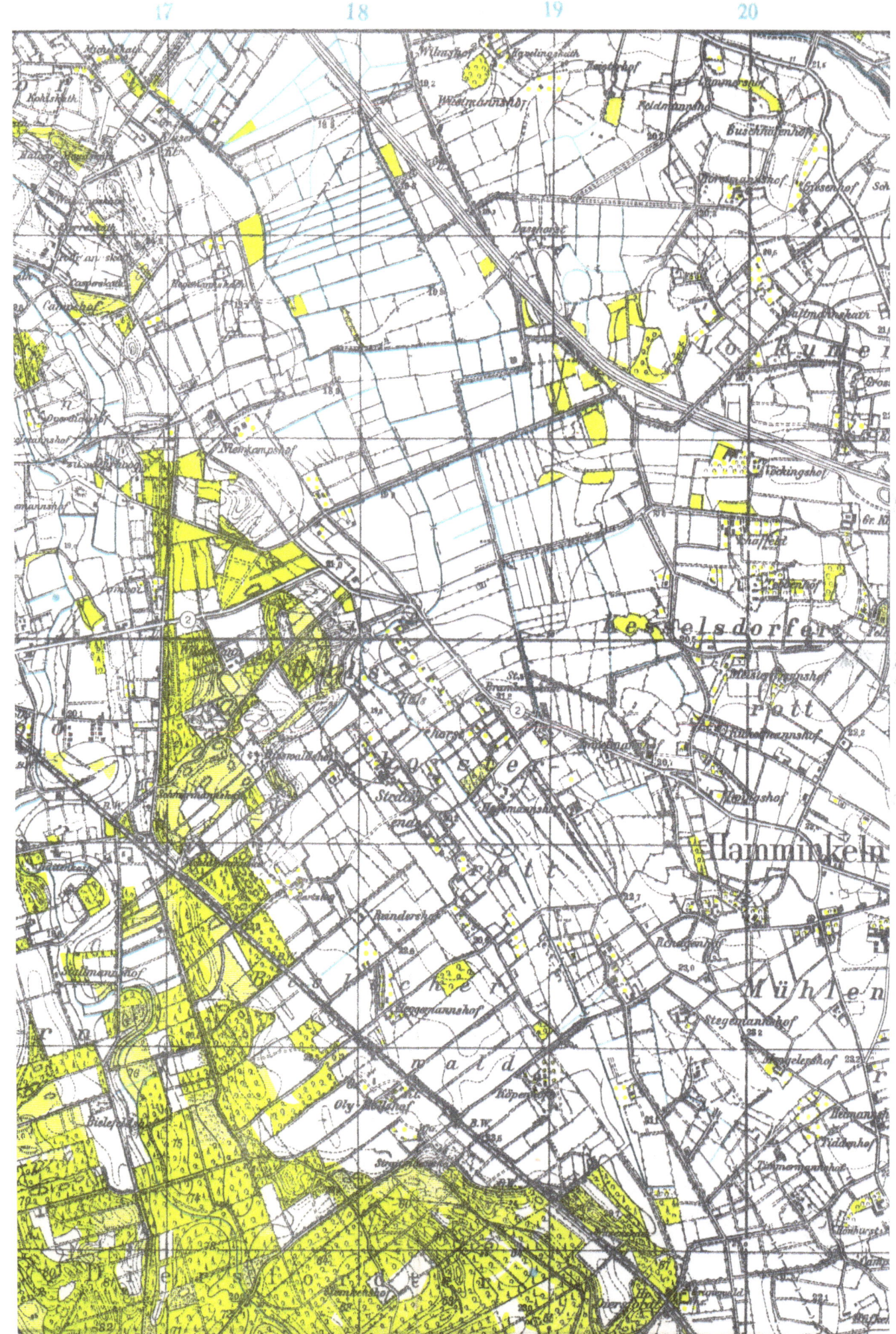

Operation Plunder 23, 24, 25 March 1945 — spread 2

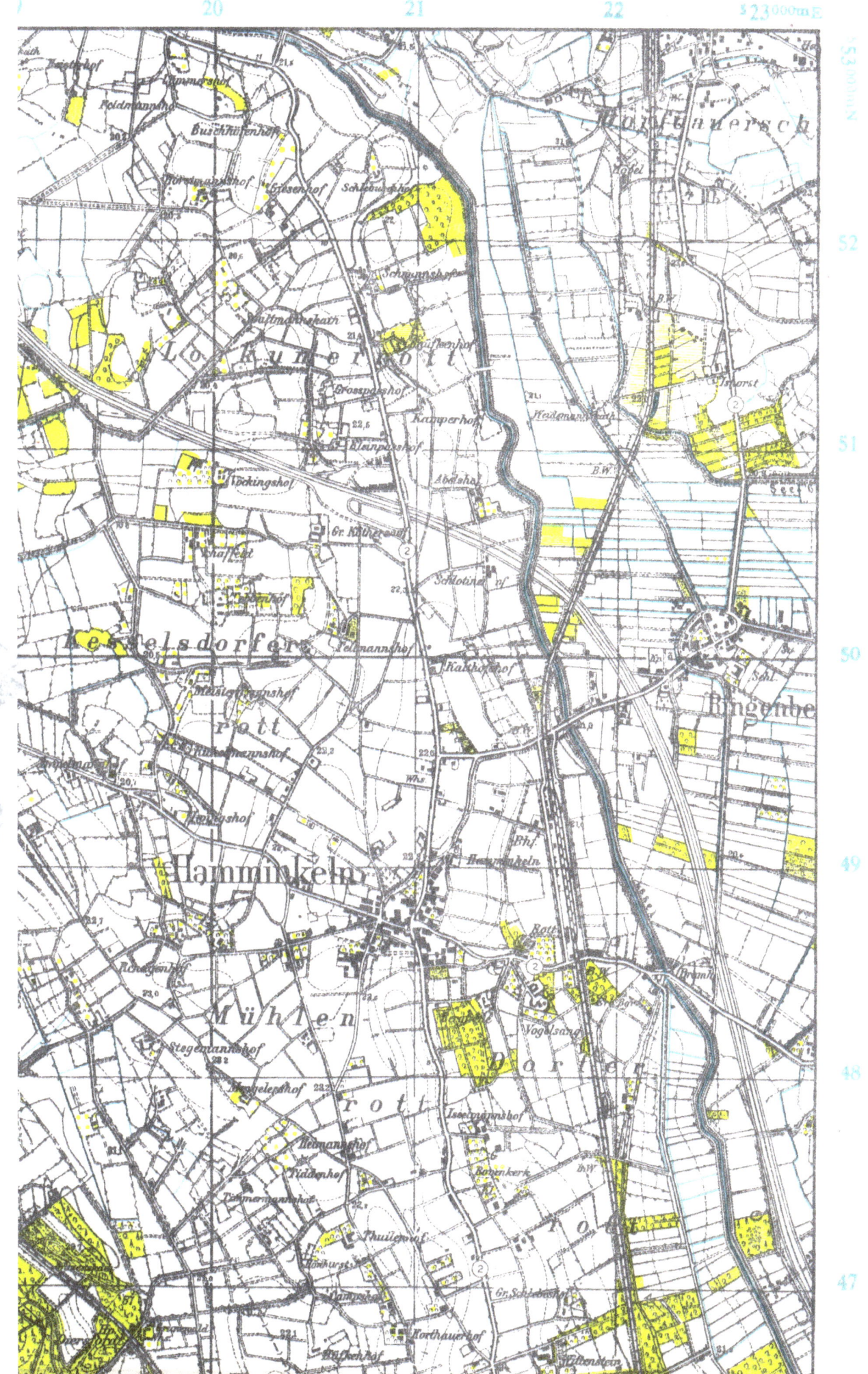

Operation Plunder 23, 24, 25 March 1945 — spread 3

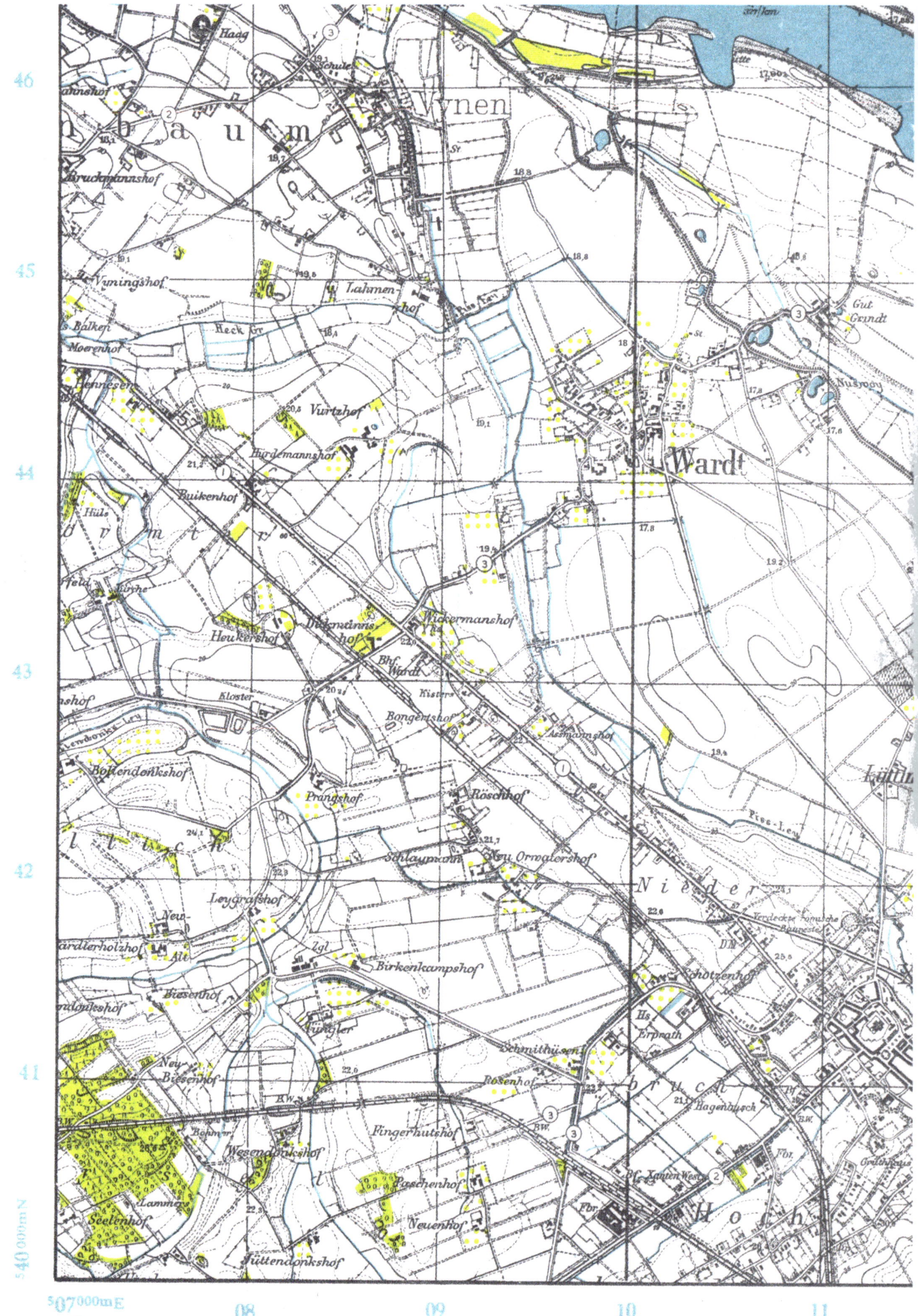

Operation Plunder 23, 24, 25 March 1945 — spread 3

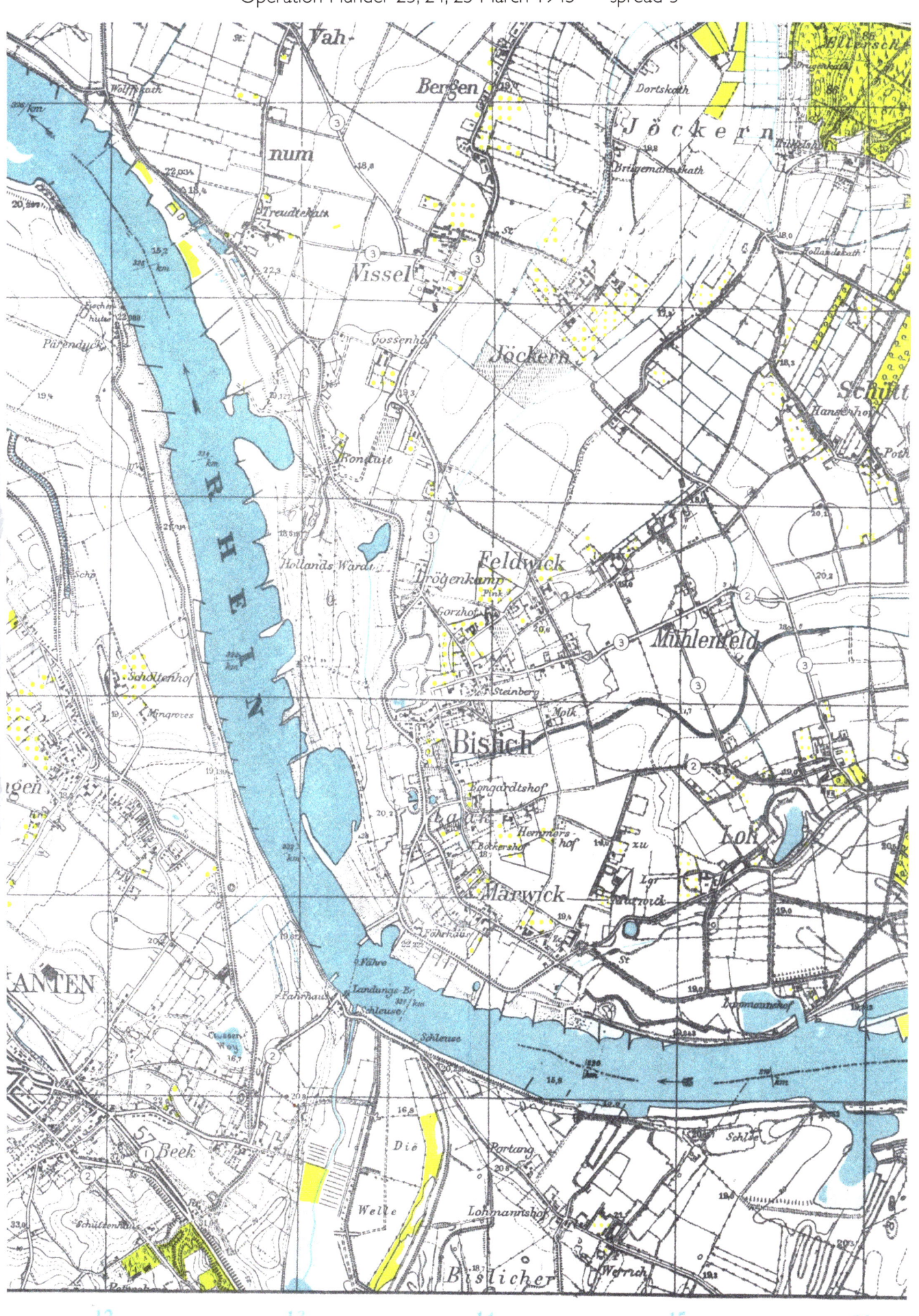

Operation Plunder 23, 24, 25 March 1945 — spread 4

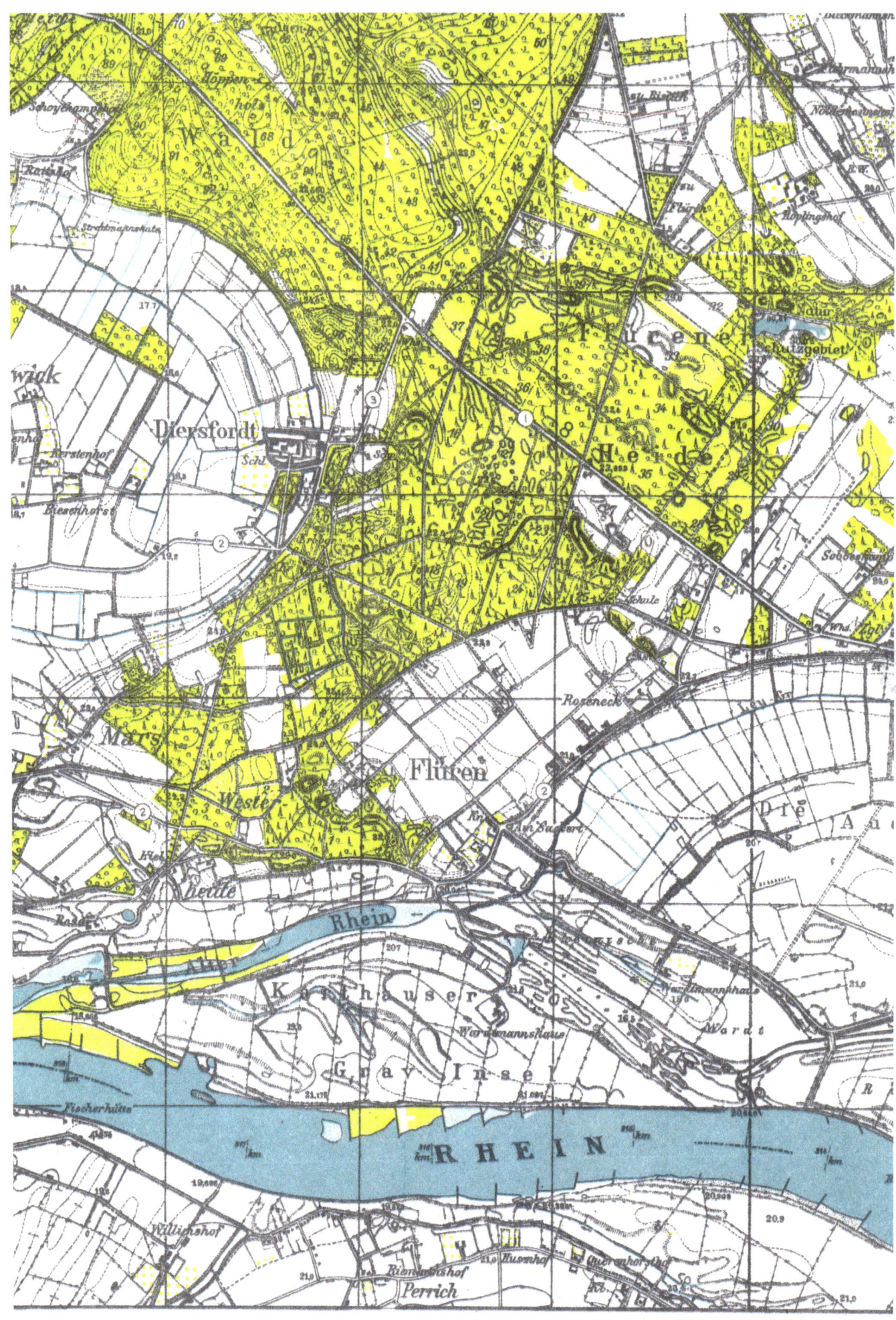

Operation Plunder 23, 24, 25 March 1945 — spread 4

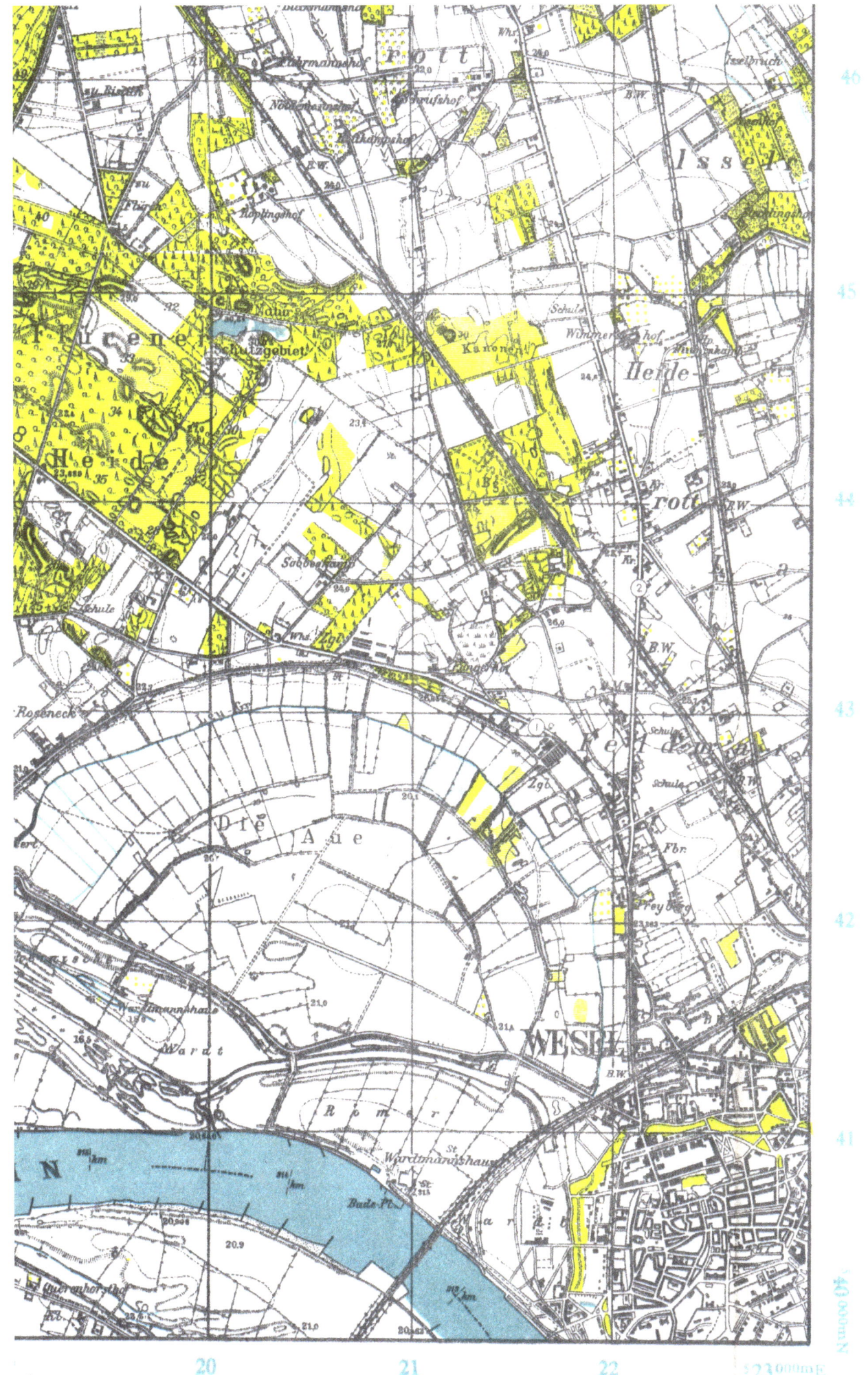

PART I

Planning the Operation

SECTION I

INTRODUCTION

A. GENERAL SITUATION

By March 1945 operations by the First Canadian and Ninth United States Armies, designed to clear the RHINE–MAAS area up to the West bank of the RHINE, had progressed to a point, at which the Commander-in-Chief 21 Army Group was able to issue firm orders to prepare for the actual crossing of the RHINE, with target date as 24 March 1945. This operation was given the name of PLUNDER.

B. 21 ARMY GROUP INTENTION

The Commander-in-Chief has stated that his intention was to secure a bridgehead, prior to developing operations to isolate the RUHR, and to thrust into the Northern plains of GERMANY. For this purpose he proposed to assault on a front of two Armies, Right Ninth United States and Left Second British, while First Canadian Army was to be responsible in the initial stages for the security of the Left flank of the Army Group.

C. PREVIOUS PLANNING

(i) **Planning at Army Group and Army Level**

Clearly 21 Army Group could not have planned and mounted an operation of this magnitude in the short time available, had not much preliminary planning already been done. In fact, study of such an operation had begun in October 1944, and in January 1945, as soon as the situation arising from the German counter-offensive in the ARDENNES had been brought under control, 21 Army Group had been directed to plan a crossing of the RHINE, North of the RUHR, with the object of isolating the Northern and Eastern sides of that great industrial area from the rest of GERMANY. This crossing was to take place at the earliest possible moment after the clearance of the West bank, and in this connection the Commander-in-Chief has written:—

The all important factor was to follow up the enemy as quickly as possible, and we were able to achieve this speed of action mainly because of the foresight and preliminary planning that had been devoted to the battle for some months.

Since both Ninth United States and First Canadian Armies were heavily involved in the operations for clearing the area up to the West bank of the RHINE, the brunt of the task of planning the assault across the RHINE fell on Second British Army.

During this period, Second Army was holding a quiet sector on the MAAS, so that its Headquarters was free to concentrate on planning the RHINE crossings. General DEMPSEY was charged with not only planning the Second Army operation, but also assisting in any way possible the preliminary planning by Ninth United States Army. Accordingly, Headquarters Second Army issued on 4 February 1945 a staff planning study of the problems involved.

(ii) **Planning at Corps Level**

Meanwhile, towards the end of January 1945, Headquarters 12 Corps was withdrawn into reserve and located South of MAESEYCK, close to the River MAAS, where topographical conditions approximated to those later to be encountered in the assault across the RHINE. It was now given the task of undertaking the detailed planning of the assault.

D. MORALE

Formidable though the task of assaulting across this major waterway undoubtedly was, everyone was sustained and inspired by the feeling that this was the "one good, strong heave all together" to end the war in EUROPE of which the Prime Minister spoke on 4 March 1945 during a visit to 21 Army Group.

Many of the formations taking part in Operation PLUNDER, however, had previously suffered considerable casualties during the operations for the clearing of the RHINE/MAAS area. The provision of reinforcements was a serious problem at this time owing to man-power difficulties at home, and little time was available for their absorption into units.

Nevertheless, morale was everywhere at a high pitch. The hard and uncomfortable winter was drawing to a close, the dangerous German counter-offensive in the ARDENNES had been broken and defeated, and, by 23 March 1945, 21 Army Group stood firmly on German soil ready to begin the final assault on the fortress of GERMANY.

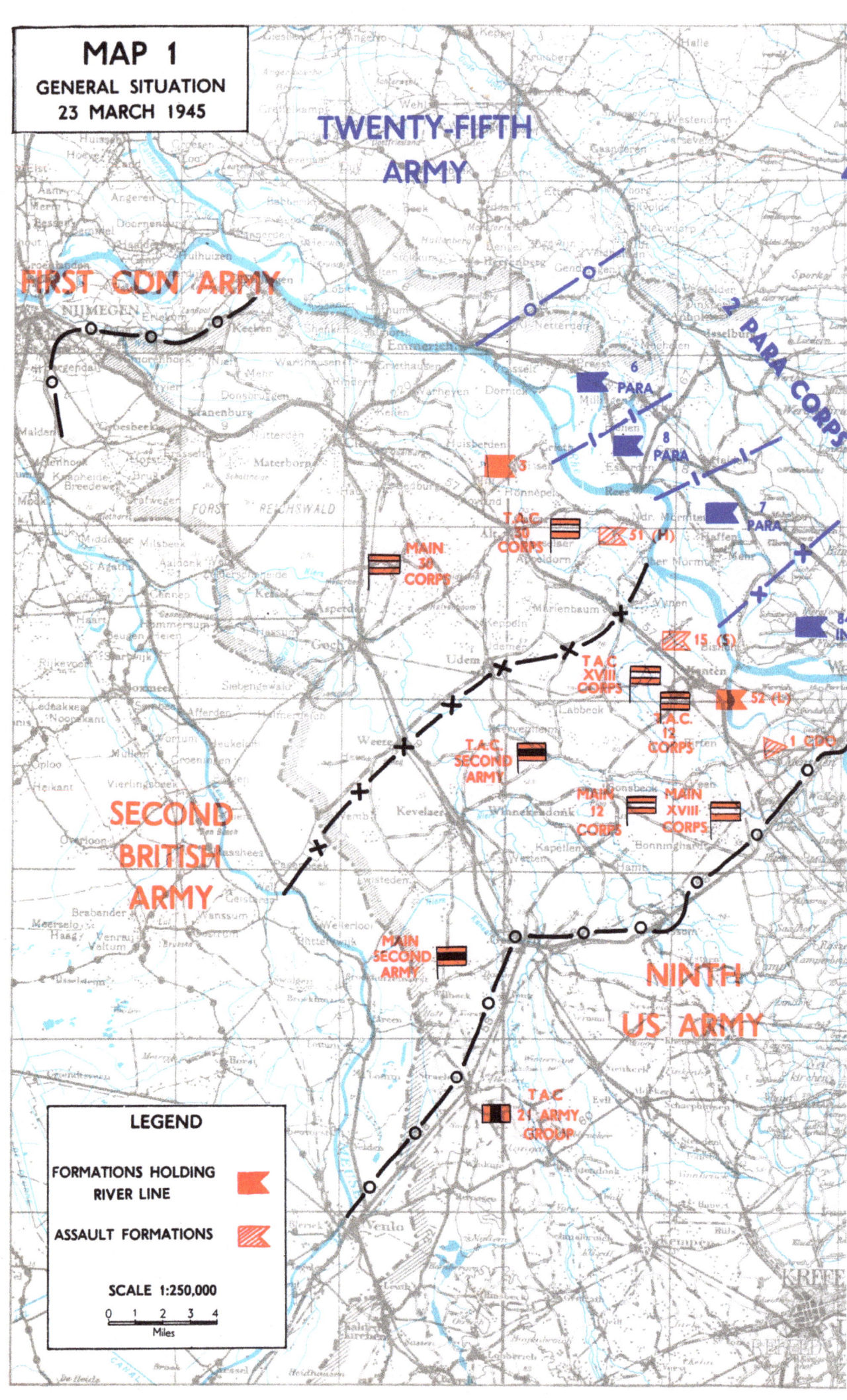

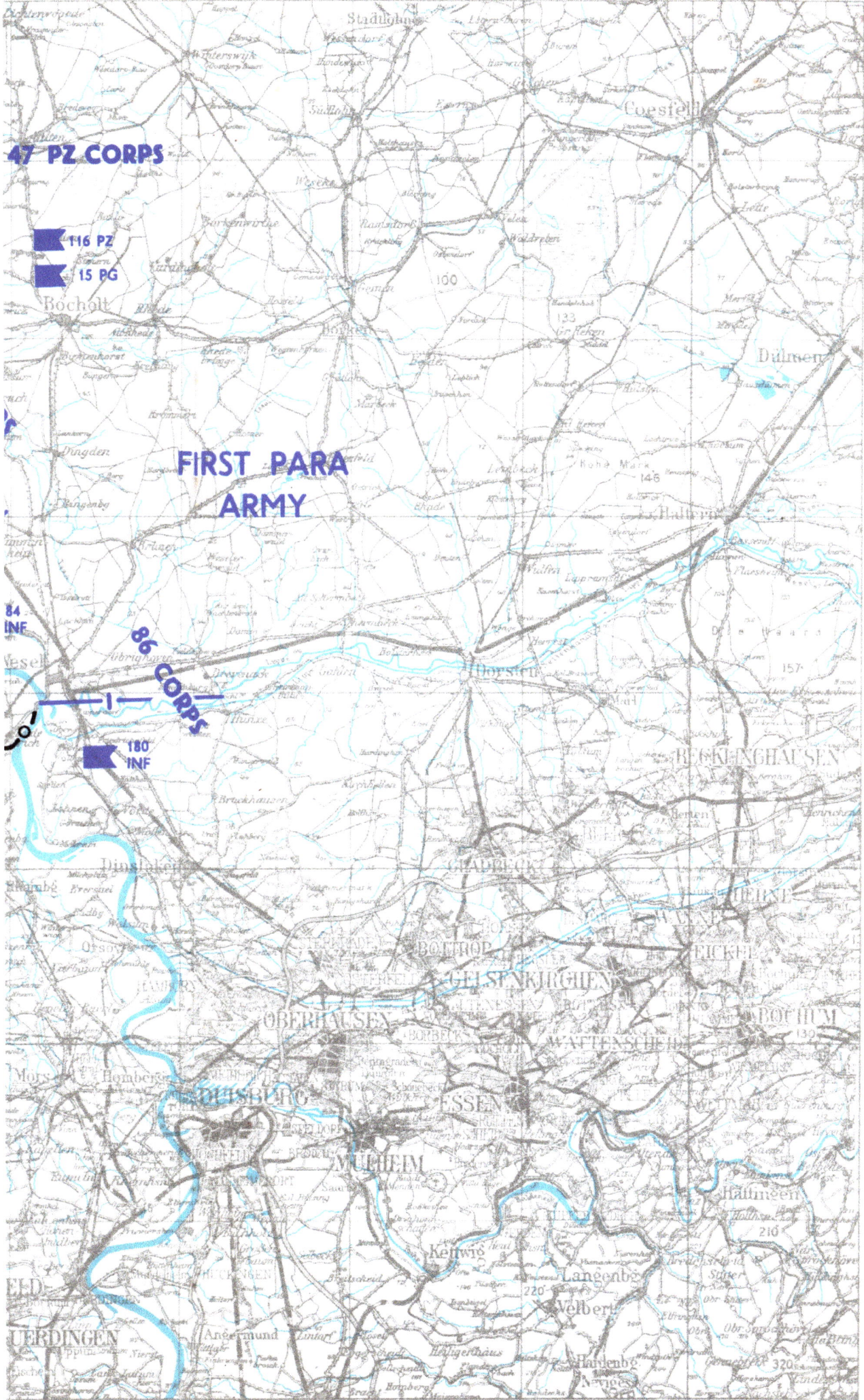

SECTION II

TOPOGRAPHY

A. THE RIVER RHINE

The area of the assault was studied in very great detail during the planning period, and a mass of data was made available to formations. This applied to the flood plain of the river, the flood banks, the approaches to the river banks, the average level of water and all other information, necessary to prepare the execution of engineer tasks. Only a short summary of this information can be given here.

In the Second Army sector, stretching from WESEL to EMMERICH, the RHINE flows through a flat, rather featureless plain five to ten miles wide. Water meadows extend on both sides of the river and the land closely resembles the Dutch Polder areas. The width of the river in this sector varies from four to five hundred yards, when flowing in its normal course, though flooding can extend it to as much as twelve hundred yards, or even more. Mean speed of flow in normal conditions at this season is about $3\frac{3}{4}$ knots. The river bed is generally sandy gravel and was expected to provide a firm bearing surface for amphibious vehicles or bridging trestles.

There are numerous meanders of the ALTER RHINE (a former course of the river) producing double water obstacles at certain places. The only commanding feature lies to the North West of WESEL and is on the West side of the WESEL-EMMERICH railway. Here the ground rises to a height of nearly 70 feet above the river level and is fairly heavily wooded in the area known as the DIERSFORDTER WALD. In general, however, possible crossing places for any considerable force are dictated almost wholly by topographical rather than tactical considerations.

B. PRECAUTIONS AGAINST FLOODING

To prevent flooding, there are two principal types of dykes:—

(i) *Summer Dykes*, that is low dykes constructed close to the river banks to retain any normal rise in water level. These were not a serious obstacle.

(ii) *Winter Dykes or "Bunds"* which are considerably larger and built at a greater distance from the river bank. Their purpose is to retain the abnormal flooding which sometimes occurs in the Lower RHINE plains during the winter and early spring. Twenty metres wide at the base, they vary from 2 to 5 metres in height and are on occasion paved with stone slabs or may carry a roadway. They could not, at most places, be crossed by a loaded LVT.

The area between the bunds is called the *Flood Bed*, while the area which would be subject to flooding in their absence is known as the *Flood Plain*.

During the winter 1944–45, the water level of the river rose to abnormal heights. All the low-lying polders within the area enclosed by the bunds were flooded. In addition, large areas of low-lying ground outside the bunds were waterlogged owing to the exceptionally heavy rainfall.

C. BRIDGES AND FERRIES

The only bridges in the Second Army sector were the railway and road bridges at WESEL, and as had been expected, these were both destroyed by the retreating enemy.

There were, however, a number of existing and potential ferry sites, and on the whole, once the problem of traversing the flood plain was overcome, which included getting vehicles over the dykes, no great difficulty in establishing ferries was foreseen, though the width and speed of the river presented their own problems of technique.

A rumoured subterranean passage under the RHINE at WESEL did not materialise.

D. EFFECT OF WEATHER

Much depended on the weather. Not only would local rain rapidly turn the whole flood plain into an impassable quagmire, but rain or abnormal melting of snow in the higher reaches of the river and its numerous tributaries might have a wholly unpredictable effect. Even if the level did not rise sufficiently to flood over the summer dykes, seepage into the flood bed could have almost equally disastrous results, since the flood bed is at this season often below river level. However, the engineer and meteorological experts calculated that, based on averages over 53 years, there was a 7 to 1 chance against flooding in April, and in the event they proved to be right, while the ground itself, so heavily water-logged in the winter months, dried out remarkably quickly.

E. ARTIFICIAL FLOODING

Consideration had also to be given to German action to demolish upstream dams. It was contended that demolition of the dams in the BASLE-Lake CONSTANCE area would have little or no effect, but that demolition of the major dams on the River RUHR might raise the level about one metre and maintain disturbed conditions for about a week. This possibility was however discountenanced in view of the economic and administrative consequences which would result from it in the vital RUHR industrial area.

F. CONCENTRATION AREAS

The area for concentration of the assaulting forces was restricted by the paramount necessity of assembling such forces, together with their immediate requirements of supply, East of the MAAS.

There was, however, a certain amount of cover available from woods such as the FORST and HOCHWALD XANTEN. The sub-soil in this area, once clear of the RHINE flood plain, is mainly sand and gravel, which dried out quickly after rain and provided reasonably good going, even for wheels.

G. APPROACHES

Good approaches to the river existed at the sites of the demolished bridges at WESEL, but this area was too restricted for an assault crossing by any but a comparatively small force. Topographical considerations therefore narrowed the choice of crossing sites in Second Army sector to a stretch of river opposite XANTEN and a second at REES.

The road RHEINBERG—XANTEN—CLEVE on the West side of the river, a 22ft metalled main road, provided good lateral communication at a distance ranging from 1500 to 5500 yards from the bank, while the main road WESEL—REES—EMMERICH fulfilled a similar function on the far side of the river. There were a number of subsidiary laterals, mostly unmetalled and suitable only for single-way traffic.

Forward from the near-side lateral, there was only one metalled access road at each site, and in neither case was this road suitable for two-way traffic. On the far side conditions were even less favourable.

There were several unmetalled tracks leading to both sites, suitable for a limited number of vehicles, but only in good weather conditions. Movement off these tracks in the flood plain was considered possible for tracked vehicles and then only if weather and flood conditions were favourable.

H. RAILWAYS AND OTHER ROADS

In addition to the East-West railway which crossed the RHINE at WESEL, railways ran on both banks roughly parallel with the main lateral roads mentioned above, that is at the edge of the flood plain, from 2000 to 6000 yards from the river banks. On the East side, at a distance of 10,000 to 12,000 yards from the river bank, ran a partially completed autobahn.

None of these presented any serious obstacle to movement, though the sandy formation of the unfinished autobahn caused some temporary delays to wheeled and light tracked vehicles.

I. OTHER WATER OBSTACLES

Between 10,000 and 15,000 yards East of the RHINE and roughly parallel to it in the sector allotted to 12 Brit Corps, ran the River ISSEL. Detailed information concerning this river was less complete than in the case of the RHINE, but it was believed to represent a tank obstacle, as it in fact proved to be. It was clear that before any breakout from the bridgehead could take place, it would be necessary to seize crossings over this river, and this requirement considerably influenced the overall operational plan.

A further water obstacle lying between the RHINE and the ISSEL in the 12 Corps sector, consisted of the two "lakes" (in reality former beds of the RHINE) just East of MEHR. These were joined mutually and to the main stream of the RHINE by minor streams or drains and thus enclosed a sort of island, opposite the XANTEN assaulting site.

SECTION III

THE ENEMY

A. GENERAL

The enemy opposition in the fighting West of the River RHINE, which came to an end on 9 March, had been intense. His parachutists had fought fanatically and he had more artillery and mortars deployed against 21 Army Group than at any other stage in the campaign.

The German losses, however, had been huge – estimates included about 40,000 men killed or wounded, to which must be added over 50,000 prisoners. The troops that he was able to withdraw to the East of the river belonged to divisions which had been badly mauled, and apart from their big material losses, their morale left much to be desired.

The decision to fight West of the river, combined with the acute weapons shortage and the crippling blows German industry and communications were receiving from the Allied Forces, meant that the enemy was never able to organise a strong defence to oppose the assault crossings of the RHINE.

Field Marshal KESSELRING took over from VON RUNDSTEDT as Commander-in-Chief, West, shortly before Operation PLUNDER. The enemy opposite 21 Army Group was mainly under command of Army Group "H" under General BLASKOWITZ.

B. ENEMY DEPLOYMENT AND ORDER OF BATTLE

The defence of the RHINE opposite the 21 Army Group sector was in the hands of First Parachute Army. This Army had three Corps on the line of the river, Right 2 Para Corps, Centre 86 Corps, Left 63 Corps. The dispositions of 2 Para and 86 Corps as appreciated by Second Army are shown on Map 1.

The reserve consisted of 47 Panzer Corps, in an area about 15 miles North East of EMMERICH with 15 Panzer Grenadier (15 PG Div) and 116 Panzer Divisions (116 Pz Div) under command.

C. ENEMY FORCES OPPOSING 12 CORPS

As will be seen from Map 2, opposition to the assault in 12 Corps sector was likely to come from 7 Para and 84 Inf Divs.

(i) 7 Para Div

This division was believed to be on the Left of 2 Para Corps. There was some evidence to support this belief, and it was in any case unlikely that 8 Para Div could be holding so long a front as to have a common boundary with 84 Div on its Left.

The following table gives the estimated strength of 7 Para Div when it was withdrawn across the RHINE after Operation VERITABLE.

It should be noted that strength given for infantry units are fighting strengths and exclude 'B' echelons, while those for divisional supporting groups (artillery, engineers, etc) include all personnel.

Unit	Estimated Strength on 12 March	Remarks
19 Para Regt		
I Bn	100	Had battalion CRAHS under command — strength 100
II Bn } III Bn }	total 250	
HQ and Regt Coys	75	
20 Para Regt } 21 Para Regt }	total 500	
7 Para Recce Coy	Destroyed	
7 Para Arty Regt	500	20 × 105 cm (possibly some 7.5 cm) 3 × 15 cm
7 Para A Tk Bn	100	4 × 7.5 cm Pak
7 Para Engr Bn	350	
7 Para Mortar Bn	350	20 × 12 cm
7 Para Sigs Bn	300	
7 Para Flak Bn	200	4 × 88 mm : 4 × 2 cm Flak
7 Para Services	700	

No information had been received about reinforcements since this date, but it was reasonable to assume that parachute formations were still at a high priority for receiving them.

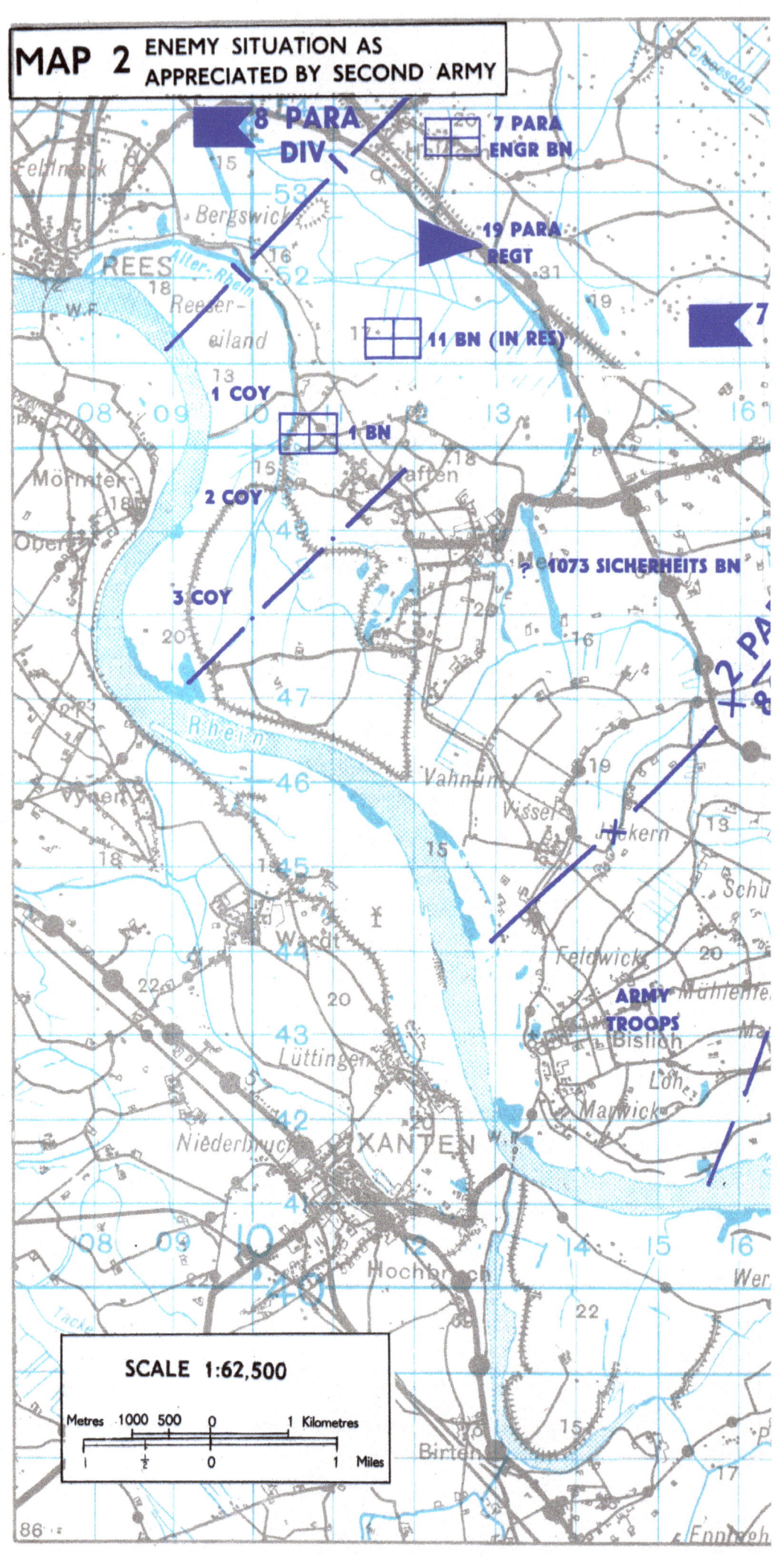

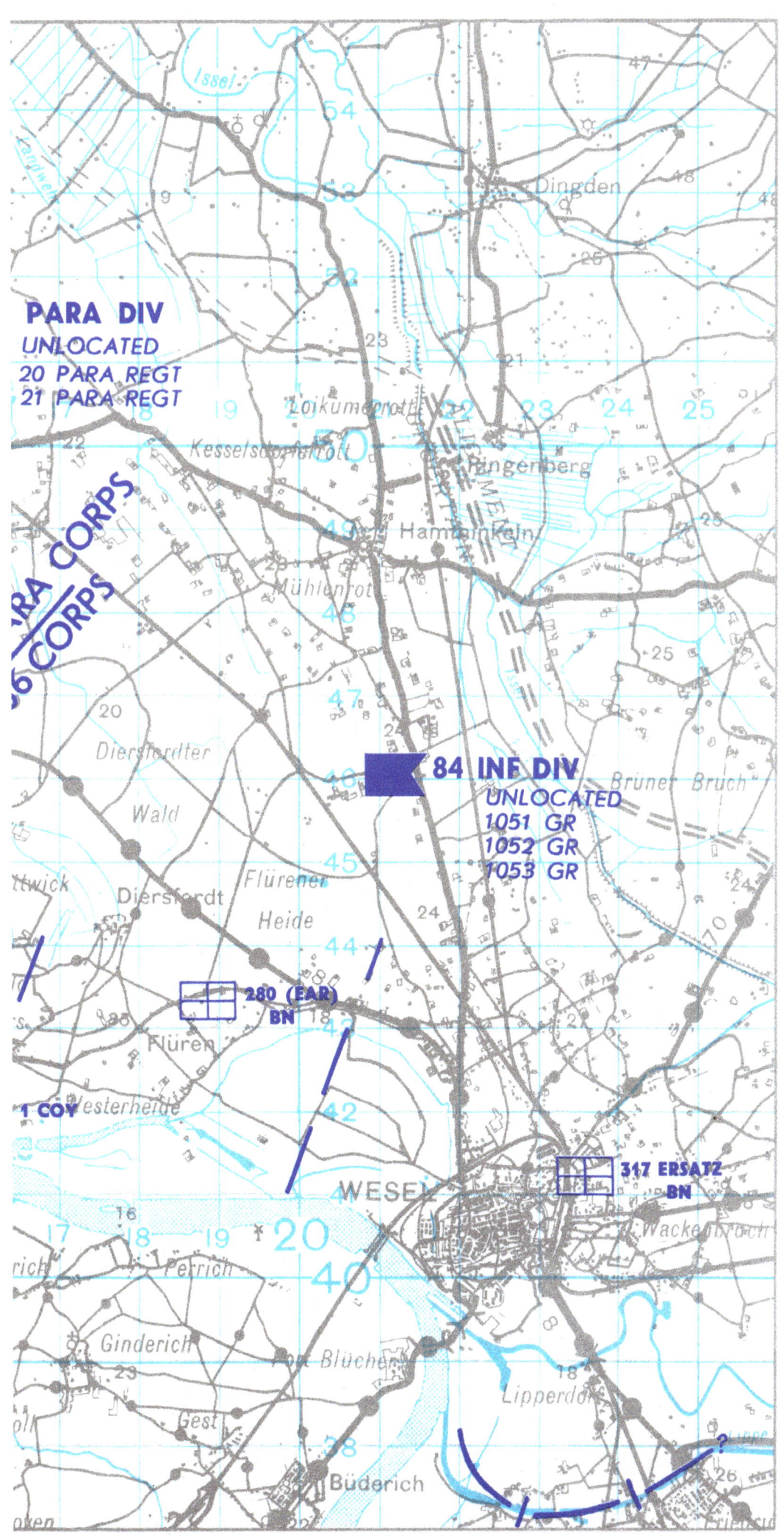

(ii) 84 Inf Div

It was almost certain that 84 Inf Div was on the Right of 86 Corps. This was a luckless formation, having been virtually destroyed at the beginning of Operation VERITABLE in February, and since reformed only to be decimated again, as a result of Operation PLUNDER. The estimated strength of 84 Inf Div on 12 March was as follows:—

Unit	Estimated Strength on 12 March	Remarks
1051 GR		Mostly newly arrived reinforcements.
1052 GR	total 500	
1062 GR		
184 Arty Regt	300	10 × 10.5 cm guns
184 Engr Coys	150	
184 Fus Bn	Destroyed	
184 A Tk Bn	100	2 × 7.5 cm Pak
184 Sigs Bn	200	
184 Services	300	

(iii) Other Troops

84 Inf Div was so weak that it was safe to assume that it was being bolstered up by certain other troops which probably included some Volkssturm (German "Home Guard") and static Wehrkreis troops. 286 'Ear' Bn, made up entirely of deaf soldiers, was also identified near WESEL. Very little was known as to the whereabouts of the static units known to form part of the Wehrkreis VI, nor of the progress of the formation of VOLKSSTURM units, but it seemed probable that most of the available men would have been drafted into the field army, if only because equipment would not be available for them elsewhere.

D. DEFENCES

The Germans had not been able to prepare a strong defence line on the River RHINE: in fact, they had little more formidable than simple earthworks with a little wire and many of these were not by any means strongly held. The defences were mainly concentrated round the possible crossing sites of EMMERICH, REES, XANTEN and WESEL and civilians were known to be helping in their construction. There was little depth in the positions and, in some cases, they proved little more than a line of automatic weapons along the bund.

E. ARTILLERY

(i) Field and Medium Artillery

On the 12 Corps front 84 Inf Div assisted by GHQ and non-divisional resources, was thought to have only about fifty medium or field guns: in fact there were probably more, and they were in any case very difficult to locate, as they were mostly sited in very enclosed country. To this figure must be added a number of guns which 7 Para Div might bring to bear against 12 Corps.

(ii) Anti-aircraft Artillery

There was no doubt that the enemy was expecting an airborne operation of some kind to be staged in connection with the river crossing.

The estimate of the number of AA guns in the EMMERICH—BOCHOLT—WESEL triangle on 17 March was 153 Light and 103 Heavy. Less than a week later, just before Operation PLUNDER began, the figures had risen to 712 Light and 114 Heavy.

F. ARMOUR

The local armoured reserve consisted of 47 Panzer Corps (47 Pz Corps) comprising 116 Pz and 15 PG Divs. Both these divisions had been employed in covering the withdrawal across the RHINE and had suffered badly. However, reliable information pointed to their having been reinforced and on 22 March 116 Pz Div was credited with up to seventy tanks and 15 PG Div with fifteen tanks and twenty to thirty assault guns. A heavy anti-tank battalion was also thought to have arrived in the area.

A figure of between one hundred and one hundred and fifty was given as the total number of AFVs at the disposal of First Para Army.

SECTION IV

THE PRELIMINARY PLANNING BY HQ 12 CORPS

A. OBJECT OF PLANNING

Preliminary planning by HQ 12 Corps began on 5 February 1945 with a two-fold object :—
 (i) to develop the proper technique for the assault across the RHINE,
 (ii) to reach solutions of certain major problems with the ultimate object of producing a specific plan for the assault crossing of the RHINE.

B. BASIC ASSUMPTIONS

Second Army planning study laid down certain basic assumptions on which planning was to proceed. The most important of these were as follows: —

(i) **Second Army Task**

The task of Second Army was, in conjunction with Ninth US Army and First Canadian Army, to establish a bridgehead over the RHINE with a view to operating towards RHEINE with Ninth US Army operating at the same time on the axis WESEL—MUNSTER—HAMM and First Canadian Army protecting the Northern flank of Second Army.

(ii) **Assault Crossing Areas**

Suitable areas for the assault crossings and their allotment to Armies were :—

RHEINBERG	:	Ninth US Army
XANTEN	:	Second Army
REES	:	Second Army
EMMERICH	:	First Canadian Army

It was foreseen that an assault crossing at EMMERICH might prove too hazardous, owing to the poor approaches in that area and to the necessity of first crossing the ALTER RHINE possibly under enemy observation from the HOCH ELTEN high ground.

Consideration was therefore to be given to an alternative plan of postponing the attack on EMMERICH until Second Army's bridgehead was established, and then capturing the town by an attack launched Westwards through the bridgehead. (This was, in fact, the plan eventually adopted, 2 Canadian Corps being placed under command of Second Army for the purpose).

(iii) **Disposition of Allied Forces Prior to the Assault**

It was assumed that Allied Forces in the whole of 21 Army Group sector would have closed up to the West bank of the RHINE sufficiently early to provide adequate time for reconnaissance of the river and the assembly and concentration of the assaulting forces.

(iv) **State of the River**

The assault was not to take place unless
 (a) the river was flowing in its normal channel,
 (b) the flood plain including the flood bed could be traversed by vehicles with a cross-country performance
 (c) weather forecasts for the first seven days were favourable.

(v) **Airborne Forces**

Airborne divisions might be available to support the crossings, but their roles and allotment had not been decided.

(vi) **Air Forces**

Normal air support from 83 Group RAF could be expected, operating from airfields West of the MAAS.

(vii) **Order of Battle**

Firm Orders of Battle could not be given at this date and planning was to proceed on the assumption that the necessary troops to form "Assault Division Groups" could be made available, at the rate of one per crossing area.

(viii) **Engineer Resources**

    (a) It was considered that the equivalent of at least twenty field companies would be required for each divisional crossing area, and that these would be made available, possibly to include a proportion of US engineer battalions.

    (b) The limiting factors in RE support were considered to be shortage of personnel and bank space for erection and operation of equipment, rather than shortage of equipment, although the supply of the latter might be restricted by the administrative problem of ferrying it forward over the MAAS in competition with other requirements.

C. THE EVOLUTION OF A CROSSING TECHNIQUE BY HQ 12 CORPS

(i) **Directive by Commander 12 British Corps**

On 5 February 1945, Commander 12 Corps issued to his staff a planning instruction which formed the basis of all subsequent planning. This instruction is reproduced in full for reference purposes at Appendix D, but the following extracts will suffice to show the general lines on which the staff were to work.

    (a) *All action will be co-ordinated towards achieving the following aims :—*
The enemy must NOT be allowed to seal off the bridgehead and it is essential that operations on the far bank should NOT congeal. Speed is therefore of the highest importance.

    (b) *This operation is in many ways akin to an assault landing on an open beach, and the problem will be tackled from this angle. The proved technique for an opposed landing will, therefore, be modified to suit this wide river problem, and so far as possible the already established and understood nomenclature employed for beach landings will be adopted.*
(*Note: For ease of reference, a GLOSSARY of the terms adopted is included at Appendix E*).

    (c) *As little time is likely to be available for the preparation of formations to undertake this operation, the technique evolved must be relatively rigid.*

    (d) *Assault on as broad a front as possible. Planning will be carried out envisaging infantry in LVsT forming the leading waves with DDs, in separate waves, to follow as soon as reconnaissance has established, and marked, the most suitable exits for them on the far bank.*

    (e) *It can be assumed that a very large scale of air support will be available if weather conditions permit. The plan will NOT be dependent for its staging upon flying conditions being suitable. It must be prepared to take place without air support.*

    (f) *Airborne operations in conjunction with the assault crossing will be superimposed.*

(ii) **Staff Planning**

    (a) HQ 12 Corps now set out to evolve a drill for the assault which could be quickly taught to the assaulting formations when these became known. It was not expected that more than a week would be available for the purpose of such special preliminary training.

    (b) On 14/15 February 1945, an indoor exercise was held with the following object :—

        To evolve a technique for an opposed crossing of a wide river.

The exercise was preceded by a demonstration of a number of the available special vehicles and devices, amphibious and otherwise. These were for the most part operated by the specialist 79 Armoured Division. Some of the problems which this exercise was designed to solve are given in Appendix F. This exercise was followed, on 2 March 1945, by a full scale brigade group trial carried out first by day and then by night on a section of the MAAS specially selected to resemble as far as possible the stretch of the RHINE already chosen for the assault. In this trial, 5th Battalion The Royal Berkshire Regiment (Princess Charlotte of Wales's) (5 R BERKS) was employed as Bank Unit (see paragraph G of this section) and continued in this role in all subsequent training and in the final assault.

    (c) The results of these studies were made available in a series of "Technique Instructions" which were issued by HQ 12 Corps during the early part of March, and provided the training doctrine for all formations and units taking part in the assault. Without these instructions it would have been very difficult for subordinate formation Commanders to put over to the junior leaders all the detailed intricacies involved in a major crossing of this nature.

D. OPERATIONAL PLANNING

Concurrently with the study of the assault technique, certain decisions had been made with regard to the grouping of forces and the employment of airborne divisions. In addition, Commander Second Army had decided to assault on a two corps front and provisional inter-Army and inter-Corps boundaries had been laid down.

Accordingly, on 8 March 1945, Commander 12 Corps held a conference at which Commanders 15 (Scottish) Infantry Division (15 (S) Div) and 1 Commando Brigade (1 Cdo Bde) were present. These formations had come under command of HQ 12 Corps the previous day, having been selected as the assaulting formations in the 12 Corps sector, that is, on the Right of Second Army.

On 10 March 1945, HQ 12 Corps issued a further planning instruction which gave the task of 12 Corps as follows :—

> *To force a crossing over the RHINE, to establish bridges across this river, and, in conjunction with XVIII US Corps (Airborne), to secure a bridgehead from which Second Army can debouch for operations to the East.*

The plans for XVIII US Corps (Airborne) and 30 Brit Corps and Ninth US Army were then outlined (see Section VI) and the instruction continued by stating that the assault on the 12 Corps front was to be made in two parts (see Map 3) :—

(i) Operation TORCHLIGHT—The assault by 15 (S) Div directed on the areas

    (a) SCHUTTWICK–LOH–BISLICH

    (b) HAFFEN–MEHR

(ii) Operation WIDGEON—The assault by 1 Cdo Bde directed on WESEL.

The relative timing of these assaults and their co-ordination with the airborne operation, for which P Hour (defined as the time troops commence dropping) was fixed for 1000 hours D Day, were left for later decision.

Based on this instruction, planning at Divisional and Brigade HQ level was able to proceed.

E. CONCENTRATION

Prior to concentration for Operation PLUNDER the majority of units of the assaulting formations of 12 Corps were located West of the MAAS.

In order to assist in the task of deceiving the enemy, it was desirable to put off final concentration until the last possible moment, and in the event, units of 15 (S) Div moved into their assembly areas by night between 21 and 23 March preceded by 1 Cdo Bde on the night 20/21 March (see Map 4).

During the intervening period, detailed reconnaissance had been undertaken for the actual crossing sites for the assault and for the great number of special areas needed for the forming-up of units and special equipment. The following is a list of such areas, as required for Operation TORCH-LIGHT, responsibility for the reconnaissance of which was delegated to 15 (S) Div :—

> Staging Areas for units under command 15 (S) Div and certain Corps and Army units, due to cross in the early stages (including land tails of the Airborne Corps).
> Marshalling Areas (two)
> Vehicle Waiting Areas (two)
> Armour Waiting Area
> DD Tank Inflation Area
> LVT Collecting Areas (four)
> LVT Loading Areas (four)
> Stormboat Waiting Areas (two)
> Forward hides for Stormboats and equipment for class 9 rafts
> RE Bridge Park and Stores Dump
> Bridge Vehicle Marshalling Areas
> DUKW Marshalling and Collecting Areas
> Sites for Bank Control HQ, Crossing Control HQ (two).
> Signal exchanges and test points
> Accommodation areas for personnel of the Bank Group and of additional RE formations under command.

Linking these various areas and the river bank, itself an elaborate network of cross-country routes for tracked vehicles and infantry, and routes passable for wheeled vehicles had also to be reconnoitred (see Map 6).

It should be noted that there was considerable urgency about the selection of these sites, owing to the extensive buried line communications required for them. For the same reason, once selected, they could not as a general rule be altered.

52 (Lowland) Infantry Division, the holding formation occupying the area up to the West bank, was ordered to conform, as far as possible, to the requirements of 15 (S) Div in the selection of sites and if necessary to re-deploy units accordingly.

The movement of guns into gun areas (see Map 4) and dumping of ammunition was co-ordinated by the CCRA. Some of the problems encountered in the concentration of the large number of guns in the restricted area of the West bank allotted to them are mentioned in Section VII.

SECTION V

THE PLAN

A. 12 CORPS INTENTION

In the final Operation Order for PLUNDER, issued by 12 Corps on 21 March 1945, the Corps task was given as follows :—

In conjunction with XVIII US Corps (Airborne) to force a crossing over the River RHINE. To establish bridges across this river and operate Eastward.

B. TROOPS AVAILABLE TO 12 CORPS

At 1200 hours on 20 March 1945, HQ 12 Corps took over from HQ 8 Corps responsibility for the front from BUEDERICH to OBER MOERMTER. In so doing, HQ 12 Corps assumed operational command of 52 (Lowland) Infantry Division. Troops available to 12 Corps for Operation PLUNDER were thus as below (for full Order of Battle, see Appendices A 1, 2, 3).

> 7 Armoured Division (7 Armd Div)
> 15 (Scottish) Infantry Division (15 (S) Div)
> 52 (Lowland) Infantry Division (52 (L) Div)
> 53 (Welsh) Infantry Division (53 (W) Div)
> 4 Armoured Brigade (4 Armd Bde)
> 34 Armoured Brigade (34 Armd Bde)
> 1 Commando Brigade (1 Cdo Bde)
> 115 Infantry Brigade (115 Inf Bde)
> Elements of 79 Armoured Division.

C. FACTORS AFFECTING THE PLAN

Many of the principal factors affecting the plan have already been noted in earlier sections. The following additional points are of interest :—

(i) WESEL

The Commander-in-Chief had laid down that one of Second Army's tasks was the capture of the communication centre of WESEL, so that Ninth US Army could bridge the river at that place, and thus open up a supply route across the RHINE.

Tactically, Commander 12 Corps considered that the whole operation, as affecting 12 Corps, depended on the assault on WESEL being successful.

It was therefore necessary to ensure the earliest possible capture of the town, which was likely to be strongly held by the enemy.

Although the main road through WESEL provided one of the few good road approaches to the river, the area was not, in general, suitable for an assault by a large force, owing to restrictions of frontage imposed by a meander of the ALTER RHINE on the near bank, and by the River LIPPE and its parallel navigation canal on the far side. It was therefore decided to use a Commando brigade which could be found without breaking into the organisation of any of the available divisions.

(ii) Airborne Assault

Contrary to the practice adopted at ARNHEM, it had been decided to drop the airborne troops comparatively close to the start lines of the ground assault with the object of widening and extending the bridgehead as quickly as possible. The airborne assault was in consequence made within range of the guns of the ground assault. The considerable advantages to be derived from this, coupled with the rapid junction with the ground troops which was thereby rendered possible, was considered to outweigh the risks due to the increased flak, the bulk of which the enemy was known to have deployed in the river area.

The problem therefore arose as to whether the land or airborne assault should go in first. Again contrary to previous practice, it was decided to lead off with the ground assault. This would still further hasten the vital link-up between airborne and ground assaulting forces. Moreover, had the air landing been made first, the presence of airborne forces on the far bank would have very seriously interfered with both artillery and bombing programmes preparatory to the ground assault.

(iii) Timing of the Assault

The timing of the assault on the various sectors of the river presented certain problems. The airborne landings could only be made by day and, owing to the take-off aerodromes being located in ENGLAND and in the PARIS area, it was calculated that P Hour could

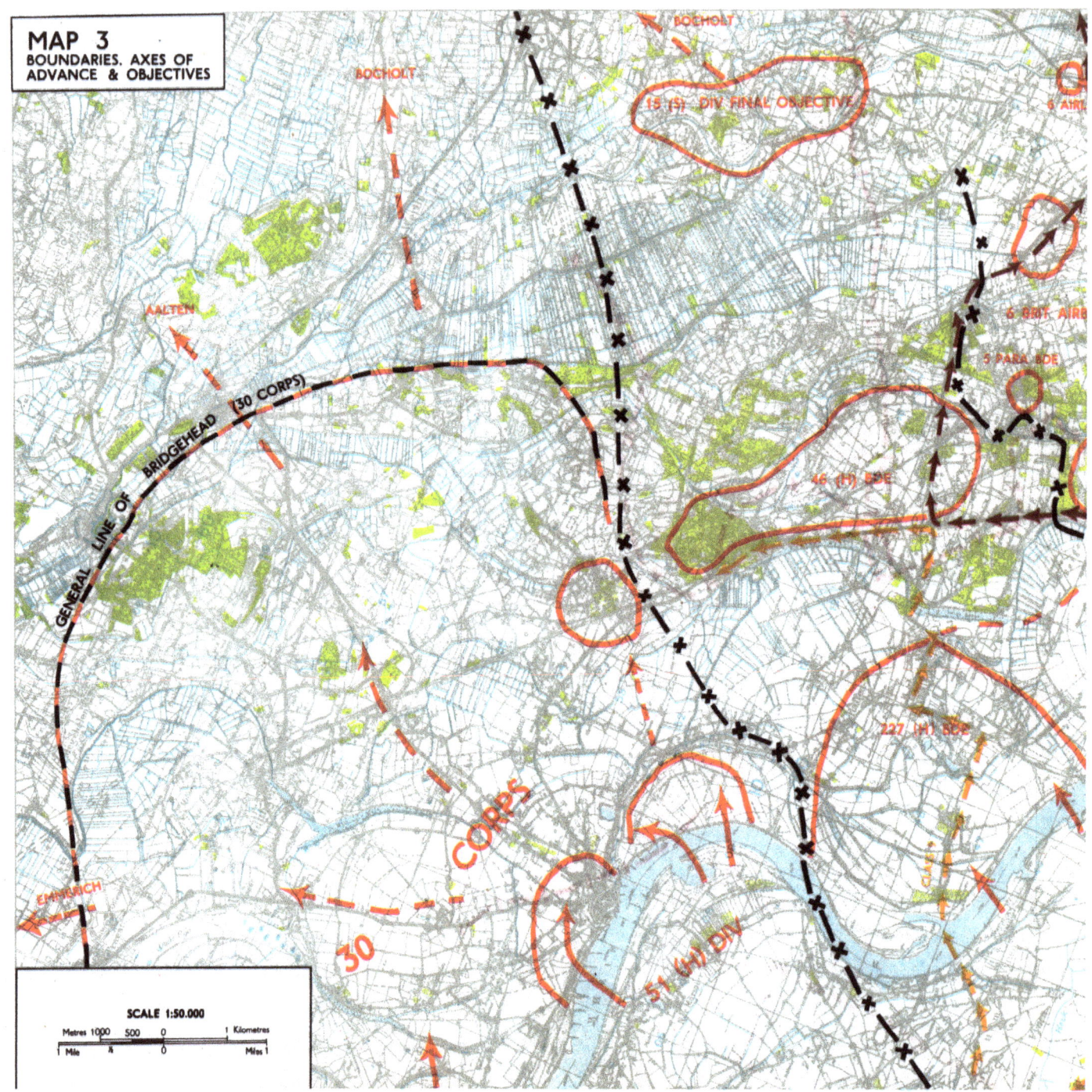

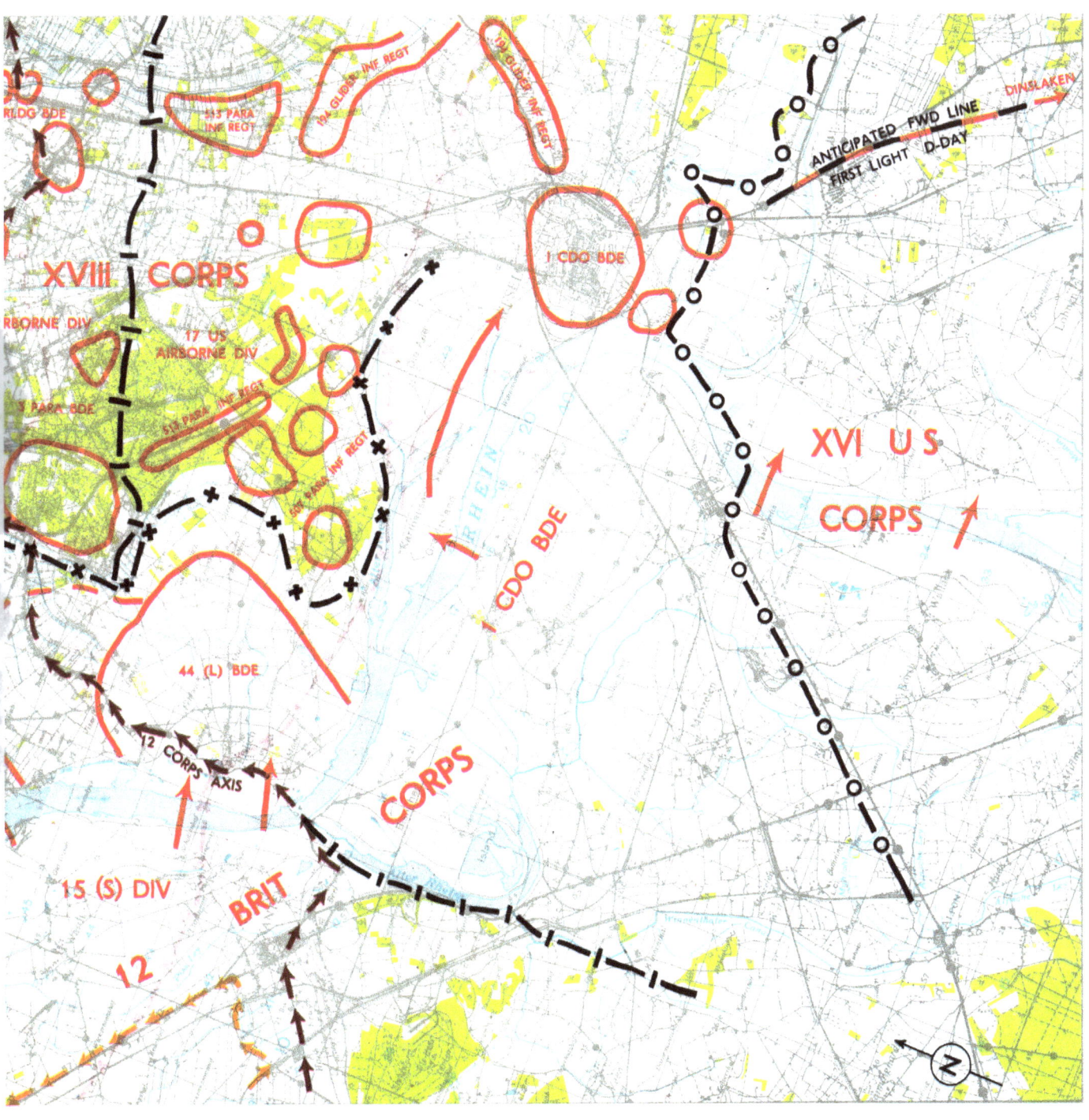

not be before 1000 hours. On the other hand a night assault by the ground troops was required for reasons of surprise, and to give the maximum cover from aimed fire during the initial crossing of the river. It was intended to offset the handicap of darkness by an extensive use of "movement light".

Having decided on a night assault by the ground troops, there were several factors which affected the final choice of H Hour.

1 Cdo Bde after crossing the RHINE, was to have the support of RAF heavy bombers for the assault on WESEL. It was estimated that about twelve hours would be needed for the resultant smoke and dust to clear. This was essential if the airborne fly-in, timed to start at 1000 hours next day, was not to be blinded. H Hour for 1 Cdo Bde (Operation WIDGEON) was therefore fixed for 2200 hours, so as to give sufficient time for final assembly and preparations on the near bank to be made under cover of darkness, while complying as nearly as possible with the airborne requirement. Last light was at approximately 1945 hours.

In the first stages of the assault, the main effort of 12 Corps artillery was to be developed in support of Operation WIDGEON and could not be made available to support the 15 (S) Div assault (Operation TORCHLIGHT) until 1 Cdo Bde was firmly established. It was essential that the leading infantry of 15 (S) Div and if possible DD tanks should be established on the far side by first light shortly before 0600 hours, and H Hour for this operation was therefore finally fixed for 0200 hours.

(iv) DD Tanks

Owing to the need for careful reconnaissance and some preparation of exits for the DD tanks, and the difficulty of manoeuvring and landing them in darkness, it was decided that it was impracticable for them to accompany the leading waves of assaulting infantry. Moreover, during their crossing, movement of other craft in the neighbourhood, particularly LVsT, would have to stop, which would have seriously affected the infantry build-up in the initial stages. As the tanks could not in any case develop their full value on the far side until they could see to shoot, their time of crossing was fixed for first light.

(v) Air Support

In his first planning instruction General RITCHIE had said that Operation PLUNDER would take place even if the weather conditions were such as to prevent the development of full scale air support.

This view came to be modified during the planning stages, and the following paragraph appeared in 12 Corps Operation Order for Operation PLUNDER :—

From D-1 onwards a very large scale of air support will be available. The operation is consequent (sic) upon flying conditions being suitable for the airborne operation. Full scale air support is therefore a "sine qua non".

As good weather was almost equally essential to the ground troops in their initial assault, it seems unlikely that serious consideration was given to the assault being undertaken without full air support, although the possibility of postponement or cancellation of the airborne operation was allowed for, in which case alternative timings were to come into use for Operation PLUNDER.

D. 12 CORPS PLAN

12 Corps plan was as follows (for details of boundaries and axes of advance, see Map 3):—

(i) 1 Cdo Bde (Operation WIDGEON)

1 Cdo Bde with

Under command :

1st Battalion The Cheshire Regiment (1 CHESHIRE)
84 Field Company Royal Engineers (84 Fd Coy RE)
One squadron, less one troop, 52nd (Lowland) Reconnaissance Regiment
  (52 (L) Recce Regt) (Bank Control)
One anti-tank troop 52 (L) Recce Regt
Anti-tank platoon, 4th Battalion The Northamptonshire Regiment
  (4 NORTHAMPTONS)
One MMG company, 7th Battalion The Manchester Regiment (7 MANCH).

In support :

77 Assault Squadron Royal Engineers (77 Aslt Sqn RE) (LVsT)

was ordered :—

(a) to cross the RHINE in the area of GRAV INSEL.

(b) to seize WESEL and the bridges over the LIPPE to the South of it, and hold the Eastern and Southern exits of the town.

(c) to come subsequently under command 17 US Airborne Div.

(ii) **15 (S) Div (Operation TORCHLIGHT)**

(Grouping for this operation is given in paragraph E below).

15 (S) Div was ordered

(a) to cross the RHINE on frontage BISLICH-VYNEN, and initially to seize and hold the areas
  1. SCHUTTWICK-LOH-BISLICH
  2. HAFFEN-MEHR.

(b) to clear the river bank between these areas, and thereafter seize and hold the area CLASENHO-MEHRHOO and the wood South East of HALDERN.

(c) to seize and hold the area GERVERSHOF-WISSMANN and the bridges over the ISSEL in that area.

(d) to relieve 6 Brit Airborne Div around HAMMINKELN and take over holding the ISSEL bridges in that area.

(e) to establish and maintain a number of ferries and bridges over the RHINE (for details see under RE Plan, paragraph F of this section).

(f) to organise an armoured mobile striking force to carry out limited exploitation.

Arrangements were made with XVIII US Corps (Airborne) for 15 (S) Div to operate over the inter-corps boundary up to P Hour, should the tactical situation require it.

Junction points with XVIII US Corps (Airborne) and with 30 Brit Corps were laid down.

(iii) **52 (L) Inf Div**

52 (L) Div was ordered

(a) to deny the line of the West bank of the RHINE to the enemy and destroy his patrols, until 15 (S) Div was established across the river.

(b) to carry out, under orders of HQ 12 Corps, very active patrolling across the river up to the time of the assault.

(c) to provide certain troops to assist 1 Cdo Bde and for control of staging areas and main routes under HQ 12 Corps: also unloading and carrying parties for such tasks as moving stormboats into their hides and thence to the river bank.

(d) to hold an infantry brigade group (less field regiment) at three hours notice from 1200 hours on D Day ready to cross the river on a Jeep and Carrier basis under operational command of 15 (S) Div.

(iv) **53 (W) Inf Div**

53 (W) Div was ordered to concentrate South West of KEVELAER on 23 and 24 March 1945 and to hold one infantry brigade ready to move on a Jeep and Carrier basis at three hours notice from 1200 hours on D Day.

The division was to be prepared to cross the river by the ferries and bridges established by 15 (S) Div, pass through 15 (S) Div bridgehead and operate towards BOCHOLT as ordered by the Corps Commander.

(v) **7 Armd Div**

7 Armd Div was ordered to concentrate in the area of WALBECK on 25 March 1945. It was to be prepared to cross the river as soon as the class 40 bridge was ready (estimated at H+70 hours), pass through 15 (S) Div bridgehead and operate towards BORKEN as ordered by the Corps Commander.

(vi) **Timings**

Timings for the various operations were fixed as under:—

H Hour: 1 Cdo Bde (Operation WIDGEON)	2200 hours D-1
H Hour: 15 (S) Div (Operation TORCHLIGHT)	0200 hours D Day
P Hour: XVIII US Corps (Airborne) (Operation VARSITY)	1000 hours D Day

H Hour was defined as the moment at which leading LVsT actually entered the water, and P Hour that at which the first parachute drops began.

(vii) **Fire Plan**

The Fire Plan is dealt with in detail in Section VII and the RA Order of Battle and grouping is given at Appendix A2.

It should be noted that the artillery support for both 12 Corps and XVIII US Corps (Airborne) was provided by artillery under command of 12 Corps, which included a group of three US field artillery battalions (each twelve 155 mm guns).

Artillery support under 12 Corps plan comprised an initial counter-battery bombardment by medium and heavy guns. Thereafter, the main effort of all guns was employed first in support of Operation WIDGEON, then in support of Operation TORCHLIGHT, and finally in support of the airborne landings (Operation VARSITY), ending immediately before P Hour.

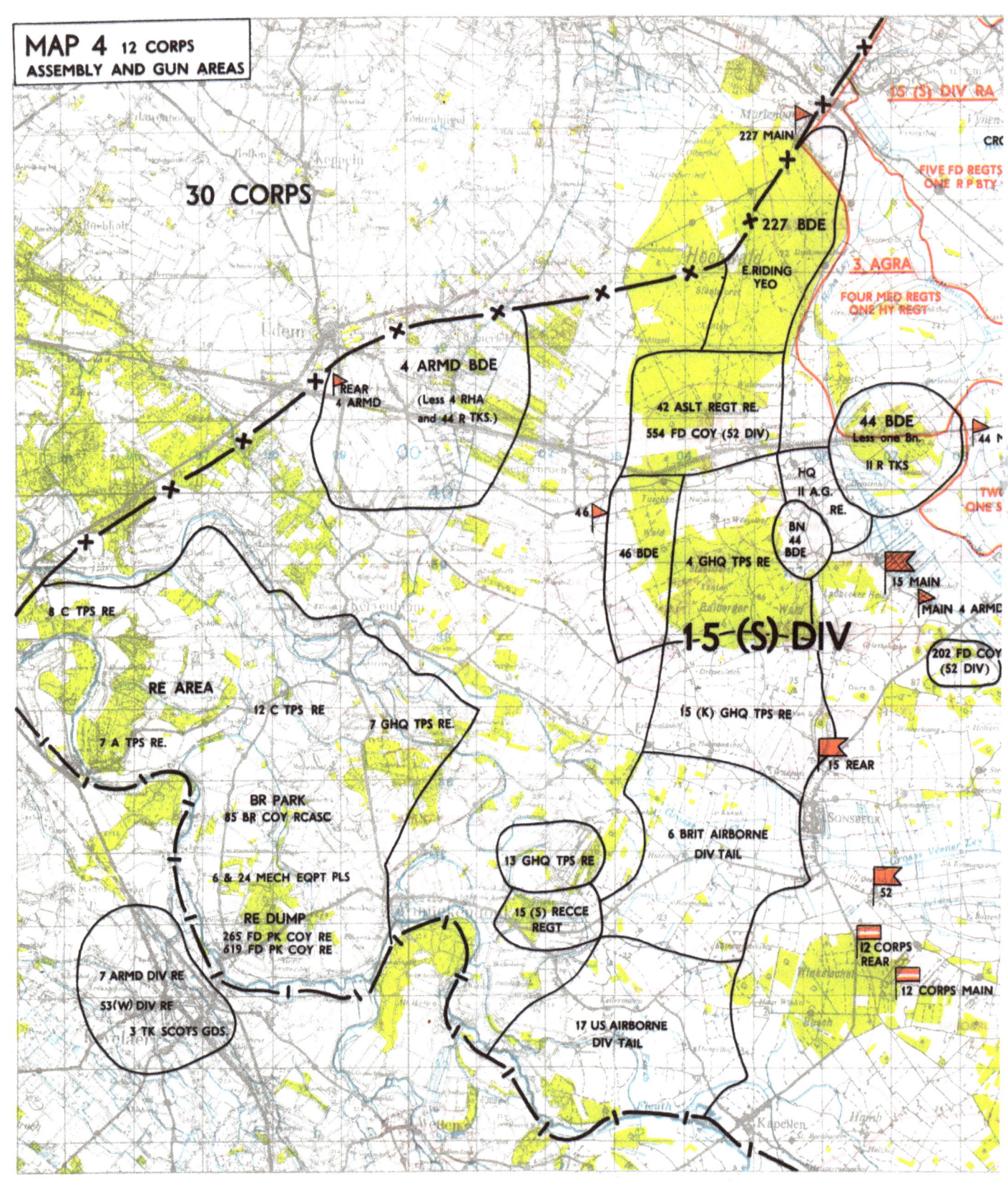

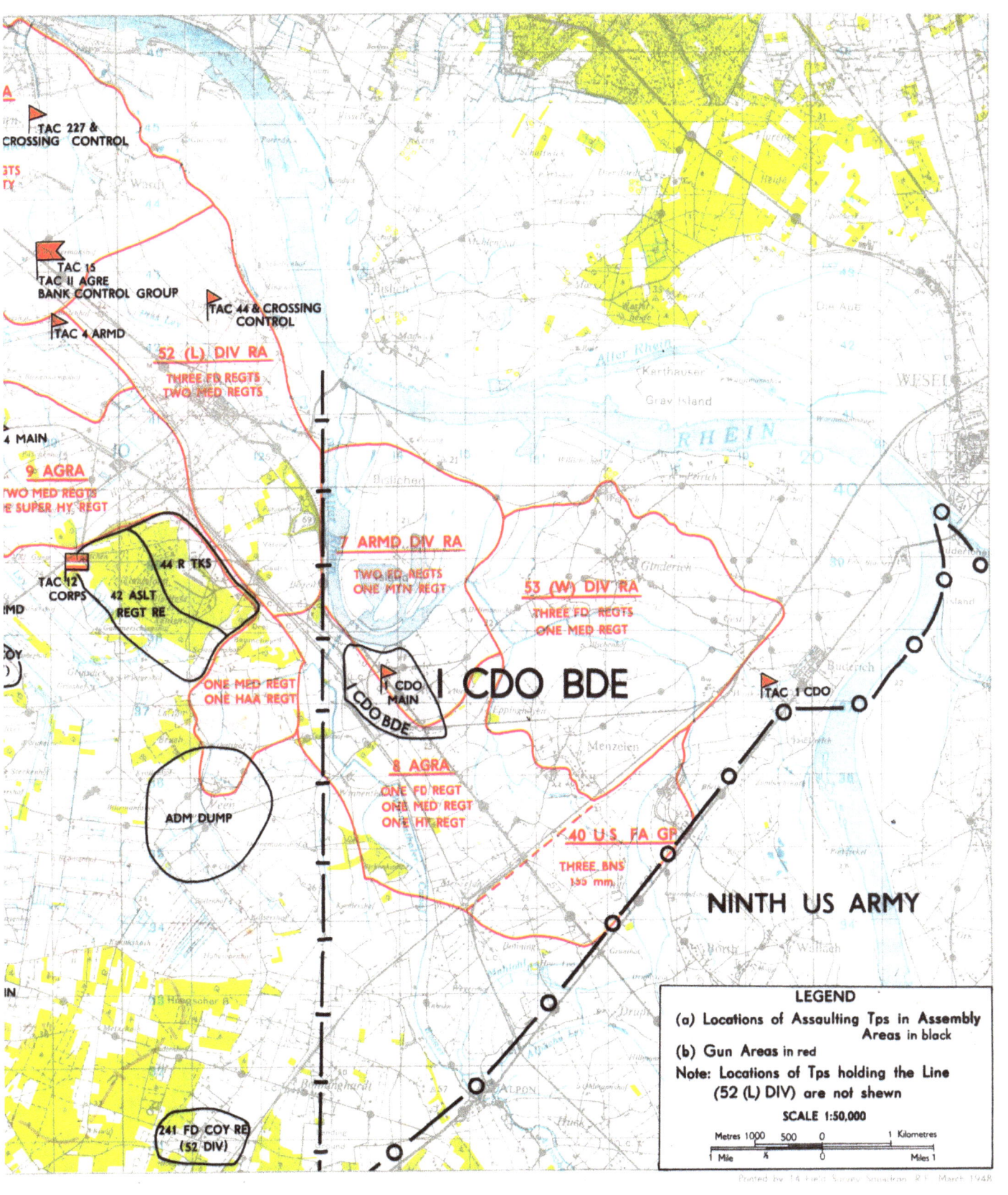

1 Cdo Bde was supported by 7 Armd Div RA Group and 15 (S) Div by 15 (S) Div RA Group respectively. These formations had prior call on the guns of their respective groups, even though the guns concerned might be engaged on other tasks under the Corps plan.

On the conclusion of the timed programme of artillery support at P Hour, a re-allotment of artillery was made (see Section VII for details) in order to provide direct support at call for the airborne formations. In addition, special priority on class 50/60 ferries was given to 4 RHA (SP 25-pounder regiment), which was primarily in support of 15 (S) Div, but was also given a secondary role in support of 6 Brit Airborne Div, as it was felt that the latter formation might be operating beyond the range of guns on the West bank. Shortage of crossing facilities, and in particular, the difficulty of supplying ammunition across the existing crossings prevented a greater number of guns being moved over the river in the earlier stages.

(viii) Defence of Bridges and Ferry Sites

(a) Anti-Aircraft

Commander 100 AA Bde was responsible for co-ordination of the AA layout on the Corps front. For the close defence of bridges and ferry sites, he had at his disposal a number of Corps and Army LAA regiments (see Appendix A2) and 15 (S) Div was ordered to give highest priority on class 9 rafts, and later class 9 FBE bridge, to the requirements of LAA on the far bank, which amounted to a total of nearly 100 guns and vehicles

(b) Ground and water-borne attack

Initially, responsibility lay with 15 (S) Div, but was to pass as soon as practicable to Commander 100 AA Bde who thus became responsible for all forms of local defence of the bridge and ferry sites. The time for this responsibility to pass was fixed by 15 (S) Div as first light on D Day. Three infantry companies of 52 (L) Div were initially allocated to 100 AA Bde for this purpose.

This responsibility included defence against floating mines and similar attacks, in which close co-ordination with the RE organisation was necessary. SP anti-tank guns and CDL tanks were allotted for this purpose and accounted for 50 mines between WESEL and XANTEN, while a further five blew up on boom defences. They were probably laid by low-flying aircraft, as no stocks were captured in the neighbourhood of the river banks.

(c) Smoke

Preparations were made to employ container smoke on the bridge sites from D Day onwards to conceal them from enemy artillery observation, but these screens were not in fact put into operation.

E. 15 (S) DIV PLAN

Extracts from 15 (S) Div Order for Operation TORCHLIGHT are reproduced as Appendix G.

(i) Troops Available

The under-mentioned additional troops were made available to 15 (S) Div. Additional RA and RE resources provided are not shown as these are dealt with fully in Section VII and Section V, paragraph F, respectively:—

Under Command
4 Armd Bde
129 SP Bty, 86 A Tk Regt, RA
5 R BERKS (including R SIGNALS, RAMC and REME elements) (Bank Group).

In Support
2nd County of London Yeomanry (Westminster Dragoons) (W DGNS) less one squadron (Flails)
7th Royal Tank Regiment (7 R Tks) less one squadron (Crocodiles)
East Riding Yeomanry (E RIDING YEO) (LVsT)
11th Royal Tank Regiment (11 R Tks) (LVsT)
One squadron 49th Armoured Personnel Carrier Regiment (49 APC Regt).

(ii) The Divisional Commander's Plan (see Map 5)

(a) The Assault

The plan of Commander 15 (S) Div involved an assault on a front of two brigades. On the Right 44 (L) Inf Bde supported by 11 R Tks (LVsT) was to capture and hold the area SCHUTTWICK–LOH–BISLICH, while on the Left 227 (H) Inf Bde, with E RIDING YEO (LVsT) in support, was to capture and hold the area HAFFEN–MEHR. The two assaulting brigades were then to clear the areas between their objectives, within their own boundaries. 44 (L) Bde was also responsible for effecting junction with 6 Brit Airborne Div and 17 US Airborne Div.

(b) 46 (H) Inf Bde, with 44th Royal Tank Regiment (44 R Tks) of 4 Armd Bde in support was to be in reserve for the assault. The brigade was to move across the RHINE in the LVT and Storm Boat ferries already established and assemble on the far side. It was then to seize and hold the woods and high ground South East of HALDERN

in conjunction with 44 R Tks. (44 R Tks was equipped throughout with DD tanks, which were to be swum across at first light). After crossing, 44 R Tks was also to be ready to support either 227 (H) Bde or 44 (L) Bde if required.

(c) A mobile striking force under command of HQ 4 Armd Bde was given high priority on class 50/60 rafts. It was expected that the force would be available for action on the far bank by 1700 hours D+1 and it was intended to use it to seize the area WISSMANN-bridge at GERVERSHOF. It was to consist of :—

> one armoured regiment
> one SP regiment, RA
> one SP anti-tank battery, RA
> one assault squadron, RE
> one squadron armoured personnel carriers
> one motor battalion.

The motor battalion was to be carried on the tanks of the armoured regiment, while an additional infantry battalion was to be provided from 44 (L) Inf Bde and picked up by the APC squadron on the far side of the river.

(d) *Subsequent Developments*

It was foreseen that 44 (L) Inf Bde would come into divisional reserve when airborne troops were firmly on their objectives and had cleared Westwards up to the divisional boundary. This brigade would then be available to seize the WISSMANN-GERVERSHOF area in conjunction with the mobile striking force, or should opposition be very light it was to be prepared to seize this area on the night D/D+1 without awaiting the latter's arrival.

If 46 (H) Bde succeeded in taking HALDERN woods, and effecting the junction with 30 Corps, 227 (H) Bde would be available to relieve 6 Brit Airborne Div ; 46 (H) Bde, together with 4 Armd Bde, would then come into divisional reserve.

(e) *Artillery Support*

Artillery support was provided in the general framework of 12 Corps Fire Plan (see Section VII). In addition from H-60 minutes to H Hour all available LAA, MMG and 4.2" mortars were to fire concentrations on known enemy localities under a centralised divisional plan. (This was a standard drill known as "PEPPERPOT".)

LAA Tracer was to be employed as a navigational aid to mark main axes of LVT crossings during the assault.

(f) The RE plan is dealt with in detail in paragraph F below.

(g) The allotment of air support tentacles is shown in Diagram 2 (Section VIII).

(h) The layout of assembly areas and approaches to the RHINE and the various ferries and bridges to be established are shown on Map 6.

F. THE RE PLAN

The RE Order of Battle and grouping for the assault are shown in detail in Appendix A3.

(i) Troops available

The task of establishing and maintaining routes across the river in the initial stages of the operation was delegated to 15 (S) Div, for which purpose the following troops were placed *under command* in addition to the divisional engineers :—

11 Army Group Royal Engineers (11 AGRE)
Six HQ RE (CsRE Div, Corps, Army or GHQ Troops Engineers)
Twenty three field companies RE (or equivalent)
One bridge company RCASC
Detachments of RASC (transport) and Royal Pioneer Corps (labour).

In support

RN parties
One HQ assault regiment RE
Three assault squadrons RE.

It was planned that as the operation developed 15 (S) Div rear boundary would be moved forward over the RHINE, and that 11 AGRE and the majority of these units would then revert to Corps control. This was timed to occur when HQ 15 (S) Div itself crossed the river.

(ii) The Task

11 AGRE was ordered

(a) To establish and maintain the following ferries and bridges (see Map 6) :—

> Two LVT Ferries (sites only)
> Two Stormboat Ferries
> Four class 9 raft Ferries
> Two class 50/60 raft Ferries
> One DUKW Ferry (site only)
> One class 9 FBE Bridge
> One class 12 Bailey Pontoon Bridge
> One class 40 Bailey Pontoon Bridge (tactical).

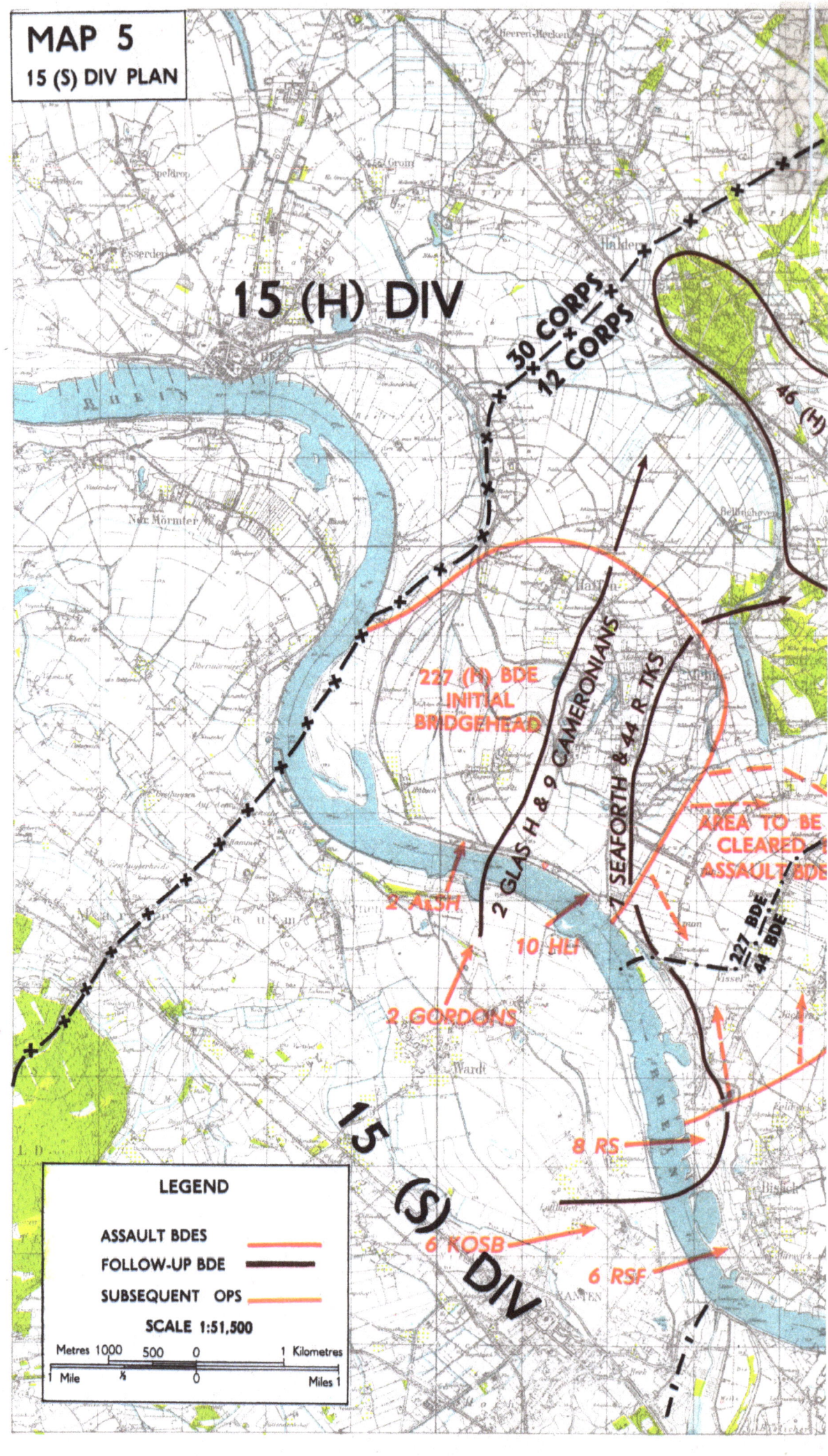

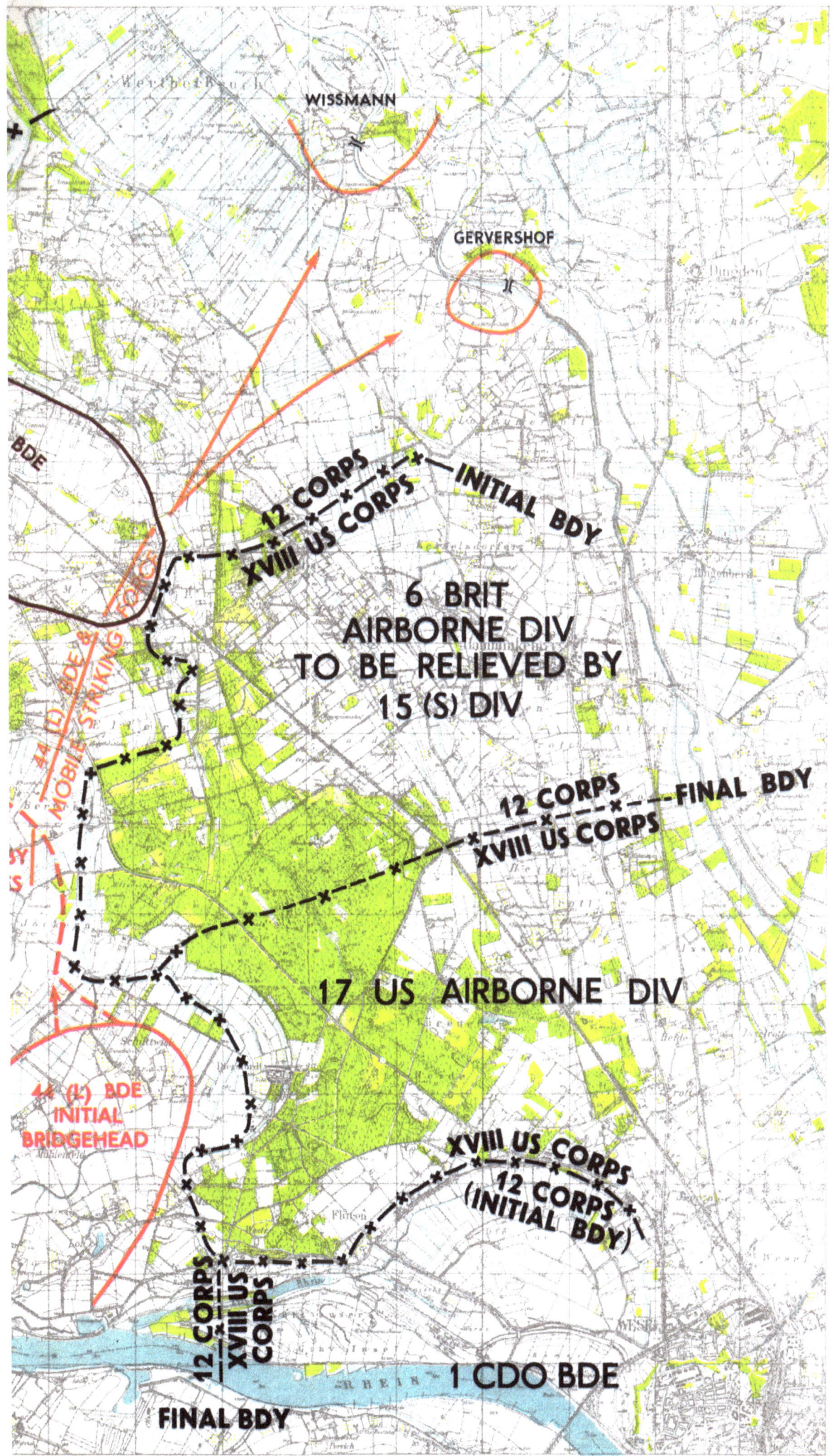

(b) To develop a class 40 route on the general line of the Corps main axis (see Map 3).

(c) To establish two routes forward from the class 9 and class 12 bridges up to the line of railway WESEL–HALDERN within the divisional boundaries, i.e. the corps boundaries (see Map 3).

(d) To establish one class 9 lateral on the far side of the river and one class 40 lateral on main road WESEL–HALDERN, within the divisional boundaries.

(e) To be prepared to start construction of a class 40 all weather Bailey Pontoon bridge (high level) in the neighbourhood of XANTEN.

(iii) **Protection of Crossings**

Elaborate precautions against floating debris, mines and sabotage swimmers were undertaken and a system of booms both up and down stream was required. Constant watch against vessels adrift or out of control was necessary to prevent damage to bridges under construction or completed.

The CAGRE was responsible for all works on the river, while, as has already been stated, Commander 100 AA Bde undertook the military defence of these works.

(iv) **Allotment of Troops**

The initial allotment of RE troops to the various tasks was as under:—

1. Right assault crossing (44 (H) Inf Bde) — one CRE (15 (Kent) GHQ Tps) five field companies
2. Left assault crossing (227 (L) Inf Bde) — one CRE (4 GHQ Tps) five field companies
3. Class 9 FBE bridge — One CRE (8 Corps Tps) three field companies
4. Class 12 Bailey Pontoon bridge — one CRE (12 Corps Tps) four field companies } RN heavy tug parties
5. Class 40 Bailey Pontoon bridge }
6. DUKW ferry landings } — one CRE (7 Army Tps) three field companies }
7. Class 50/60 raft ferries — one CRE three assault squadrons } 42 Assault Regiment RE
8. Booms — one field company, RN boom party
9. Route Maintenance near side of RHINE — one CRE (52 (L) Div) one field company two field squadrons
10. Engineer work forward of RHINE — one CRE (15 (S) Div) three field companies (includes one field company each from serials 1 and 2 on completion of assault task)
11. Reserve — one field company
12. Stores (under CE 12 Corps) — two field park companies

CRE 7 GHQ Tps Engineers acted as deputy to the CAGRE.

(v) **Areas of Responsibility**

(a) Before the start of the operation 52 (L) Div RE, under 11 AGRE, with five additional companies in support was responsible for engineer preparatory work on the near side of the river. This included route development, provision of a forward dump of track material and the considerable engineer assistance to other arms required at this stage. Plans were also made by CsRE Assault Crossings to breach the bunds to allow passage of LVsT, but the actual work could not be undertaken until shortly before H Hour in order to preserve surprise.

(b) Once established across the river, the area under control of 11 AGRE divided itself into three parts:—

1. East of the river, forward of, inclusive, the class 9 lateral, where CRE 15 (S) Div assumed responsibility.
2. The river area including the immediate approaches and exits, where several CsRE, each responsible for a particular crossing or crossings, were operating under 11 AGRE.
3. West of the river, where responsibility was delegated by Commander 11 AGRE to CRE 52 (L) Div.

(c) 11 AGRE's rear boundary was fixed approximately 6,000 yards from the West bank, and behind this CE 12 Corps assumed responsibility for engineer work—chiefly road and bridge maintenance. Forward airfield construction was under control of CE Second Army, a forward airfield with 3,600 foot pierced steel plank runway having been completed at GOCH on 20 March 1945.

(d) The great number of RE units required for the assault had strained Second Army's resources to breaking point, and in order to provide engineers for the maintenance of routes in the Army area, it was necessary to call upon outside assistance. Between the end of February and 14 March therefore, seven battalions of US Combat Engineers took over maintenance of the MAAS bridges and a large mileage of main road on both sides of the river in Second Army's area, while considerable aid was provided by the DUTCH and BELGIAN civil authorities. The problem of road maintenance was a very real one, owing to the serious damage caused to the road system by the exceptionally severe winter, and the vast amount of traffic.

(vi) **Stores Organisation**

The main 12 Corps engineer dump, containing upwards of 5,000 tons of engineer stores on wheels, was established in the KEVELAER area, choice of site being largely dictated by the need for good road access (Map 4). This dump was stocked with all the bridging equipment and other RE stores estimated to be required for the assault in 12 Corps sector. It was fed from Second Army dump near GOCH, where nearly 25,000 tons of material had been placed during the period 4 to 23 March. Most of this vast quantity was carried by road, but the dump at GOCH was rail-served from 21 March.

Prior to H Hour only assault equipment, including class 9 rafts and stormboats, was dumped forward in carefully concealed "hides" (see Map 6). Class 50/60 rafts were held back on wheels or sledges owing to the impossibility of concealing them. A US camouflage unit assisted in forming the hides but it was not possible to do more than conceal the nature of the stores and the existence of dumps would have been apparent from the air.

Other bridging equipment was called forward when required by Commander 11 AGRE, into special Bridge Vehicle Marshalling Areas, and as the situation permitted fed forward to the bridge or ferry sites. Bridging vehicles were as far as possible allotted special routes.

(vii) **Communications**

As HQ AGRE, Army and GHQ Troops Engineers were not equipped with wireless, all necessary nets had to be found from outside resources of the Royal Corps of Signals, who also provided line communications to the various ferry and bridge sites.

(viii) **Forecast Timings of Readiness of Crossings**

It was planned to have the crossings in operation at times shown in column 3 of the table below. Actual times are shown in column 4 for comparison.

1 Crossing	2 Bridge length	3 Estimated time of readiness	4 Actual time of readiness	5 Remarks
Class 9 rafts	—	H+5 hours	44 Bde sector H+4¼ hours 227 Bde sector H+10¼ hours	Times in column 4 are for establishment of ferry service (minimum two rafts). Individual loads were carried over earlier
Class 50/60 rafts	—	H+5 hours	H+16½ hours	Start of construction delayed by shelling of sites
DUKW ferry	—	H+12 hours	H+13 hours	
Class 9 FBE	1320 feet	H+29 hours	H+21 hours	Damaged and put out of action for 13 hours, three hours after opening
Class 12 Bailey Pontoon	1940 feet	H+53 hours	H+55 hours	Two sections of, 1,580 and 360 feet respectively
Class 40 Bailey Pontoon (Tactical)	1102 feet	H+70 hours	H+38½ hours	
Class 40 Bailey Pontoon (high level all weather)	2085 feet	D+8 days	D+10 days	

(ix) **Stormboat Ferries**

48 Stormboats per assault brigade were to be employed as ferries for men of the reserve battalions of the assaulting brigades and the follow-up brigade. This allowed 100% spares, 24 boats only being in operation at each ferry site at any one time. They were not for use in an assault role. A few spare boats were also allotted for rescue service and similar tasks.

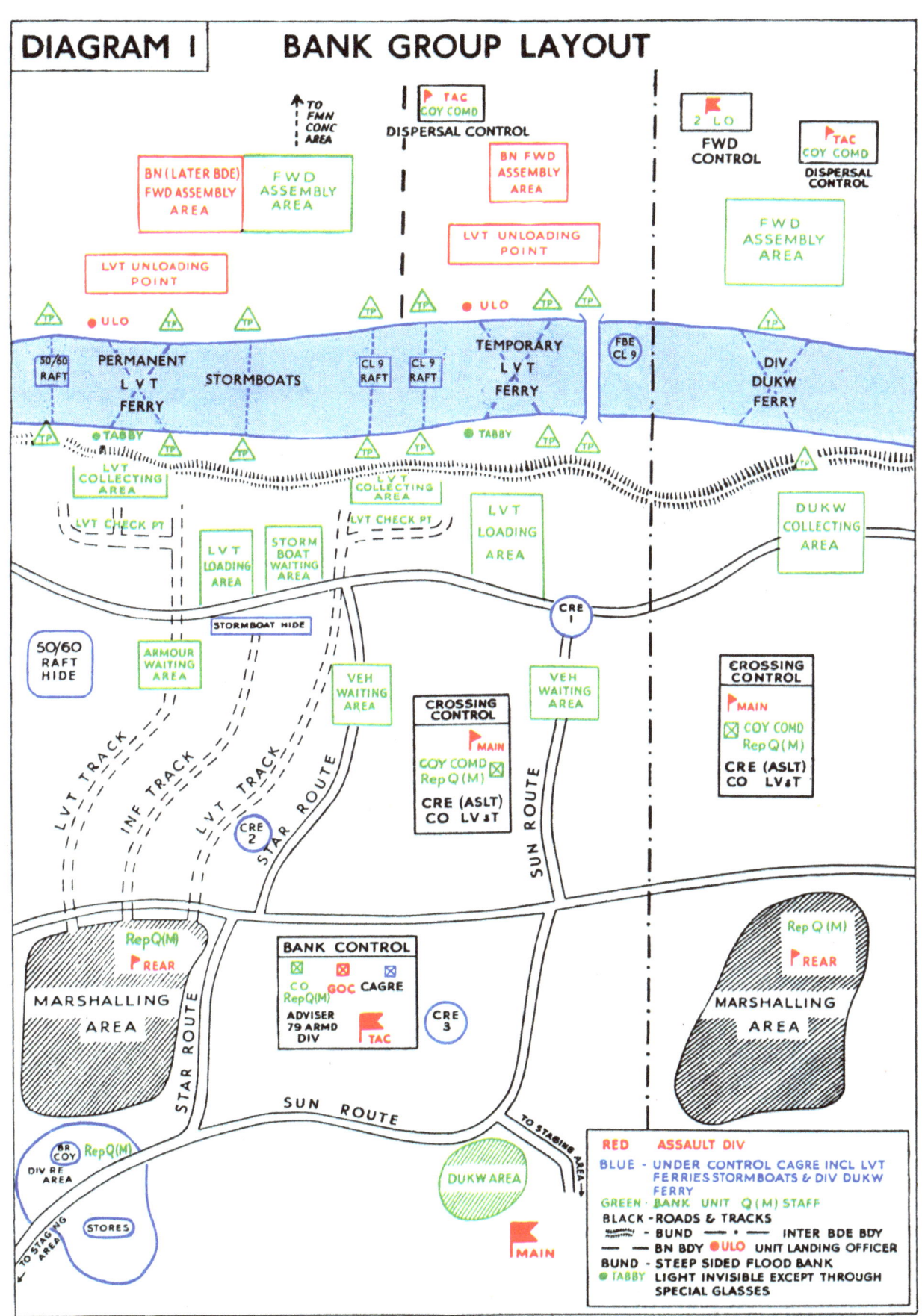

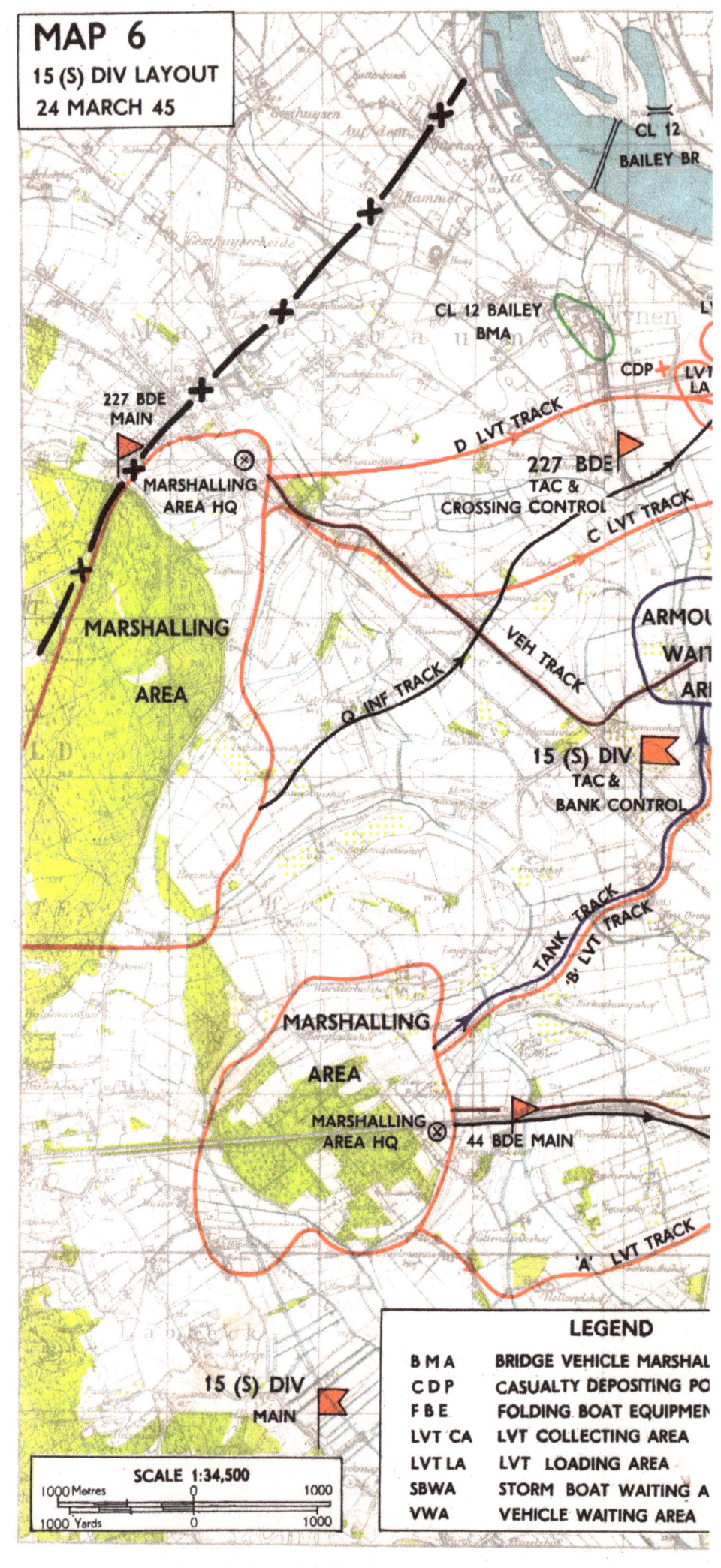

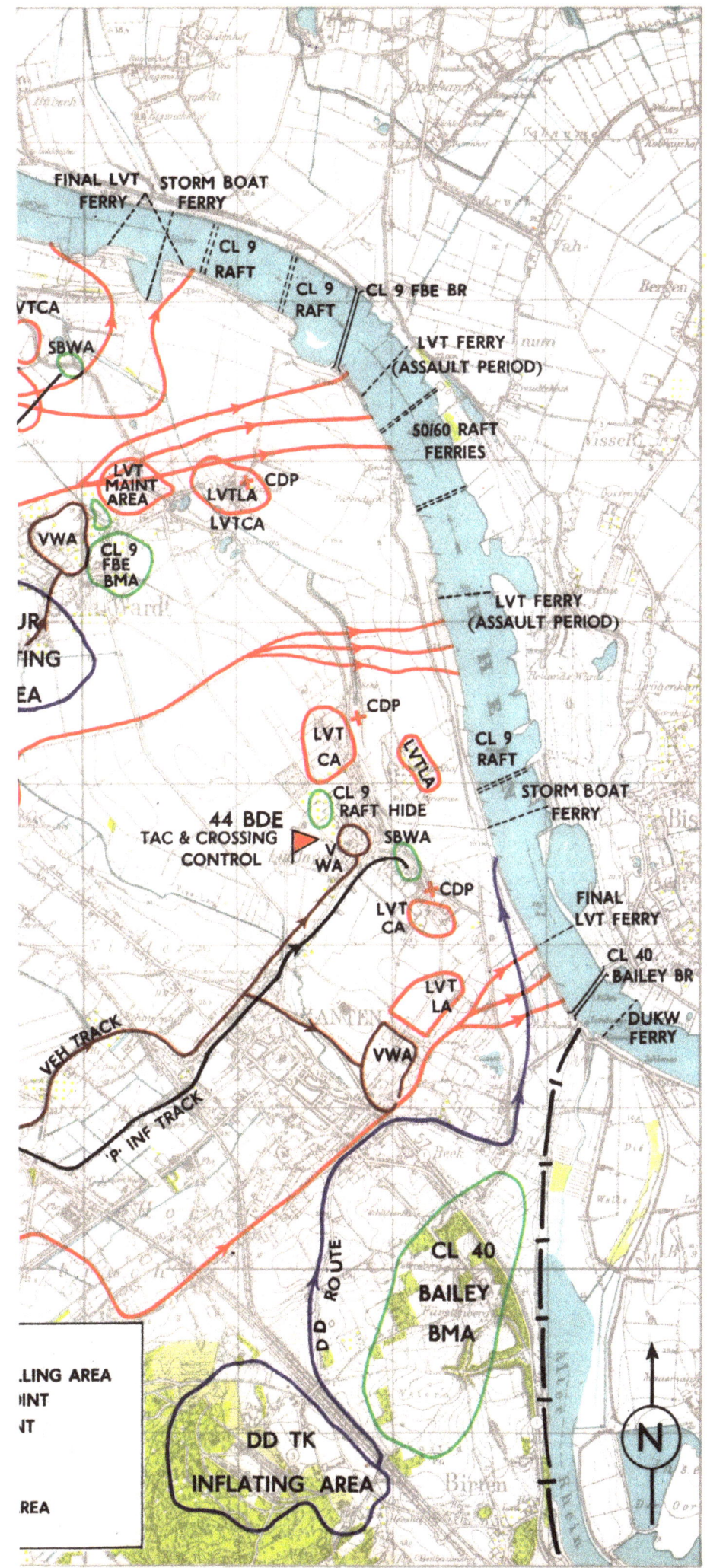

G. TRAFFIC CONTROL

(i) Concentration and Assembly

HQ 12 Corps in conjunction with HQ Second Army controlled all movement from rear concentration areas into assembly areas. Assaulting formations were moved direct by night into their marshalling areas (Map 4), while build-up formations were to be moved forward into staging areas East of the MAAS whence they could be called forward to the RHINE crossings as the situation permitted or as they were required. The whole concentration plan required most careful co-ordination since the capacity of the available bridges over the MAAS, over which the whole administrative traffic had also to pass, was strictly limited. In Second Army area there were only three one-way and one two-way class 40 bridges, though limited running rights were granted over the class 70 bridges at GRAVE and VENLO in First Canadian and Ninth US Army areas respectively; yet between 17 and 24 March 1945, operational moves alone totalled 32,022 wheeled vehicles, 662 tanks and 4,049 transporters.

(ii) Control of movement over the River

In the initial stages, all control of movement over the river was delegated to the assaulting formation. For this purpose, a special Bank Group organisation was set up, and placed under command of 15 (S) Div. It was intended that this organisation should revert to control of HQ 12 Corps as the battle moved forward, but not until bridges over the RHINE had been established. The special organisation would then be replaced by normal working. This actually occurred on D+4.

(iii) Bank Group

The special bank group organisation consisted basically of an infantry battalion or equivalent, with additional signals communications and a special movement control staff provided from Q (Movements) at Corps HQ. Its function was to ensure that crossings were made in accordance with the priorities laid down and to prevent any undue congestion near the river or in the neighbourhood of ferries and bridges.

The layout is illustrated in Diagram 1 (*facing page* 17).

In this organisation, Crossing Control HQ was responsible for calling forward serials in accordance with priorities given by Bank Control HQ, which was in close touch with the headquarters of the assaulting division concerning such priorities. Situation reports were forwarded from Crossing Control HQ to Bank Control HQ every 10 to 15 minutes. Bank Control HQ, in addition, kept a complete record of all material crossing the river.

In the Marshalling Areas all vehicles except tanks were parked in their serial priorities waiting to be called forward through Vehicle Waiting Areas. These acted as a cushion and could hold up to six serials at one time. Thence, the vehicles were directed as required to one of the six Traffic Control Points on the banks of the river which were responsible for loading the vehicles on to craft or ferry. Tanks and SP guns were called forward from concentration areas either direct to traffic control points or through a special Armour Waiting Area (see Map 6), and were embarked on class 50/60 ferries, until the class 40 bridge opened.

On the far bank of the river a Forward Control HQ was established to direct serials to Forward Assembly areas, whence they passed to their formations as required.

Intercommunications throughout the Bank Control Group was provided by wireless, and on the near bank by an elaborate network of buried cable. By this system the whereabouts of any serials could be ascertained at any time and priorities of crossing adjusted up to the last moment.

(iv) Priorities

In the initial stages, HQ 15 (S) Div had complete control of priorities, and by means of the Bank Group organisation, was able to keep itself informed of the progress of all vehicles from the Marshalling Areas across the river. From the evening of D Day, land tails of the airborne corps, including 3rd Tank Battalion Scots Guards (3 Tk SG) in support of 6 Brit Airborne Div, were to be phased over the river in accordance with priorities laid down by HQ XVIII US Corps (Airborne). This involved nearly 5,000 vehicles of all types, of which 1,300 were to cross by ferries, and the remainder when bridges were open.

SECTION VI

PLANS OF OTHER FORMATIONS
(see Map 3)

A. XVIII US CORPS (AIRBORNE) (OPERATION VARSITY)

(i) The intention of XVIII US Corps (Airborne) was as follows :—

To disrupt the hostile defence of the RHINE North of WESEL by seizure of key terrain by airborne attack in order to rapidly deepen bridgehead, facilitate crossing by Second British Army and link-up with Ninth US Army : then be prepared for further offensive action Eastward on Second British Army orders.

(ii) XVIII US Corps (Airborne) comprised 17 US Airborne Div and 6 Brit Airborne Div.

Both divisions were to drop during daylight D Day beginning at P Hour (1000 hours).

(a) *6 Brit Airborne Div*—was then to seize, clear and secure the divisional area, with priority to the high ground in the general area of the West end of the DIERSFORDTER WALD, the town of HAMMINKELN and the two bridges over the ISSEL East of it.

(b) *17 US Airborne Div*—was to seize, clear and secure the divisional area with priority to the high ground East of DIERSFORDT and the bridges over the ISSEL North East of WESEL.

B. NINTH US ARMY (OPERATION FLASHPOINT)

XVI US Corps of Ninth US Army, operating on the Right of 12 Corps, was to force a crossing on a two division front, 79 US Div on the Right and 30 US Div on the Left. The most Northerly Regimental Combat Team of 30 US Div was to cross immediately South of BUEDERICH.

H Hours for these operations were :—

    30 US Div :   D Day :   0200 hours
    79 US Div :   D Day :   0300 hours.

It was anticipated that XVI US Corps would reach the line of the road DINSLAKEN-WESEL by first light D Day.

C. 30 BRITISH CORPS (OPERATION TURNSCREW)

30 Brit Corps, operating on the Left of 12 Corps, was to assault on a one division front on both sides of REES and North of HONNEPEL.

HQ 30 Brit Corps, estimated that they would be in possession of HALDERN by 0900 hours D Day and of REES three hours later. It was then intended to expand this bridgehead, as soon as build-up permitted, to the general line REES-HALDERN-ISSELBURG-DORNICK preparatory to breaking out on the axes ISSELBURG-BOCHOLT-WINTERSWIJK and ANHOLT-AALTEN-GROENLO.

H Hour for Operation TURNSCREW was 2100 hours D—1.

SECTION VII

THE 12 CORPS FIRE PLAN

A. ARTILLERY RESOURCES AND GROUPING

A very great weight of artillery was made available to 12 Corps and was to be used in support of Operations WIDGEON, TORCHLIGHT and VARSITY. All artillery was under command of the CCRA, 12 Corps, and grouped under CsRA and CsAGRA as shown in Appendix A2. During the planning stage, some difficulty was experienced due to the great distance separating the various artillery formations from HQ 12 Corps, one formation being as far distant as BRUSSELS, while others had not been re-deployed since the conclusion of the operations in the REICHSWALD area, at which time they had been under command of First Canadian Army.

The total number of guns by types is shown in Table 1 (*page 25*).

B. DEPLOYMENT

An extremely forward deployment in the flood plain of the RHINE was adopted, in order to obtain maximum range on the far side of the river without the necessity of moving the guns, with consequent loss of fire power, during the initial stages. Guns could not in any case cross the RHINE during the early stages, owing to the limited ferrying resources likely to be available, and certainly could not have been supplied with sufficient ammunition on the far bank. The deployment areas are shown on Map 4.

This forward deployment and the dumping of the large quantity of ammunition required, presented serious problems of concealment, since some positions were in full view from enemy ground observation on the DIERSFORDTER WALD high ground. Some of the steps taken to overcome this difficulty are discussed in Section X.

Figures of ammunition expenditure are given in Table 2 (*page 26*). They give an indication of the dumping problem involved, while the concentration of the great number of guns presented very serious problems of movement, which have already been mentioned under Traffic Control in Section V paragraph G. Guns had to be moved up early in the planning stages, in order to relieve pressure on the MAAS crossings, but owing to the concealment problem, it was frequently necessary for them to move into temporary staging areas before final deployment.

4 RHA, which was to be the first regiment to cross the RHINE, was deployed as near as possible to the Armour Waiting Area. The guns would thus be able to continue firing until the last possible moment before being called forward to the ferries.

C. THE TIMED PROGRAMME

The programme and allotment of artillery for the period up to P Hour are shown in the following table :—

12 CORPS

Operation PLUNDER

Allotment of Artillery

Day	Time	Event	Resources employed	Remarks
D—1	1800—2000 hours	Counter battery bombardment (code name BLOTTER)	Eleven medium regiments Two heavy regiments One super-heavy regiment One HAA regiment Three US field artillery battalions (155 mm)	Programme arranged by Commander 9 AGRA to cover all located hostile batteries. To start only on orders CCRA 12 Corps.
D—1 D	2000—0100 hours	Counter battery bombardment (continued) (code name BLOTTER)	One medium regiment Four heavy batteries (155 mm) One super-heavy battery (8") One HAA regiment Three US field artillery battalions (155 mm)	Programme arranged by Commander 9 AGRA, on most likely positions. To start only on orders CCRA 12 Corps

Thereafter, programme continued until 0400 hours by heavy batteries only.

Operation WIDGEON
(Assault by 1 Cdo Bde)
H Hour 2200 hours D—1

Day	Time	Event	Resources employed	Remarks
D—1	2030—2130 hours	Softening bombardment	Ten medium regiments Four heavy batteries (7.2″) One super-heavy battery (240 mm)	Programme arranged by CRA 7 Armd Div.
D—1	2130—2230 hours	Initial covering fire (barrage and concentrations)	Seven field regiments	From 2230—2245 hours 200 heavy bombers were to attack WESEL. If for any reason this bombing could not take place, one Heavy Artillery Group of Ninth US Army was at call for bombardment of the same targets.
D—1 D	2230—0800 hours	Subsequent covering fire at call	Two field regiments One mountain regiment Two medium regiments One heavy battery (7.2″)	

Note: Thereafter, Operation WIDGEON had priority call on all regiments of 7 Armd Div RA Group, and on one medium regiment of 9 AGRA irrespective of the tasks allotted to any of these regiments in the VARSITY support programme.

OPERATION TORCHLIGHT
(Assault by 15 (S) Div)
H Hour 0200 hours D Day

Day	Time	Event	Resources employed	Remarks
D—1 D	2330—0030 hours	Softening bombardment	Ten medium regiments Four heavy batteries (7.2″) One super-heavy battery (240 mm)	Programme arranged by CRA 15 (S) Div.
D	0100—0530 hours	Covering fire	Twelve field regiments Nine medium regiments Three heavy batteries (7.2″) One super-heavy battery (240 mm) Three HAA batteries One rockets-projector battery	Figures include three field regiments at priority call for Corps smoke screens if required and one medium regiment at call of 9 AGRA for CB/Arty R.
D	0530—0730 hours	Pre-arranged concentrations at call		

Note: Thereafter, Operation TORCHLIGHT had priority call on all regiments of 15 (S) Div RA Group and on two medium regiments of 3 AGRA, irrespective of the tasks allotted to any of these regiments in the VARSITY support programme.

Operation VARSITY
(Airborne landings by XVIII US Corps (Airborne))
P Hour 1000 hours D Day

Day	Time	Event	Resources employed	Remarks
D	0820—0920 hours	Bombardment of localities (code name CLIMAX)	Nine field regiments Eleven medium regiments One heavy regiment Two heavy batteries (7.2″) Two heavy batteries (155 mm) One super-heavy battery (240 mm) One HAA regiment Three US field artillery battalions (155 mm)	Programme arranged by CCRA 12 Corps. Targets selected by CsRA 6 Brit and 17 US Airborne Divs. VT fuses to avoid cratering on LZs. Includes three field regiments at priority call for Corps smoke screens. Includes one medium and one HAA regiment, two heavy batteries at call for CB/Arty R.

Day	Time	Event	Resources employed.	Remarks
D	0930—0958 hours	Anti-flak bombardment (code name CARPET)	Eleven field regiments Eleven medium regiments Two heavy regiments One super-heavy regiment One HAA regiment Three US field artillery battalions (155 mm)	Programme arranged by CCRA 12 Corps. Targets from HQ Second Army and from 83 Group RAF. Includes three field regiments at priority call for Corps smoke screens. Includes one medium regiment at call for CB/Arty R.

D. TARGETS

Fire Plan details were overprinted on 1/25,000 maps for issue to supported arms, and the overprints for Operation TORCHLIGHT and WIDGEON are reproduced as Maps 7 and 8.

The selection of targets, particularly counter-battery targets, presented certain problems. Air cover of the enemy area was good, but observation by ground OPs was made difficult by the smoke screen which was maintained almost continuously on the front for the purpose of screening the artillery deployment (see Section X). In consequence, flash spotting was virtually impossible.

E. SMOKE

Corps smoke screens to blind the high ground East of the RHINE were arranged from first light on D Day (see Maps 7 and 8). Three field regiments were at priority call of the CCRA for this purpose, but in the event they were not required.

F. COUNTER-BATTERY AND ARTILLERY RECONNAISSANCE

Commander 9 AGRA, who had been responsible for the timed counter-battery programme, was allotted a proportion of medium, heavy and HAA guns at priority call for counter-battery and artillery reconnaissance purposes from 0100 hours D Day.

G. ARTILLERY REGROUPING AFTER P HOUR

(i) At P Hour, the following RA regrouping was to take place :—

(a) To pass under command of XVIII US Corps (Airborne) (but remaining West of the RHINE) :—
RA 52 (L) Div Group — in direct support of 6 Brit Airborne Div.
RA 53 (W) Div Group — in direct support of 17 US Airborne Div.
8 AGRA Group — in general support.

It should be noted that these arrangements were to last only until it became possible to pass guns across the RHINE. When this occurred a further comprehensive regrouping took place (see paragraph H below).

(b) To remain in support of 12 Corps :—
RA 15 (S) Div Group
RA 7 Armd Div Group
3 AGRA Group

(c) To be at call of either XVIII US Corps (Airborne) or 12 Corps :—
9 AGRA Group

(ii) When 1 Cdo Bde passed to under command of XVIII US Corps (Airborne), command of 1 Mountain Regiment (1 Mtn Regt) RA was also to pass. In the event, this change of command occurred at 1400 hours on D Day. (1 Mtn Regt RA formed part of 52 (L) Div RA but was allotted for the assault to 7 Armd Div RA Group).

(iii) Subsequently, as the situation developed, the Corps plan intended that :—

(a) RA 52 (L) Div and RA 53 (W) Div should revert to under command of their respective divisions, remaining in support XVIII US Corps (Airborne) until required to move in support of their own divisions.

(b) 6 Fd Regt should pass from under command 15 (S) Div to under command XVIII US Corps (Airborne).

H. REGROUPING ON 25 MARCH 1945 (D+1)

In the event, the regrouping at this later stage was extremely complicated, as can be seen from the order issued by RA 12 Corps on 25 March 1945 (D+1), which, inter alia, included the following :—

As soon as they reach the East bank

(a) *6 Fd Regt will pass from under command RA 15 (S) Div to under command 6 Brit Airborne Div.*

(b) *25 Fd Regt will pass from under command 8 AGRA to under command 6 Brit Airborne Div.*

(c) *90 HAA will pass from under operational command 9 AGRA to under command 100 AA Bde for AA role.*

As soon as (a) and (b) are complete, and 692 US Fd Arty Bn has joined 17 US Airborne Div

    (a) 63, 77, 146 Med Regts* will revert to under command 8 AGRA (or earlier if ordered by XVIII US Corps (Airborne)).

    (b) 52 and 53 Div Arty will revert to under command of their respective formations.

* At the time, these regiments were grouped under command of 52 and 53 Div RA (see Appendix A2).

I. SAFETY PRECAUTIONS AND THEIR EFFECT

Stringent safety precautions were adopted by order of Second Army in order to safeguard the aircraft bringing the airborne troops as they passed over the area of the land battle.

The overriding principle is that NO GUN MUST FIRE ALONG OR ACROSS THE ROUTE TAKEN BY ANY AIRCRAFT during the fly-in or fly-out.

The ultimate responsibility for ensuring that this instruction by RA 12 Corps was obeyed, lay with Gun Position Officers (GPOs). They were to stop the fire of their guns if they considered that any aircraft was flying into their line of fire, and a look-out was to be posted on every troop position.

No anti-aircraft gun was allowed to fire other than in a ground role between P—1 and P+4 hours.

The anti-flak bombardment (CARPET) was timed to finish just before the leading aircraft passed over the general line of the gun areas, but GPOs were to be prepared to stop it earlier if necessary. Once they had been stopped, all guns were to remain silent until CCRA 12 Corps authorised them to start shooting again.

As an additional precaution an observer on the CCRA's net was stationed ten miles behind the gun areas to give advance warning of the arrival of the aircraft, and another observer on the same net was posted in an observation tower in XANTEN woods. In practice, the leading aircraft arrived eight minutes early, and the latter observer gave the order "STOP" to all the Corps artillery.

A "NO SHOOTING" line was laid down between 12 Corps and XVIII US Corps (Airborne) to be observed from the time that the airborne troops had landed. Shooting over this line by 12 Corps guns was permitted only on call from the formation concerned or on observed and recognised hostile targets within 1000 yards of the observer.

The ban on firing while aircraft were overhead which was imposed by Second Army, meant that:—

(i) There could be no fire support at the time of landing of the airborne troops, nor subsequent response to calls for fire as long as the fly-in and fly-out lasted. (The North fly-in route was expected to be clear by P+70 minutes and the South by P+210 minutes).

(ii) The anti-flak bombardment was only effective for the leading waves of aircraft, and thereafter the enemy could shoot undisturbed: and, in the event, this bombardment had to be stopped before it had been completed, owing to aircraft arriving early.

In practice there was some relaxation of these precautions after about 1½ hours, by which time the stream of aircraft had thinned out and it was possible to see when the line of fire was clear from individual gun positions.

J. COMMUNICATIONS

(i) **12 Corps**

RA communications, FOOs and OPs were normal except that the special grouping involved the provision of a number of additional LOs at the HQs concerned.

(ii) **XVIII US Corps (Airborne)**

6 Brit Airborne Div and 17 US Airborne Div each had a Forward Observer Unit. These units provided complete wireless communication between FOOs dropped with the airborne troops and the guns of 12 Corps, where they had their own representatives trained to work with the FOOs concerned.

US parties were specially trained to interpret US fire orders to the British gunners.

12 CORPS
NUMBER OF GUNS (BY TYPES) IN FORMATIONS

TABLE 1

Formation	Mtn 3.7"	Fd 25 pdr	Med 4.5"	Med 5.5"	Hy 155 mm	Hy 7.2"	S Hy 8"	S Hy 240 mm	HAA 3.7"	Rocket Bty	Remarks
7 Armd Div	24	48									
15 (S) Div		120								12(a)	(a)—Projectors each of 30 barrels
52 (L) Div		72	16	16					8		
53 (W) Div		72		16					8		
3 AGRA				64	8	8			8		
8 AGRA		24		16	44	8					
9 AGRA				48			2	4	24		
100 AA Bde									48		
TOTALS	24	336	16	160	52	16	2	4	96*	12	

*=48 in AA role, 48 in ground role

TABLE 2

12 CORPS

ARTILLERY AMMUNITION EXPENDITURE

D Day = 24 March 1945

Figures show total expenditure of rounds up to date and hour stated

Period D—3 up to :—	25 pr HE	25 pr Smoke	4.5"	5.5"	155 mm (Brit)	155 mm (US)	7.2"	240 mm	8"	3.7" AA (ground role)	3.7" Mtn
23 March 1800 hours	9,169	132	—	—	—	—	—	—	—	—	—
24 March 0600 hours	87,092	132	3,439	35,543	852	2,165*	2,203	212	34	8,325	1,656
1800 hours	123,819	247	4,556	42,362	1,284	—	2,459	292	60	12,097	4,312
25 March 0600 hours	131,720	247	6,012	45,785	2,064	—	2,475	368	64	13,715	6,224
1800 hours	148,692	816	6,303	49,497	2,501	—	2,817	420	76	13,751	5,832
26 March 0600 hours	159,924	1,238	6,837	52,147	3,041	—	3,157	444	96	15,491	5,832
Total expenditure D—3 to 28 March 1800 hours	222,274	2,787	7,602	69,607	4,335	—	3,964	576	176	16,573	5,832
Allotment for Operation PLUNDER	393,120	105,840	17,280	172,800	7,200	—	7,920	600	280	43,200	—
Balance not fired	170,846	103,053	9,678	103,193	2,865	—	3,956	24	104	26,627	—
% of allotment expended	56%	2.7%	44%	40%	60%	—	50%	96%	62%	38%	—

* further figures for US Formations not available.

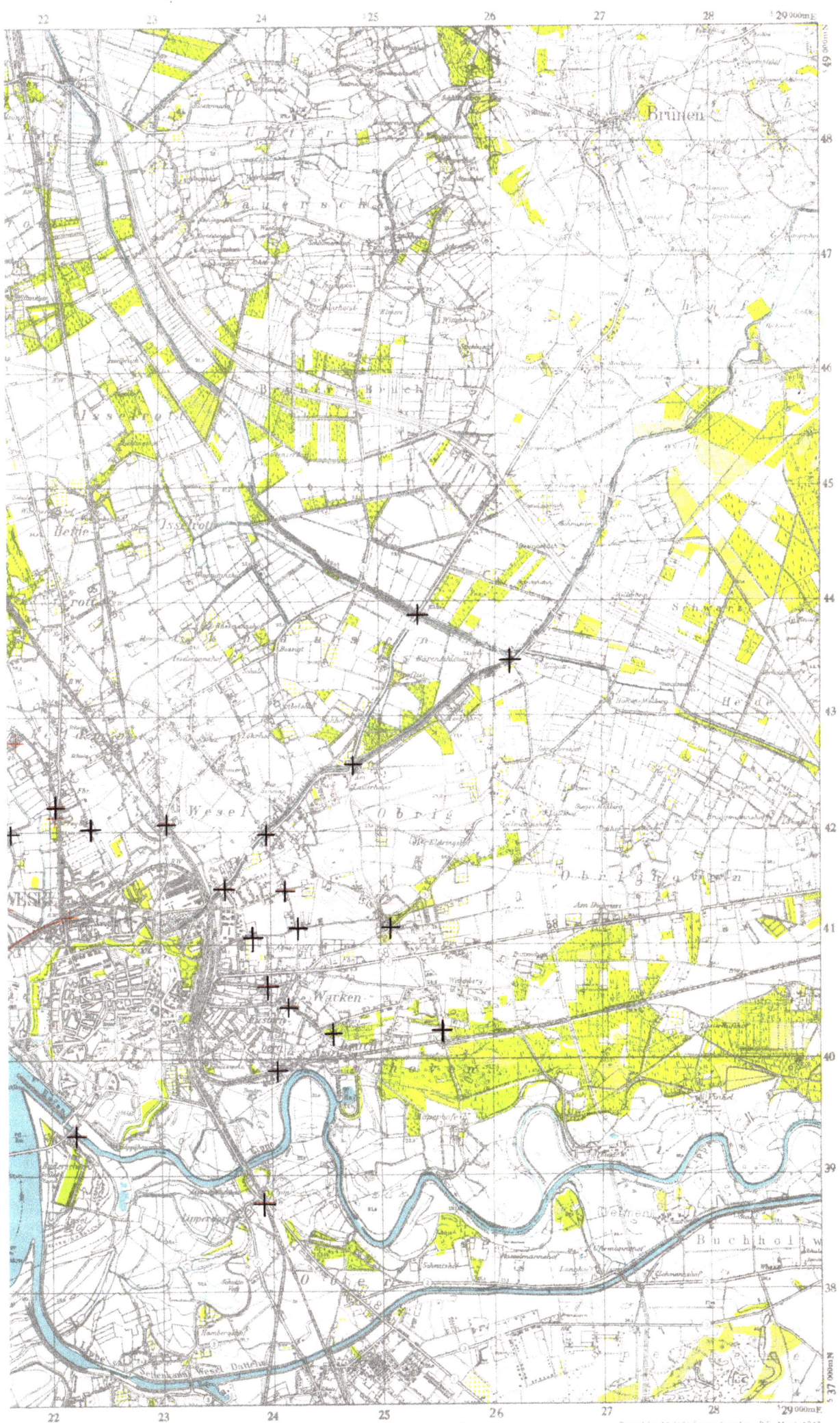

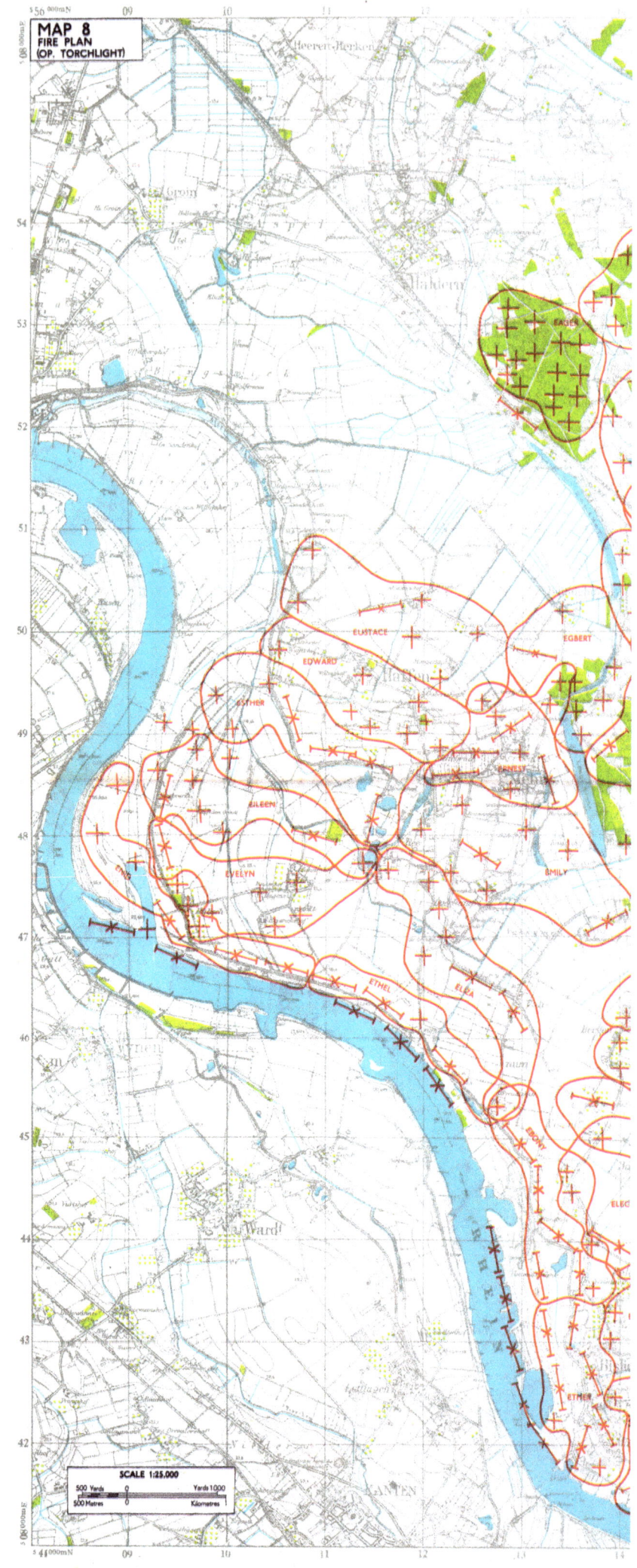

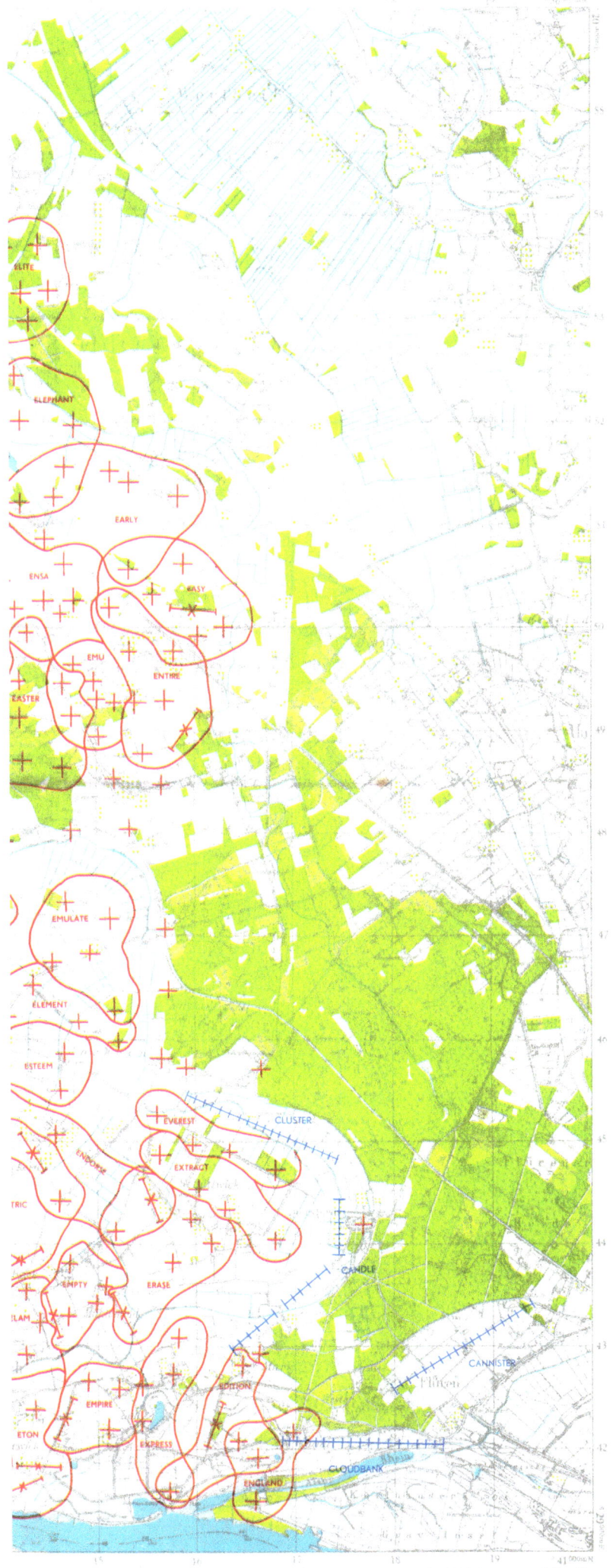

SECTION VIII

THE AIR PLAN

A. INTRODUCTION

Air operations in connection with Operation PLUNDER started on 9 February 1945, and although these operations cannot be said to have been intimately connected with PLUNDER in the early phases their results had an appreciable effect on the actual operation. Thus, the air support for Operation PLUNDER can be divided into five phases :—

Phase I. The interdiction programme which was designed to isolate the RUHR — operations commencing on 9 February 1945 (see Map 9).

Phase II. The interdiction programme specially designed for PLUNDER. These operations commenced on 10 March 1945, with the object of isolating the battlefield North and South of the RUHR, and West of a line ZWOLLE—LINGEN—RHEINE—MUNSTER—HAMM—SOEST—SIEGEN—BONN (see Map 10).

Phase III. A programme of harassing bombing extending over a period of three days, starting on D—3. In general terms the object was to reduce the enemy's will to fight, to hinder the preparation of his defensive system, and to disrupt his communications. The targets were both North and South of the RUHR in the rear areas (see Map 11).

Phase IV. The main air plan for Operation PLUNDER. This included a pre-arranged programme of major air operations in support of the RHINE crossings as follows :—

    (a) The establishment and maintenance of air superiority over the assault areas and dropping zones/landing zones.

    (b) The neutralisation of Flak.

    (c) The provision of fighter protection for the airborne forces.

    (d) The close support of the assault and airborne forces.

    (e) The prevention of enemy movement into and within the battle areas.

Phase V. The day-to-day support provided from D Day onwards.

B. PRELIMINARY AIR OPERATIONS
(PHASES I, II AND III)

Air operations were designed from the outset to provide the maximum assistance to the actual crossing of the RHINE. As the planning for Operation PLUNDER became more settled and detailed, so then did the air operations become more confined to the actual battlefield area selected for PLUNDER. Preparatory air operations were those included under Phases I, II and III above, and in order to appreciate the way in which the planning proceeded until the formulation of the main air plan for the crossing itself, it will be necessary to study briefly the air operations of these preliminary phases.

Isolation of the RUHR (Phase I)

In January 1945, in conjunction with outline plans that were being formulated by Supreme Headquarters Allied Expeditionary Force (SHAEF) for a possible crossing of the RHINE, SHAEF (Air) produced a plan designed to isolate the RUHR by the attack of eighteen railway bridges on the most important routes from central GERMANY. The attack on these targets was apportioned between the medium bombers on the continent and the strategic bombers in UK, and the targets selected are shown on Map 9. The coordinated attacks of RAF Bomber Command and IXth United States Army Air Force (IX USAAF) were reasonably successful, so that by D Day of the operation, a maximum of four and a minimum of three of the eighteen railway bridges only remained in use.

Interdiction to isolate the battlefield area (Phase II)

As detailed planning for Operation PLUNDER progressed, it was considered necessary to augment the interdiction programme outlined above by a further interdiction plan designed to isolate the area East of the selected river crossings. Thus HQ 2nd Tactical Air Force (HQ 2 TAF), in conjunction with HQ 21 Army Group and HQ Second Army, formulated a plan based on the selection of the minimum number of road and rail communications bottle-necks, necessary to cover all the main axes of approach to the battle area. Aided by good weather, however, the Air Forces were able to deliver a larger number of attacks than were scheduled in this programme, and particularly North of the RUHR an intensity of bombing was maintained that brought movement almost to a standstill. Among the targets outside the programme, the heavy attacks by Bomber Command on the RUHR towns of ESSEN, DORTMUND, BARMEN and WITTEN contributed to the difficulty of the enemy in moving troops

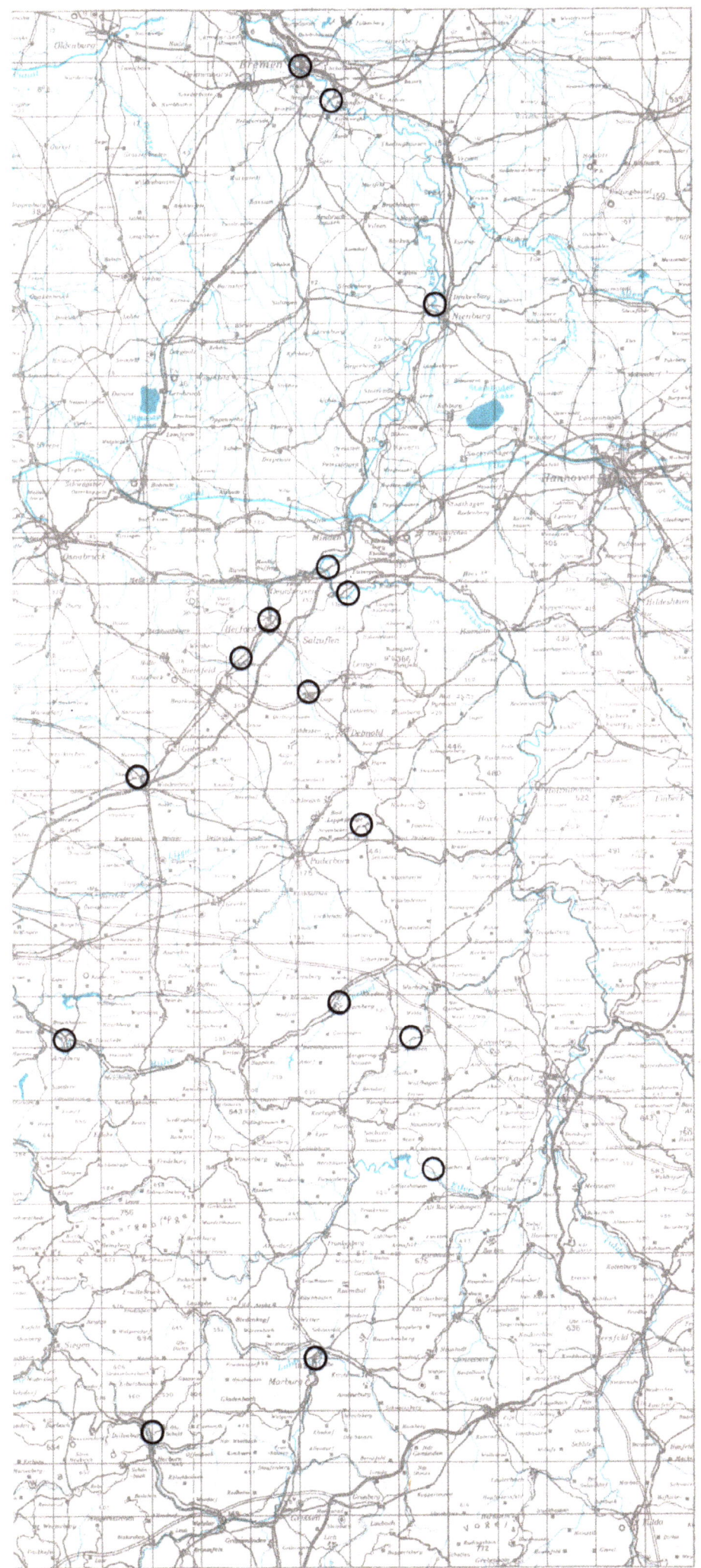

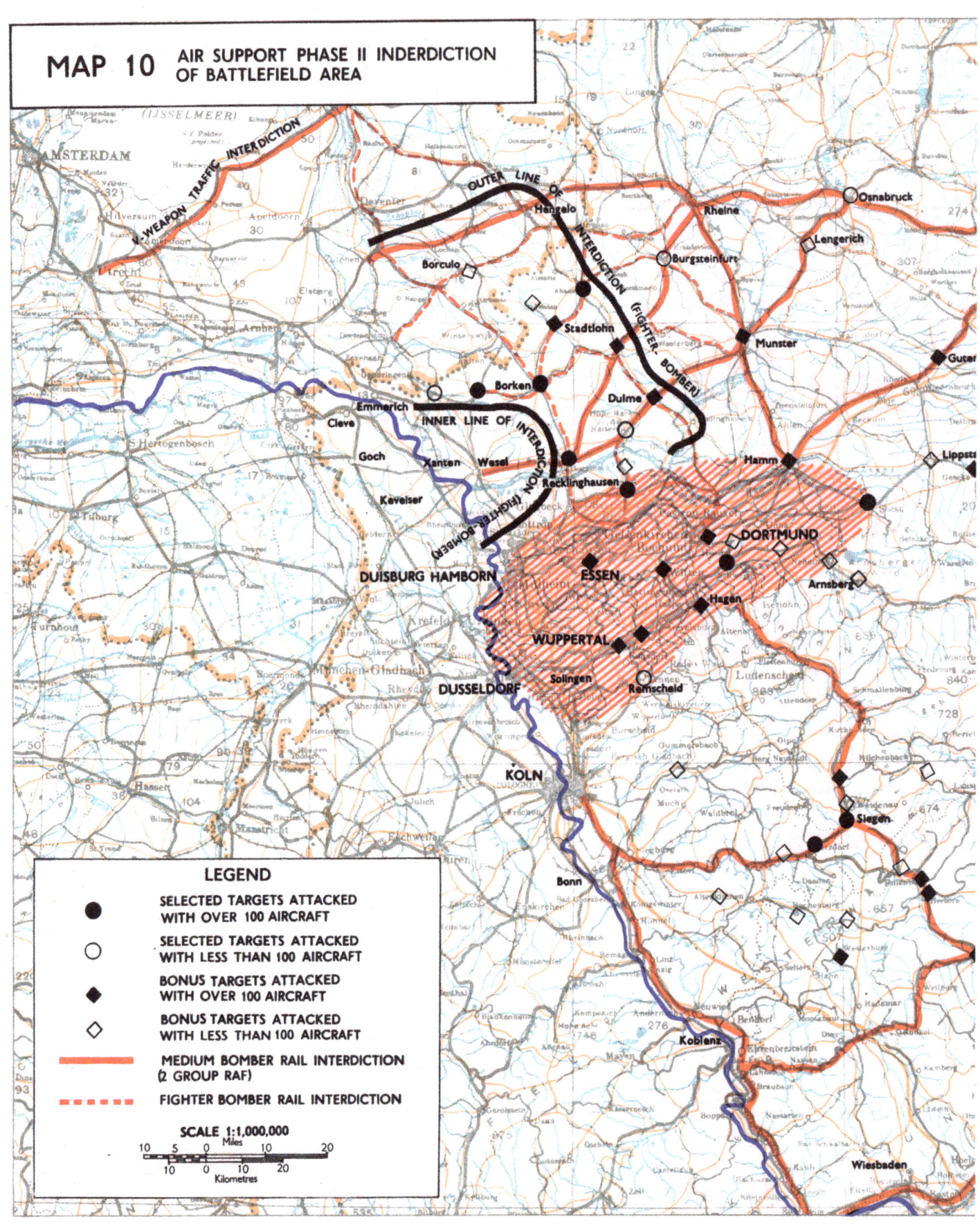

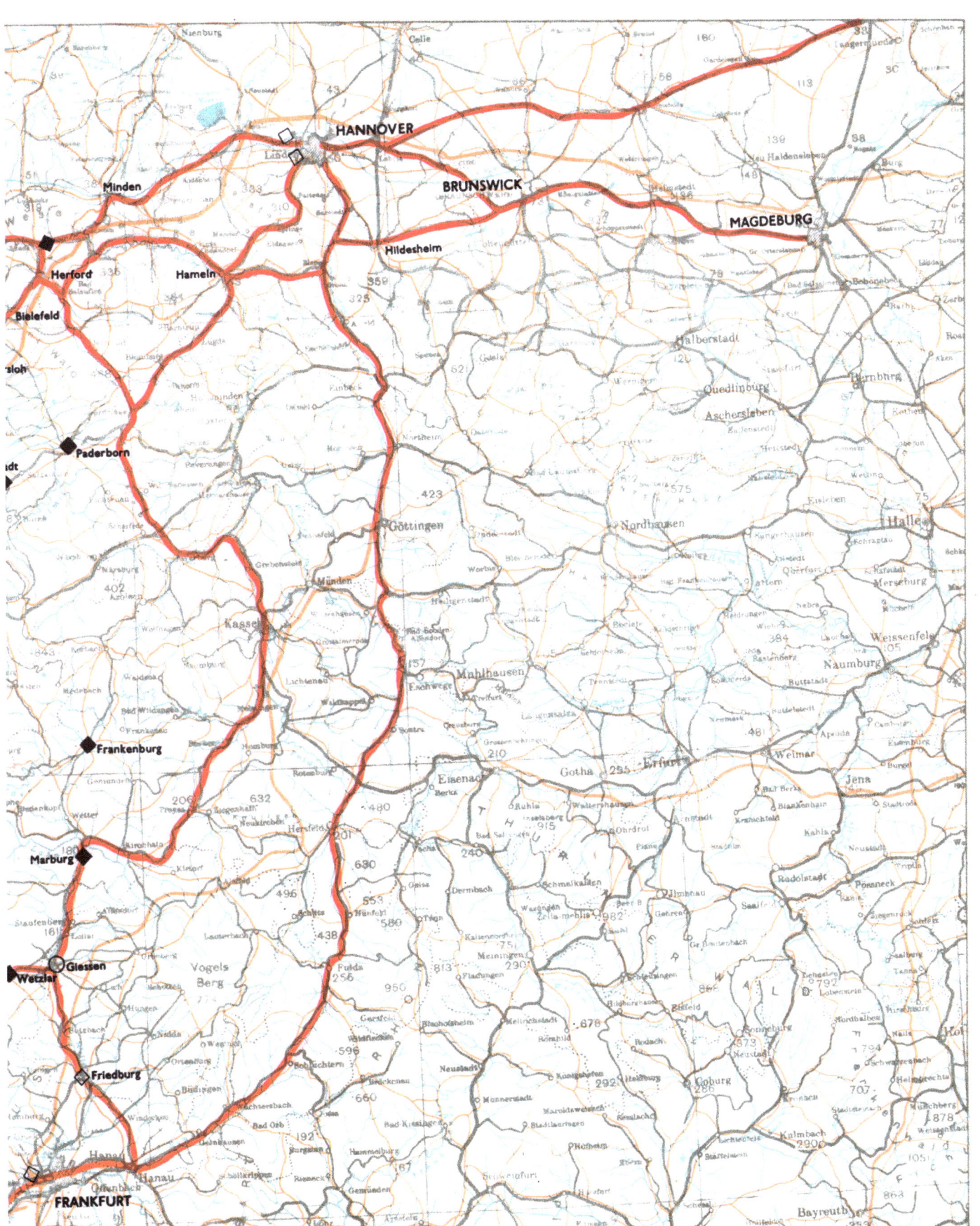

by road through the RUHR area, but never prevented it entirely. Rail movement was brought practically to a standstill in the RUHR area by the accumulation of cuts made by the fighter bomber aircraft of 2 TAF; and to complete the picture, the night Mosquitos of 2 Group RAF were given the task of patrolling the railway system deep into GERMANY. The measure of success of the other Air Forces was proved by the fact that very few moving train targets were found West of OSNABRUCK and SIEGEN, and the only notable night movement seen was in the HANNOVER—MAGDEBURG—STENDAL area. Illustrations of the areas selected for attack by the various Air Forces are shown on Map 10.

Pre-D Day Bombing (Phase III)

By D—7 it was apparent that the overall effect of the interdiction programme was such that it had reduced the enemy's ability to move by road and rail to a very low ebb. It was also apparent at this stage that the enemy was aware of our intentions in broad terms, and had been able to locate the forthcoming offensive as being launched somewhere between DUISBURG and EMMERICH, with the subsequent reduction in the need for security. As a result of these considerations, it was decided by 2 TAF, in consultation with 21 Army Group, to switch the available air effort from interdiction tasks to a programme of harassing bombing within the tactical area. The plan decided upon, therefore, was to commence on D—3 for the attack of a number of tactical targets both North and South of the RUHR with the object of:—

(i) Harassing the enemy in his known billeting areas.

(ii) Delaying the work which was known to be taking place in the key defensive positions.

(iii) Attacking the communication system within the projected battle area.

The programme, as planned finally, involved attacks on twenty targets on the Second Army front and nine on Ninth US Army front. In the event, the latter targets were eventually assigned to VIIIth United States Army Air Force (VIII USAAF) and a proportion of those in the North to RAF Bomber Command. This formidable and unexpected increase to the medium bomber effort was outside the effort as planned and as a result all targets were attacked with great success (see Map 11).

C. THE MAIN AIR PLAN (PHASE IV)

The air plan for Operation PLUNDER was the responsibility of HQ 2 TAF and also included details for Operations VARSITY and FLASHPOINT. Apart from the airlift operation in connection with VARSITY, all air operations came under the control of the AOC-in-C 2 TAF. AOC-in-C 2 TAF had, in turn, delegated to AOC 83 Group RAF the responsibility for coordinating the fighter cover and anti-flak operations of 83 and 84 Groups RAF and of 29th United States Tactical Air Command (29 USTAC) in connection with Operation VARSITY.

Air Forces employed

The following Air Forces were employed in this operation (for organisation of command see Appendix A 4):—

(i) *Royal Air Force*
2 TAF including 29 USTAC (IX USAAF)
Bomber Command
Fighter Command
Coastal Command

(ii) *United States Army Air Force*
VIII USAAF
IX USAAF (less 29 USTAC)

(iii) *Troop-carrying aircraft for Operation VARSITY*
38 and 46 Groups RAF
IXth United States Troop Carrier Command (IX US Tp Carrier Comd)

Air Tasks

The general tasks of the various Air Forces in this phase were as follows:—

(i) Establishment and maintenance of air superiority over the assault areas and dropping zones and landing zones.

(ii) Neutralisation of Flak.

(iii) Fighter protection of the airborne forces while in the air.

(iv) Close support of the assault and airborne forces on the ground.

(v) The prevention of enemy ground movement in and towards the battle area.

Allocation of Tasks

Tasks were allocated to the various Air Forces as follows:—

2 TAF

(a) *83 and 84 Groups RAF and 29 USTAC*

(i) Fighter protection for the assaulting troops of Second Army and Ninth US Army (including the airborne troops on the ground).

(ii) Fighter protection of the airborne forces' aircraft and supply aircraft while East of the River RHINE.

(iii) Anti-flak fighter patrols during the period of the drop.

(iv) Close support for Second Army and Ninth US Army.

(v) Armed reconnaissance.

(b) *2 Group RAF*

Medium bomber attacks against flak positions and communications centres, and night armed reconnaissance.

(c) *85 Group RAF*

Night fighter defence, in particular for the assault forces of Second Army, Ninth US Army and the airborne corps.

RAF Bomber Command

RAF Bomber Command was to attack focal road and rail communications centres and also defence positions at WESEL.

Fighter Command and Coastal Command RAF

Aircraft of these commands were detailed to supply escort to troop-carrying operations of 38 and 46 Groups RAF and to provide Air/Sea Rescue facilities.

VIII USAAF

Aircraft of this command were to carry out the following tasks:—

(i) Bomber attacks on selected enemy airfields.

(ii) Initial supply for airborne force.

(iii) Armed reconnaissance.

(iv) Fighter sweeps over selected enemy airfields.

IX USAAF

IX USAAF fighters were to carry out fighter protection of IX US Tp Carrier Comd up to the RHINE. Medium bombers were to carry out attacks against flak positions and road and rail communications centres.

D. THE PROGRESS OF AIR OPERATIONS DIRECTLY CONCERNED WITH OPERATION PLUNDER UP TO D DAY

(i) Maintenance of Air Superiority

It was feared that there would be a revival in operations by jet aircraft of the German Air Force, and to counteract such a possibility a heavy effort was employed by Allied Air Forces to ensure that the crossing of the RHINE should be unimpeded by enemy air interference. Accordingly, on D—3, and again on D Day immediately prior to the dropping of the airborne troops, VIII USAAF carried out a programme of attacks on selected enemy airfields, involving over 1,400 heavy bombers on each day. In addition, 2 TAF and fighters of VIII USAAF carried out periodic sweeps over the key airfields from first light on D Day until 1400 hours.

The success of these air missions was complete, and enemy air activity remained negligible throughout D Day.

(ii) Heavy Bombers in Close Support

To provide direct assistance to the task allotted to 1 Cdo Bde, RAF Bomber Command was to attack the communication centre and strong point of WESEL on the night of 23/24 March (see Map 12). The Commando crossing was timed for 2200 hours and thus the Bomber Command attack was timed to finish at 2245 hours. A two stage attack took place consisting of twenty-seven aircraft in the first wave, bombing at last light, followed by two hundred heavy bombers during the hours of darkness, bombing on visual markers. No errors occurred and the whole plan was carried through by all concerned with great success, the bombing providing a fine illustration of accuracy and concentration. WESEL was penetrated within an hour or two of the last bomb falling.

(iii) Tactical Interdiction

Other targets directly connected with the bridge-head operations, which were mainly communication centres near the assault area and which for local security reasons had not been engaged earlier, were attacked on D—1 and D Day. The important communication centres and the strong point at DINSLAKEN, South of WESEL, and clearly connected with the early phases of Ninth US Army operations were heavily attacked by IX USAAF on the morning and the afternoon of D—1. BRUNEN and RAESFELD, where reserve elements of the divisions in the line opposite the Second Army crossings were known to be located, were bombed by 2 Group RAF day mediums as turn-round targets on D Day. Similarly, during the night of D—1/D Day, and on several succeeding nights, 2 Group RAF carried out a series of attacks by single Mosquitos under control of Mobile Radar Control Posts on the villages of ISSELBURG and ANHOLT. Further afield, heavy bombers from VIII USAAF and RAF Bomber Command attacked rail and road centres of GLADBECK and the rail centre of STERKRADE, both in the Northern limits of the RUHR, while IX USAAF mediums completed the tactical interdiction programme with attacks at BOCHOLT, BORKEN and DORSTEN.

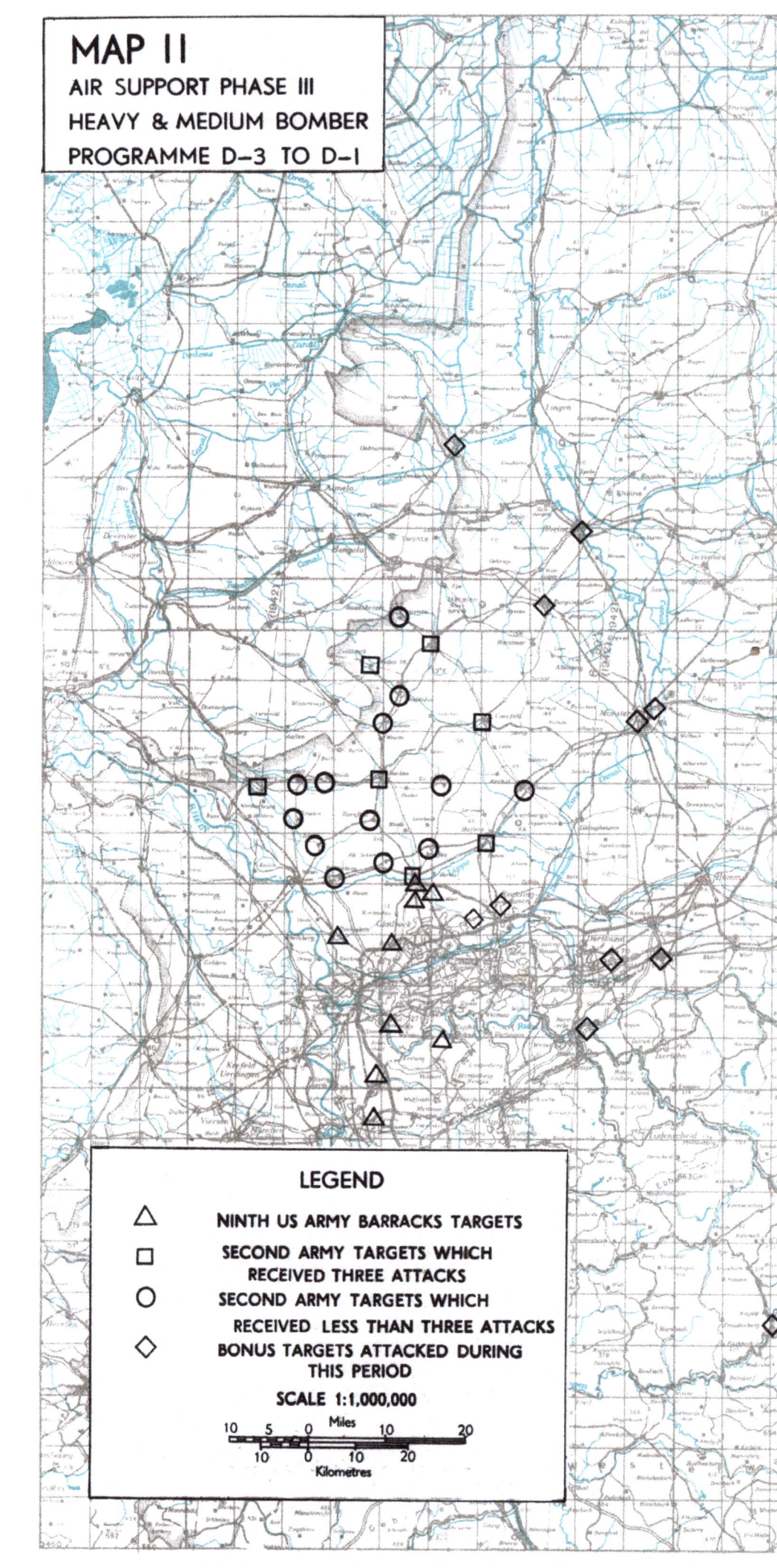

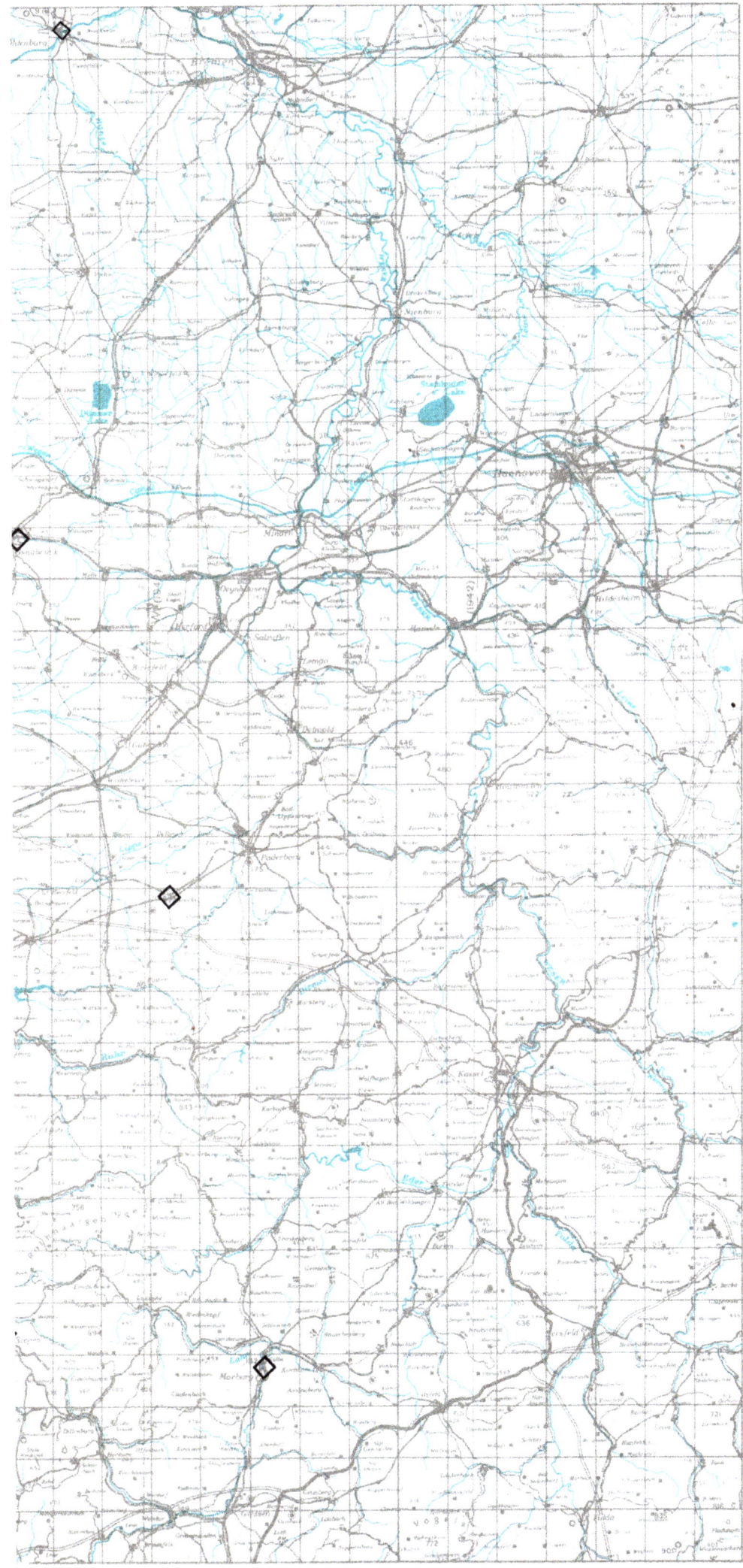

MAP 12 HEAVY BOMBER CLOSE SUPPORT FOR ASSAULT BY I CDO BDE

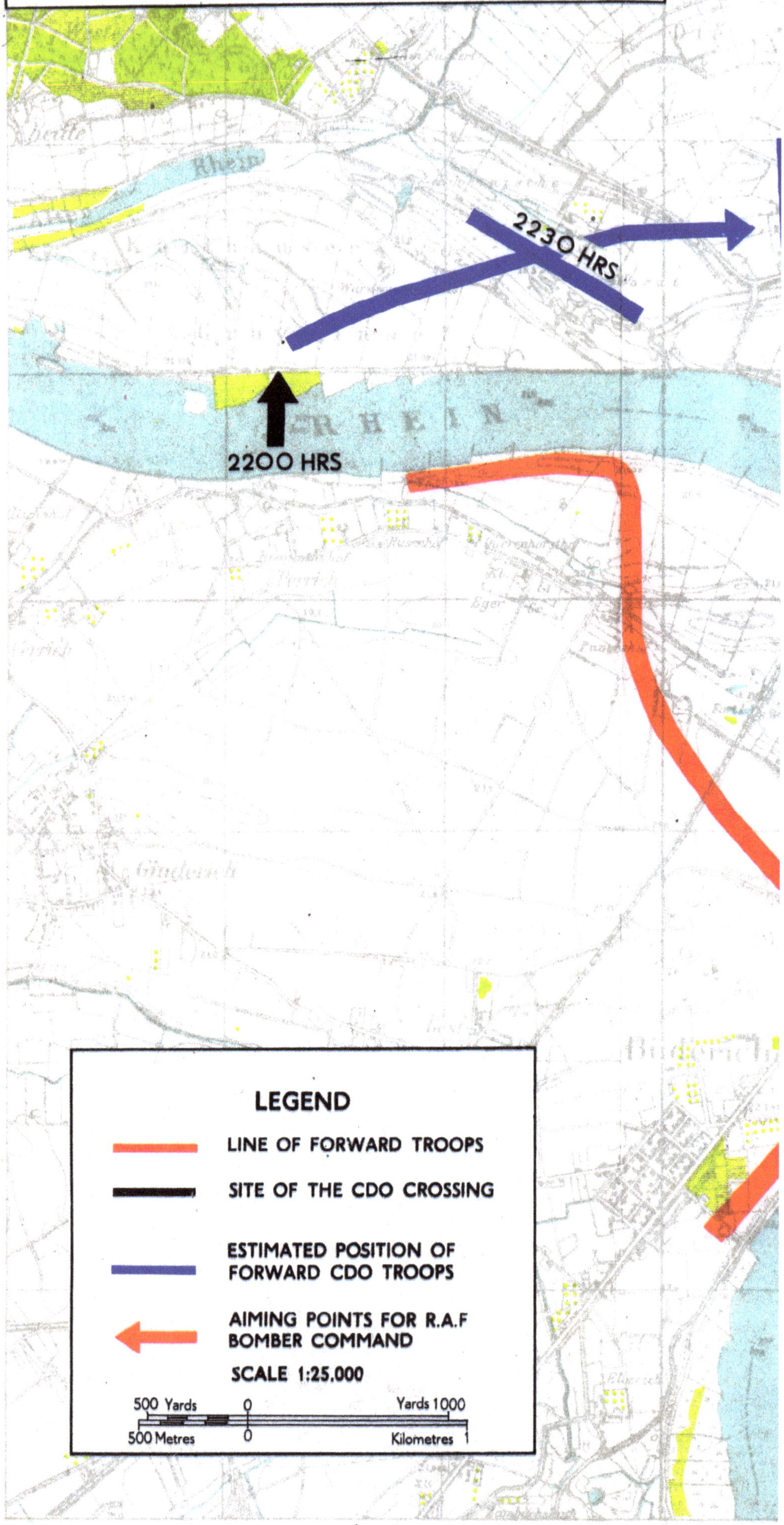
2230 HRS
2200 HRS
RHEIN
LEGEND
LINE OF FORWARD TROOPS
SITE OF THE CDO CROSSING
ESTIMATED POSITION OF FORWARD CDO TROOPS
AIMING POINTS FOR R.A.F BOMBER COMMAND
SCALE 1:25,000
500 Yards
0
Yards 1000
500 Metres
0
Kilometres 1

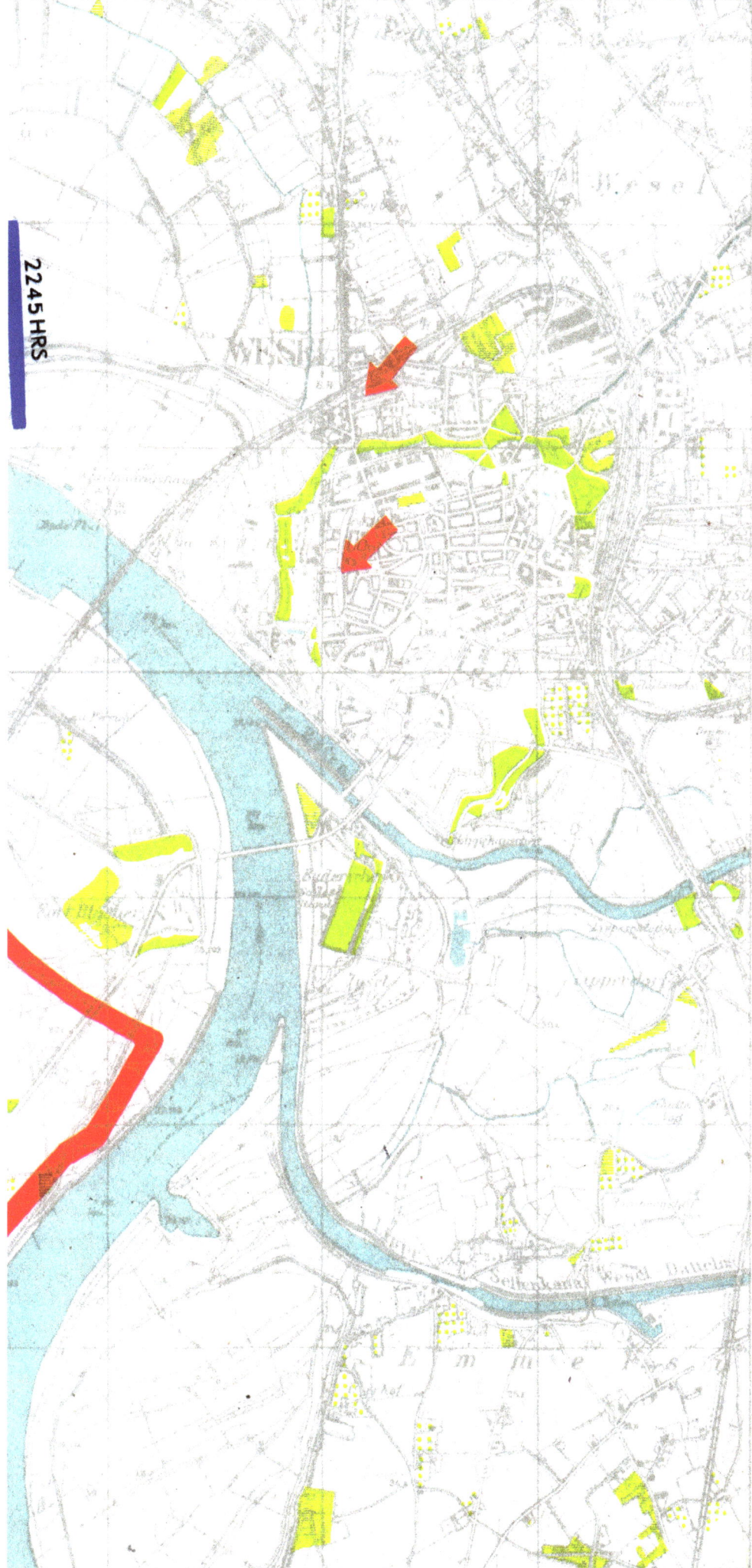

2245 HRS

E. DAY-TO-DAY SUPPORT FROM D DAY ONWARDS (PHASE V)

The main contribution by the Air Forces from D Day onwards, consisted of fighter bomber support controlled by the Forward Control Posts (FCP). In addition an extensive programme of heavy and medium bomber attacks was arranged in direct support of the advance.

F. AIR SUPPORT SIGNALS ORGANISATION FOR OPERATION PLUNDER

(i) In order to provide the most effective immediate support for the crossing of the RHINE, modifications to the normal air support equipment were necessary. It was essential to provide tentacles to serve the assaulting brigades and airborne formations on a scale which would guarantee air support communications until they could be replaced by normal tentacles.

(ii) **Provision of Special Equipment for Assaulting Brigades**

It was decided to provide three special types of outstations for the assault:

(a) The *"Assault Tentacle"* consisting of a jeep fitted with the normal tentacle facilities, which was designed to be ferried across the river in LVsT. This precluded the use of trailers.

(b) The *"Contact Jeep"* consisting of a jeep fitted with the normal facilities of a Contact Car, but capable of being ferried in a LVT. A second jeep accompanied the contact jeep to carry the Air Liaison Officer and RAF Controller.

(c) The *"DD Contact Tank"* consisting of a DD tank with the normal facilities of a Contact Tank.

A DD Contact Tank with a Contact Jeep to act as reserve in case the tank failed to cross was allotted to one assault brigade of each division. An assault tentacle was allotted to each of the other assault brigades, to 1 Cdo Bde and to the Armoured Mobile Column operating under 15 (S) Inf Div. The layout of tentacles and contact cars in 12 Corps sector is shown in Diagram 2 (*facing page* 31).

(iii) **Deployment of the Air Support Signals Unit**

Only one network was provided for each corps owing to the shortage of tentacles, lack of frequencies and limitations in the number of nets on which the FCP could intercept. In addition to the contact jeeps and VHF teams already mentioned, air to ground communication was provided to headquarters of each assaulting infantry division and each armoured division by allotment of contact cars briefed initially in a "reconnaissance" role only. The FCP was required to handle air support for three corps in this operation. On account of this extension of its normal responsibilities, it was decided to amplify its normal facilities and to establish an advanced section of 83 Group RAF Control Centre (GCC) alongside it. This expanded version of the FCP was located as far forward as possible in a good wireless site West of the RHINE, but not alongside any Army formation headquarters.

(iv) **Operation of the Air Support Signals Unit**

During the operation communications were effectively maintained with all outstations. Watch was opened at 0600 hours on D Day on the 12 and 30 Corps nets and all assault tentacles were in communication with Control and being fully intercepted by 0645 hours.

The DD Contact Tank was preceded in the assault by Contact Jeeps and did not, in fact, have a fair trial.

G. FORWARD CONTROL OF AIRCRAFT DURING OPERATION PLUNDER

(i) The expanded version of the FCP/Advanced GCC rendered necessary by the exceptional number of tentacles deployed on the operation and the extensive scale of air effort available to support the Army, has already been referred to. The location of the Advanced GCC alongside the FCP, provied sufficient VHF communications to control all aircraft supporting the operation, and landline facilities to all Wings, Army Headquarters and to the headquarters of both assaulting Corps.

(ii) **Method of Operating**

The main feature of the control exercised by the FCP was the ability of all tentacles at any time to flick on to an alternative frequency and talk by R/T direct to the Army Air Liaison Officer at the FCP. For a normal target, where speed was not vital to a successful attack, the tentacle submitted its demand by W/T to Control at HQ Second Army in the usual way, and any resulting air strike was laid on through the Tactical Headquarters of 83 Group RAF. The FCP intercepted all messages, and when it was clear that the engagement of a particular target depended on speed for its success, the FCP took the decision to handle that particular request. Many short term targets, however, were passed initially over R/T to the FCP and handled entirely by it, which resulted in a marked decrease in the number of support demands received at Army HQ.

(iii) **Use of the Contact Car for Strikes**

When a call for support came from a Contact Car, a check on priority and suitability was made at the FCP, and, if accepted, the Car was authorised to call down the next section in the cab rank and control the attack itself. This procedure provided a relief to the FCP during pressure periods.

(iv) Special Forms of Air Attack

In some cases, forward troops put down a smoke screen to mark their positions, and aircraft were given a free hand to attack targets beyond it. When considerable lateral movement was taking place within the bombline, arrangements were made for the road to be indicated with alternate red and white smoke at intervals of half a mile on a ten to fifteen mile stretch. As flying weather was not always good during this operation, considerable use was made of the Mobile Radar Control Post. Its use to control fighter bombers on to targets in conditions of 10/10th cloud was well known and readily employed. In addition, 2 Group RAF, by day and night, made use of this instrument to carry out blind bombing in close support.

(v) Intensity of Fighter Bomber Attack

The early targets each day were dealt with by aircraft scrambles from runway readiness. As soon as demands appeared likely to warrant it, a cab rank was started : at first one section every twenty five minutes and later stepping up to one every fifteen minutes. This continued throughout the day until the supply of aircraft began to exceed the demand when cab rank was gradually reduced, and ultimately one squadron remained at runway readiness again.

Some details of the close air support actually provided will be found in Part II, Section V.

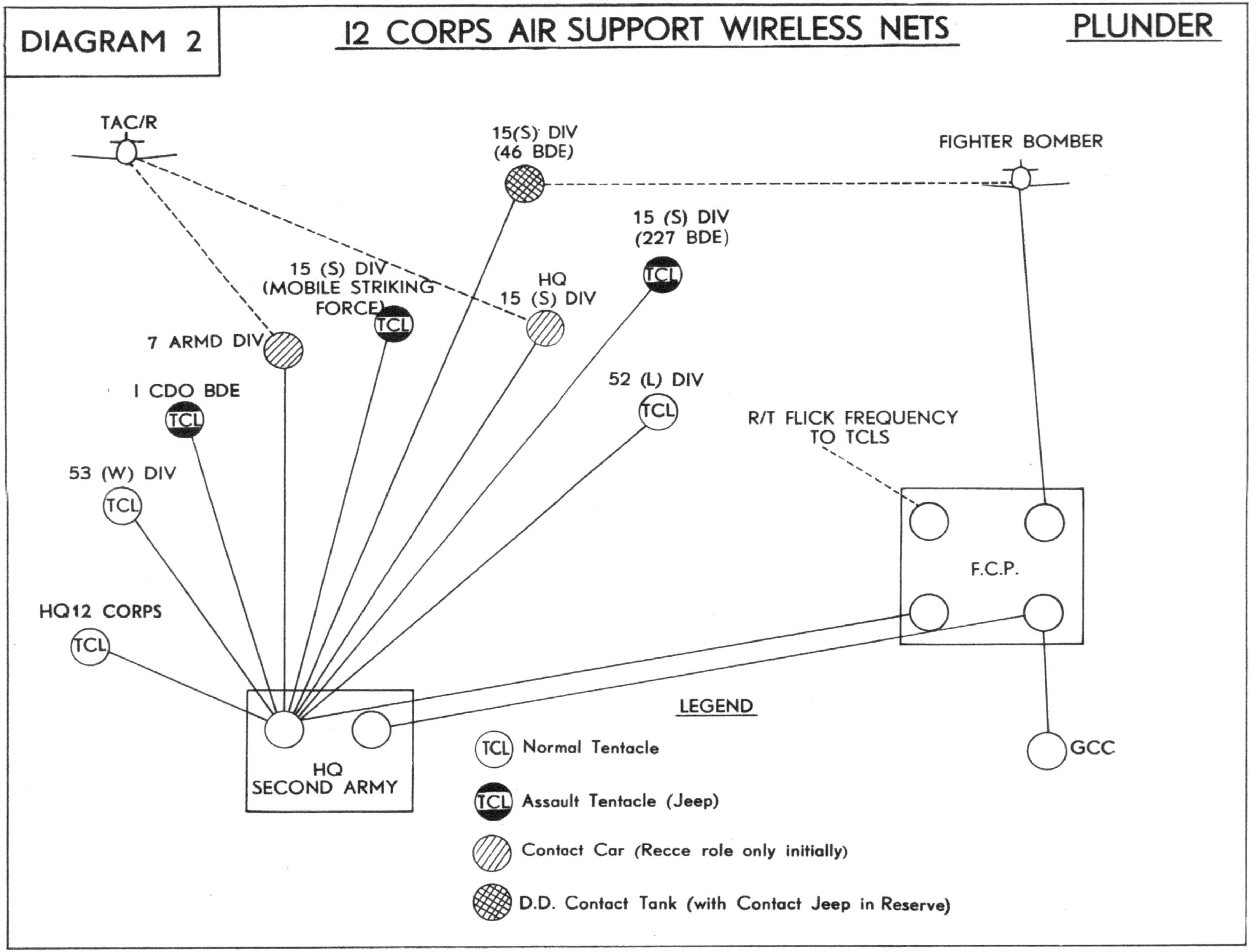

DIAGRAM 2

12 CORPS AIR SUPPORT WIRELESS NETS

PLUNDER

FIGHTER BOMBER

F.C.P.

GCC

R/T FLICK FREQUENCY TO TCLS

15 (S) DIV (227 BDE)

52 (L) DIV

15(S) DIV (46 BDE)

HQ 15 (S) DIV

15 (S) DIV (MOBILE STRIKING FORCE)

TAC/R

7 ARMD DIV

1 CDO BDE

53 (W) DIV

HQ 12 CORPS

HQ SECOND ARMY

LEGEND

- (TCL) Normal Tentacle
- (TCL) Assault Tentacle (Jeep)
- Contact Car (Recce role only initially)
- D.D. Contact Tank (with Contact Jeep in Reserve)

Printed by 14 Field Survey Squadron. R.E. March 1948

SECTION IX

PRELIMINARY TRAINING

The period available for preliminary special training of the assaulting formations was relatively short and training was correspondingly intensive.

HQ 12 Corps issued a seven day syllabus of training for an assault brigade group, which is reproduced at Appendix H, and training of the brigades of 15 (S) Div began on 9 March 1945, on the MAAS between MAASTRICHT and MAESEYCK. Each assaulting brigade group carried out one full-scale rehearsal by day and a second by night. At these rehearsals all supporting arms and units took part grouped exactly as they were to be in the final operation. Thus, for example, every infantry soldier embarked in the very LVT in which he was to cross the RHINE on D Day, and the closest possible liaison was established between the men who were to go together into the battle. It is interesting to note that practically everything went wrong at the rehearsal, while practically everything went right on D Day iself.

Several units had to be converted to new equipment during this relatively short training period, in order to provide for example, sufficient LVT crews. In particular, 44 R Tks which had been engaged in some hard fighting up to the end of Operation VERITABLE as a normal armoured regiment, completely re-equipped and trained in DD tanks during the ensuing fortnight.

The training of RE units provided a particular problem. As has been noted, the RE resources of Second Army alone were insufficient and US Engineers had to be lent to relieve British units employed on the rearward communications. Even when these reliefs were complete, it was still exceedingly difficult to spare RE units from essential tasks to enable them to concentrate on training, and certain RE formations were obliged to take part after only one or two day's special training in their allotted tasks.

For security reasons and because of the smoke screen (see Section X), only very limited reconnaissance of the assault area was possible. Company and platoon commanders of the assaulting battalions were in some cases only able to undertake one reconnaissance of the river and the ground beyond, and that from a distance of several thousand yards. Moreover, the configuration of the ground itself made the selection of good view points even for this limited scale of reconnaissance extremely difficult. The problem was, however, partially solved by the issue of very complete and accurate models down to brigades, together with a generous allocation of excellent air photos.

SECTION X

THE COVER PLAN

Once 21 Army Group was established on the West bank of the RHINE it was clearly only a matter of time before the Army Group attempted an assault across the river. The situation in this respect from the enemy's point of view was in fact similar to that in NORMANDY before D Day in 1944. Just as then, he appreciated that invasion was inevitable, but did not know when or where, so on the RHINE, he expected the assault, but lacked the necessary detailed knowledge to meet it with his limited resources.

Every effort of deception was therefore directed towards preventing him obtaining this vital information, in order that the assault might be made with the advantage of tactical surprise.

The steps taken to this end were numerous and varied and only a brief resume can be given here. Their overall object was to draw attention to First Canadian Army sector, and away from Second Army and Ninth US Army.

Every precaution was taken to conceal the date fixed for D Day, and briefing was therefore postponed until the last possible moment.

First Canadian Army undertook the construction of dummy dumps in their area, and carried out a dummy build up of gun positions, including ammunition dumping, tracks and cable laying. Similarly both First Canadian Army and Ninth US Army maintained a level of reconnaissance and patrolling at least equivalent to that on Second Army front, so that these activities were being carried out concurrently along the entire bank of the RHINE in Allied possession.

Laying of buried cable routes, being easily detected from the air, was delayed as long as possible, while extensive dummy cable-ploughing was arranged by HQ Second Army, with a general bias towards the First Canadian Army sector.

Careful selection of marshalling and RE areas, forward dumps, equipment hides and similar areas was insisted on, particular attention being given to approaches, so that vehicles might enter and leave without making visible tracks. Forward movement of special bridging and other equipment was delayed as long as possible, as were troop movements into their assembly areas.

Work on forward LVT tracks and preparations on the near bank were not permitted until darkness on the actual night of the assault.

The necessarily forward deployment of artillery has already been mentioned. This was carried out under orders of HQ 12 Corps, and all ammunition dumping and moves into battle positions were supervised by teams of camouflage experts provided by HQ 21 Army Group. In addition smoke-containers were used to create a screen from enemy ground observation over the entire front of the assault, a distance of some 50 miles, for a period of seven days before D Day. Registration was not permitted, and only the guns already deployed for the last stages of the operations of clearing the West bank maintained normal activity in the period prior to the opening of Operation PLUNDER.

Arrangements were made for flanking formations, including Ninth US Army to open bombardment concurrently with the artillery of 12 Corps in the opening stages of the operation.

All wireless deception was directed by HQ Second Army and directed to creating the illusion that no regrouping had taken place since the conclusion of the operations to clear the West bank, during which time the majority of Second Army's formations had been under command of First Canadian Army. Wireless silence was maintained by formations and units of 12 Corps, with the exception of certain RA nets, until three hours before the respective H Hours.

Sonic equipment designed to deceive the enemy by the use of loud speakers broadcasting recorded sounds of movement of troops and vehicles, was operated under arrangements of HQ 21 Army Group.

Finally a policy of educating the enemy to the sound of LVsT and the sight of movement light for a considerable period before D Day was adopted, so that the amount of noise and light immediately before the assault should appear to him as nothing unusual.

PART II

Account of the Battle

INTRODUCTORY NOTE

D Day

The Commander-in-Chief had given 24 March 1945 as the target date for D Day, but was prepared to accept postponement up to five days if required, to ensure favourable weather conditions for the airborne assault. From 12 March onwards weather conditions had generally been fine and clear. On 23 March weather forecasts were still favourable and at 1700 hours the Commander-in-Chief finally confirmed 24 March 1945 as D Day. One hour later, the counter-battery bombardment opened.

D Day in fact was fine and clear, with practically no wind. Conditions were therefore ideal for the airborne operation. Generally speaking the weather was excellent up to the end of March, though occasional periods of light rain and drizzle sometimes affected air operations and there was often ground mist during the first two hours of daylight. There was a sharp rain storm in the evening of 26 March, and on 2 April high wind and rain caused the FBE bridge on 12 Corps front to be swamped, and 400 feet of bridge sank.

Under the threequarter moon, aided by the searchlights, movement by night was not difficult.

SECTION I

OPERATIONS OF 12 CORPS 23/25 MARCH 1945

A. 1 CDO BDE (OPERATION WIDGEON)

Concentration and Crossing

1 Cdo Bde moved to its concentration area South West of WESEL (see Map 4) on the night 20/21 March. Leading elements of the brigade began to cross the RHINE in LVsT at 2200 hours on 23 March under cover of an artillery barrage, and established themselves with very little opposition on the far bank.

Bombing of WESEL

At 2230 hours, when leading troops of 1 Cdo Bde were on their start line only 1,500 yards distant (Map 12), the pre-arranged bombing of the town of WESEL by 200 heavy bombers of the RAF began, the town having already been attacked by 27 heavies at last light. The bombing lasted ¼ hour, and was carried out with great accuracy.

Capture of WESEL

1 Cdo Bde then attacked with great energy and determination and by first light 24 March, the whole brigade, less 1 CHESHIRE, was in the town and over 400 prisoners had been taken, although much mopping up remained to be done. During the afternoon 24 March, a ferry was established opposite WESEL and 1 CHESHIRE crossed over. By midnight, 1 Cdo Bde reported the town itself clear (a report which later proved to be somewhat premature), and work was begun in clearing a way through the debris. Ninth US Army had not however been able to start bridging as planned, owing to the continuance of enemy shelling on the proposed bridge sites.

Operations on 25 March

During the early hours of 25 March a strong enemy counter-attack developed in the North East sector of the brigade positions in WESEL, accompanied by continuous shelling by SP guns. This counter-attack was repulsed by 45 Royal Marine Commando (45 RM Cdo), and the enemy sustained losses from artillery fire. Meanwhile, owing to shelling, 1 Cdo Bde was having some difficulty in maintaining its ferry service and getting heavy weapons over the river, especially as the LVsT had been working some 24 hours continuously. Crews required a rest and machines were in need of maintenance.

In order to tidy up the position, 507 Parachute Infantry Regiment (507 Para Inf Regt) of 17 US Airborne Div was ordered to make firm contact with 1 Cdo Bde North West of WESEL and the link-up took place at 1330 hours 25 March. 46 Royal Marine Commando (46 RM Cdo) then pushed South through the town in order to link up with 1 CHESHIRE, who were engaged in clearing the South West part. At 1400 hours 1 Cdo Bde passed to under command of XVIII US Corps (Airborne), but it was not until 2100 hours on 25 March that WESEL was finally reported clear of the enemy, and 46 RM Cdo had made contact with the Americans South of the River LIPPE. 850 prisoners had been taken and the German garrison commander, General DEUTSCH, killed.

B. 15(S) DIV (OPERATION TORCHLIGHT)

44 (L) Inf Bde

Concentration

44 (L) Inf Bde, the Right assaulting brigade of 15 (S) Div, moved to its concentration area during the night 22/23 March. Battalions moved direct into the brigade Marshalling Area (Map 6), where they linked up with 11 R Tks (LVsT). The Brigade Commander held a final conference at 1400 hours on 23 March, and at 1645 hours Bde HQ was informed by divisional HQ that Operation PLUNDER would take place as planned.

The Brigade Plan

The intention of 44 (L) Inf Bde was given by the Brigade Commander as follows:—

44 (L) Inf Bde will establish a bridgehead on the East bank of the River RHINE in the area BISLICH in order to enable 12 Corps to advance to BERLIN.

As the first step in this ambitious project, the brigade was to assault two battalions up, with Right 6th Battalion The Royal Scots Fusiliers (6 RSF) and Left 8th Battalion The Royal Scots (The Royal Regiment) (8 RS), with initial objectives to clear the line of the bund immediately West of BISLICH, between FAHRHAUS and RONDUIT, and to occupy the Western half of BISLICH itself (see Map 13).

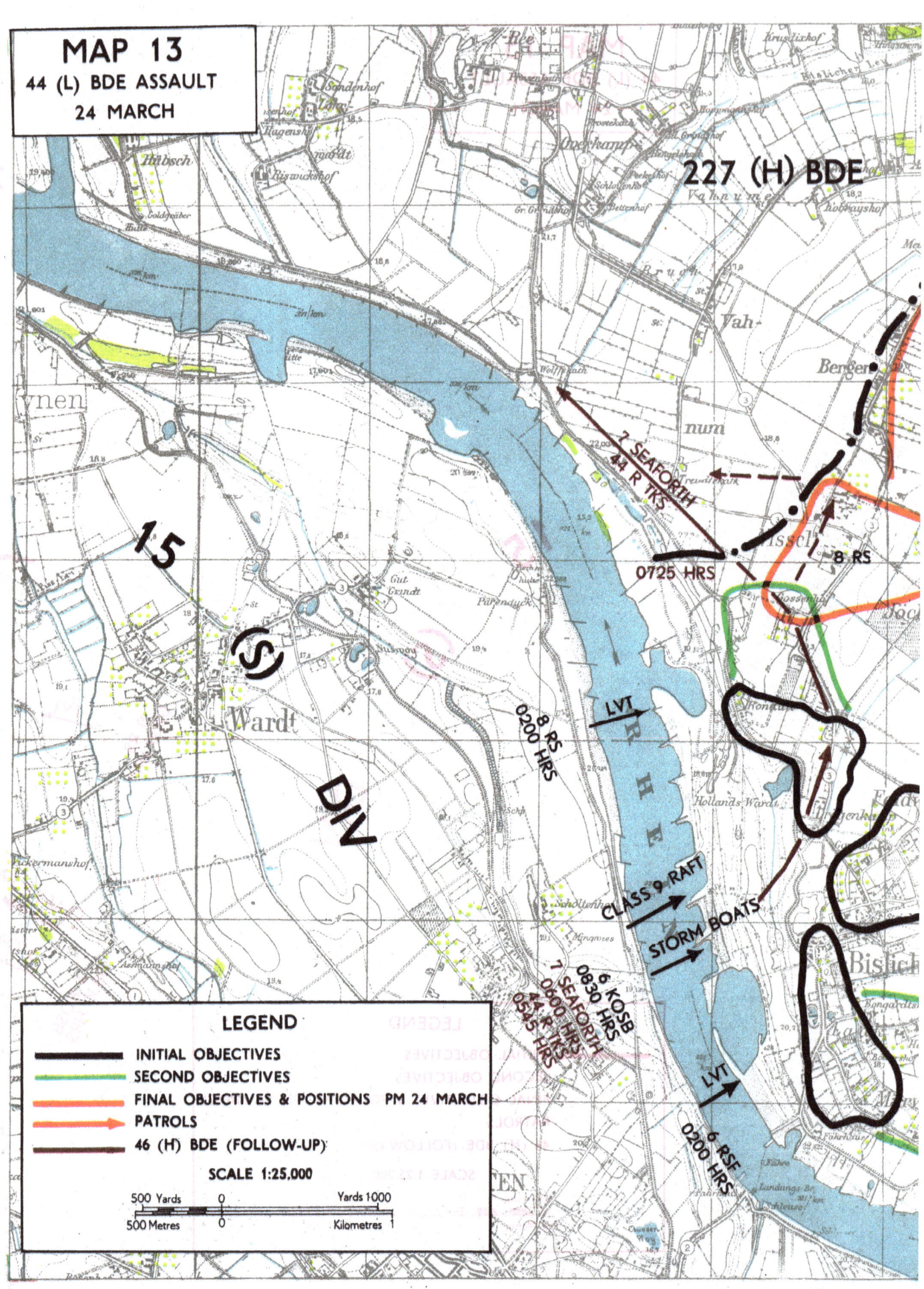

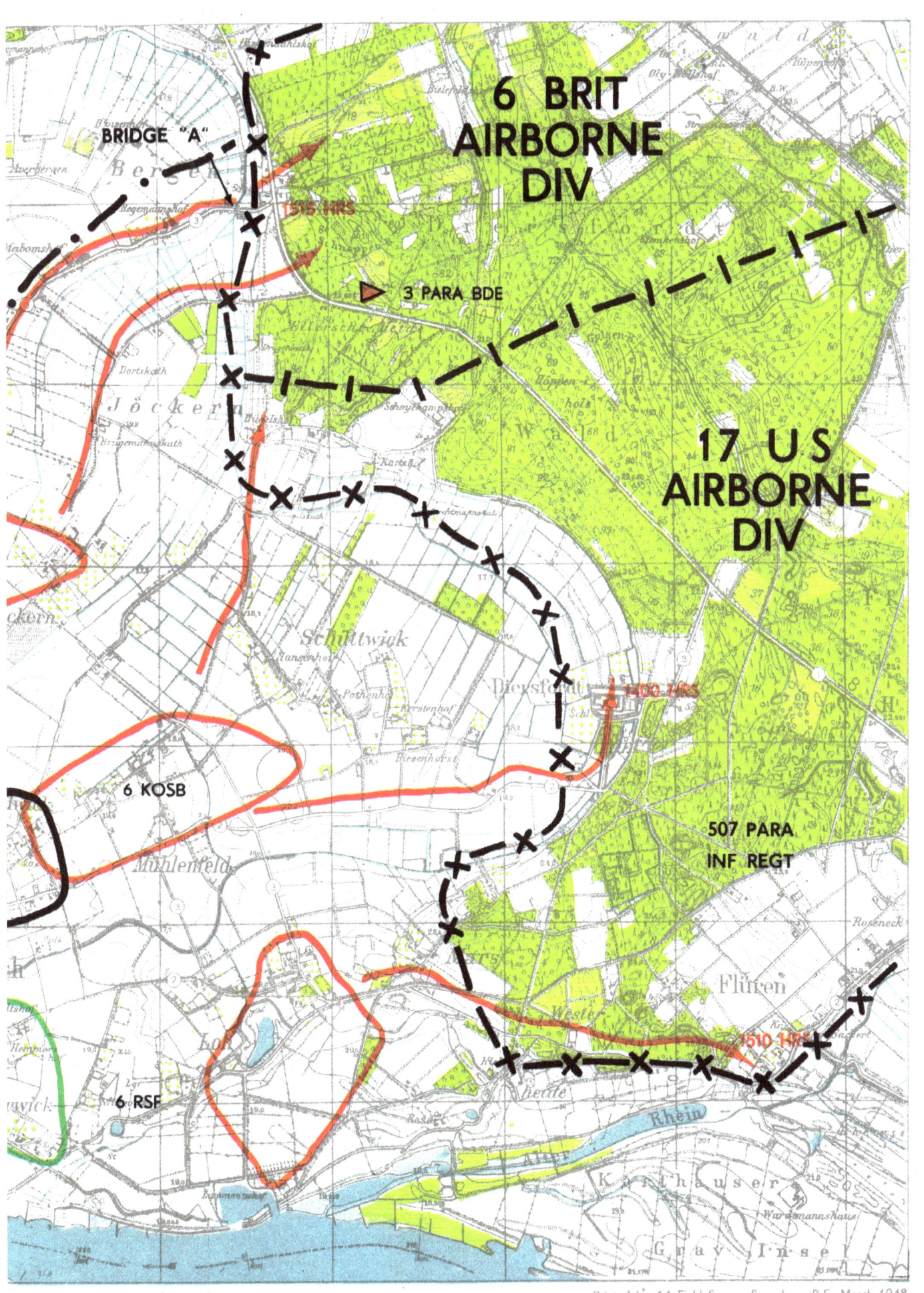

6th Battalion The King's Own Scottish Borderers (6 KOSB) was then to pass through 6 RSF and seize the remainder of BISLICH, after which the whole brigade was to advance to the general line LOH–MUHLENFELD–VISSEL.

The Approach to the River

Soon after midnight 23/24 March the assaulting battalions embarked in their allotted LVsT in the Marshalling Area, six LVsT to an infantry company, with a further twelve per battalion carrying Bn HQ and supporting weapons, including detachments of medium machine guns of 1st Battalion The Middlesex Regiment (Duke of Cambridge's Own) (1 MX). In addition, the assault wave LVsT carried RA OPs, advanced parties of the Bank Group (5 R BERKS) including medical personnel, RE and RAC (DD) reconnaissance parties.

Prior to arriving in the Marshalling Area, a proportion of LVsT had been stowed with the minimum vehicles essential in the assault stages of the operation. The stowage of LVsT in the assault waves had been worked out in detail by HQ 12 Corps and though there was some slight variation between battalions, the following allotment of vehicles was generally adopted.

Vehicles Carried in Assault Wave LVsT
(per assaulting battalion)

6-pounder A Tk guns and towers	4
Jeeps	3 (one each for CO, battalion MO and RE reconnaissance officer)
Carriers	4 (two for reserve ammunition, one each for RA OP party and battalion signal officer)

The Assault

At about 0030 hours 24 March, LVsT set out from the Marshalling Area in single file, under movement light, each battalion on a separate route marked with shaded lights (see Map 6). Meanwhile, sappers had breached the bund to enable the heavily loaded LVsT to pass through.

The columns paused momentarily at the bund to check timings, and then the first flights, comprising three companies per assaulting battalion, passed through the gaps, fanned out into line and entered the water at H Hour (0200 hours). At this time our artillery fire was falling on the far bank, whence it lifted at H+2½ minutes to the bund and again at H+5 minutes to the area beyond the initial objectives: there it was to stand until called off by FOOs.

By 0220 hours, the leading companies were all across, having been disembarked dry shod on the far bank. There was some desultory shelling and mortaring and both 6 RSF and 8 RS reported a certain amount of trouble from light automatic fire (spandaus). 6 RSF sustained casualties from anti-personnel (schuh) mines, and also in a sharp hand-to-hand struggle for a house, which ultimately yielded some forty prisoners.

The second flight LVsT followed as soon as the leading companies were established ashore and by 0305 hours all initial objectives were in our hands, though mopping up was still continuing, some enemy parties having gone to ground in cellars. 6 RSF was however able to report initial objectives cleared and consolidated at 0330 hours, and 8 RS shortly afterwards.

Establishment of LVT Ferries by 11 R Tks

Meanwhile the empty LVsT of 11 R Tks were returning across the river to the LVT Collecting Area and thence to the LVT Loading Area (see Map 6). From 0230 hours 24 March until 0800 hours 26 March they were continuously employed on the ferrying of vehicles across the river, carrying a total of 407 vehicles on 24 March and a further 726 on 25 March. At 0400 hours LVsT of this regiment carried over the equipment for the specially prepared "carpet" on the far bank of the river designed to provide exit facilities for the DD tanks of 44 R Tks, together with the laying party. This task was successfully accomplished though casualties were sustained. Over the whole ferrying period, however, 11 R Tks had only two men killed and eleven wounded.

Crossing of the follow-up battalion

While the assaulting battalions were moving down to and across the river, 6 KOSB had moved on foot from the Marshalling Area to the Stormboat Waiting Area (Map 6), where they sheltered from the desultory shelling in the houses and cellars of LUTTINGEN. At 0310 hours orders were received to cross the river, and the battalion began to cross in Stormboats at approximately 0330 hours. The battalion was all across by 0430 hours, and by first light had secured its initial objectives, taking a number of prisoners (see Map 13).

By 0415 hours, 6 RSF were on their second objective (see Map 13) and were beginning to receive their vehicles from the LVT Ferries, preparatory to a further advance Eastward. A little earlier, a chance shell unfortunately caused twenty casualties in one company of this battalion, including all three platoon commanders, but casualties were otherwise very light, and a considerable number of prisoners was taken.

At 0700 hours 24 March the Brigade Commander crossed the river and saw all his Battalion Commanders in turn. Progress was everywhere satisfactory.

Traffic Control

At 0830 hours 24 March, 5 R BERKS on Bank Group duties reported that all their wireless links were ready to operate on the far bank, and the full forward control came into operation at 1000 hours. Up till this time each unit had provided its own unit landing officer who had been responsible for directing vehicles to their destination on landing. On the near side, Crossing Control was established next to Brigade Tac HQ at the outset, and serials were called forward from the Marshalling Area to LVT ferries (and later to other crossings) in a pre-arranged sequence subject to such variation as the tactical situation demanded.

Advance to Final Objectives

At 0945 hours, 8 RS launched attacks to clear VISSEL and JOCKERN (Map 13). The attack on VISSEL was supported by a squadron of 44 R Tks which was moving West along the bund in support of 46 (H) Bde, and which was temporarily diverted to assist 8 RS. VISSEL was cleared by 1000 hours yielding 28 prisoners.

At the same hour, the airborne landing began (see Section II, paragraph A) and led to a very noticeable loosening on the 44 (L) Bde front, resistance gradually fading away as the airborne troops overran the enemy gun and rear defence areas. All battalions were able to advance to their final objectives without difficulty by the early afternoon.

Contact with Airborne Formations

First contact with the airborne troops was reported in the neighbourhood of DIERSFORDT, where 6 KOSB linked up with 17 US Airborne Div at 1400 hours. This was followed by 6 RSF at 1510 hours and 8 RS who contacted 6 Brit Airborne Div at 1515 hours, at the bridge 2,000 yards North East of BERGEN (marked A on Map 13), which was captured intact. Finally the Brigade Commander and the Commander 8 RS drove up to HQ 3 Para Bde (6 Brit Airborne Div) at 1545 hours, receiving a rousing reception from the parachutists.

Preparation for further advance

At 1800 hours 24 March, orders were issued for 6 KOSB to concentrate in BERGEN with a view to operating North Eastwards early the next day. This was completed by 1900 hours.

Remaining battalions concentrated in the areas which they had reached, and all battalions were ordered to obtain maximum possible rest that night. Over a thousand prisoners had been taken during the day (24 March).

Brigade Commander's Orders for 25 March

Brigade HQ was established in BISLICH at 2200 hours and at 2230 hours the Brigade Commander held an 'O' Group.

44 (L) Bde was to be the leading brigade of 15 (S) Div. The Divisional Commander's intention was to secure exits from the bridgehead for 53 (W) Div, which was expected to pass through about first light D+2 (26 March). 44 (L) Bde was directed on the bridge over the ISSEL at GERVERSHOF (marked B on Map 14).

For this operation 44 R Tks (less one squadron, which had been placed under command 6 Brit Airborne Div) came under command 44 (L) Bde. The Brigade Commander's plan envisaged an advance to contact. 6 KOSB, with under command 44 R Tks (less one squadron) and elements of 15 (S) Recce Regt, with one troop SP anti-tank guns and RE parties in support, was to form the advanced guard, and 8 RS and 6 RSF were to follow in that order. The general line of advance was as shown on Map 14. 4 RHA was in support, though in the event, its crossing over the RHINE was delayed and did not take place until the evening of 25 March. 6 KOSB were to move off at first light, 25 March.

The Advance to Contact

Owing to unforeseen delay in completion of the regrouping necessary before the advance, 6 KOSB did not move off until 0850 hours. They were preceded by reconnaissance patrols of 15 (S) Recce Regt and the two leading companies were carried on the tanks of 44 R Tks. The remainder of the battalion followed on foot, clearing the woods alongside the road and protecting the route until relieved by the main body. Contact was made at 0930 hours with 5 Para Bde of 6 Brit Airborne Div at the point where the WESEL-HALDERN railway crossed the brigade axis (marked C on Map 14).

By 1020 hours leading elements had arrived at the cross roads marked D on Map 14, thirty prisoners having been taken. Opposition up till this time was negligible, but at this point there was considerable enemy fire, including some anti-tank guns from the area South and East of MEHRHOO station, and the infantry were obliged to deploy.

A Sqn, 44 R Tks, which was leading the advance, redeployed at 1150 hours, facing West, under cover of smoke, while artillery concentrations were brought down on the suspected enemy positions. Meanwhile C Sqn was ordered to pass through under cover of A Sqn's fire, and to continue the advance along the axis. By 1335 hours the leading troops of C Sqn, with the loss of one tank, had almost reached the partially constructed autobahn, where they were heavily engaged; four tanks were then knocked out by SP guns, and at 1544 hours the squadron was ordered to withdraw under cover of smoke. This withdrawal was completed at 1700 hours. Meanwhile A Sqn from its position West of the wood was getting a number of good targets, and knocked out an enemy SP gun. This squadron remained in position in this area all day.

During the whole day of 25 March 8 RS remained under cover of the woods North East of BERGEN, where they were subject to spasmodic enemy mortar fire. 6 RSF moved into a defensive position in the area HULSHORST, where they sustained some casualties from accurate and fairly heavy shelling.

Plan for Night Attack

It had proved impossible for infantry to debouch from the woods and advance over the open ground to the autobahn by daylight, and it was therefore decided that a night attack by 6 KOSB should be undertaken with the object of securing the brigade objective, i.e. the bridge at GERVERS-HOF (marked B on Map 14). Meanwhile 44 R Tks (less one squadron) was to concentrate, refill with ammunition and petrol, and then pass through HAMMINKELN in time to rejoin 6 KOSB on their objective at first light 26 March.

8 RS was ordered to take over the area of the autobahn astride the axis after its capture by 6 KOSB.

Start of the Night Attack

6 KOSB moved forward to the attack at 2100 hours, and by 2245 hours had reached its initial objectives a thousand yards beyond the autobahn, against light opposition. Resistance was afterwards to stiffen, and the enemy was able to destroy the bridge over the ISSEL before its capture. The subsequent assault crossing of the ISSEL is outside the scope of this narrative.

227 (H) Inf Bde

Concentration and Plan

227 (H) Inf Bde, the Left assaulting brigade of 15 (S) Div, concentrated in its Marshalling Area (see Map 6) on the night 22/23 March, where it joined up with E RIDING YEO (LVsT).

The Brigade Commander held a final co-ordinating conference on the evening of 22 March, to confirm the written orders issued on 18 March. The Brigade Commander's plan was to assault with two battalions up, Right 10th Battalion Highland Light Infantry (City of Glasgow Regiment) (10 HLI) and Left 2nd Battalion Argyll and Sutherland Highlanders (Princess Louise's) (2 A & SH). The objectives of these battalions are shown on Map 14. 2nd Battalion Gordon Highlanders (2 GORDONS) was initially in reserve, and was to cross the river on orders of Brigade HQ, when OVERKAMP and LOHR were reported clear, relieving 10 HLI and 2 A & SH respectively in those places: the latter battalions were then to exploit to BELLINGHOVEN and WISSHOF.

The Approach to the RHINE

The method of approach to the RHINE was similar to that employed by 44 (L) Bde, which has already been described.

The Assault

First flights of LVsT carrying the assaulting battalions entered the water at or soon after 0200 hours 24 March. The leading companies of 10 HLI crossed without casualties, but were unfortunately landed several hundred yards too far to the Right, causing some confusion in the darkness and opening a wide gap between 10 HLI and 2 A & SH. They found the bund strongly held by three companies of 1/21 Para Regt, with a strongpoint at WOLFFSKATH, and suffered considerable casualties, including all the officers of A Coy, in attempting to clear it.

B and D Coys following in the second flight of LVsT started to push on to their objectives, under the impression that the bund was cleared, and Bn HQ which had also landed too far to the Right was temporarily left unprotected in 'no man's land', where it was attacked and only extricated with some difficulty at 0500 hours.

B Coy meanwhile was ordered to clear the bund Westwards, while D Coy formed a firm base, from which A and C Coys were to press on to their original objectives in OVERKAMP.

B Coy cleared the bund as far as the battalion boundary i.e. the sluice gates (marked E on map 14) and eventually made contact with 2 A & SH at 1200 hours. At dawn A and C Coys were entering the outskirts of OVERKAMP, and the third flight of LVsT, containing most of the support company and essential vehicles was then ordered to cross.

Meanwhile 7th Battalion Seaforth Highlanders (Ross-shire Buffs, The Duke of Albany's) (7 SEAFORTH), of 46 (H) Bde, supported by 44 R Tks, had crossed the RHINE into 44 (L) Bde bridgehead, and advancing Northwards made contact with 10 HLI at about 1200 hours. At 1300 hours 7 SEAFORTH supported by 44 R Tks began to pass through 10 HLI in the general direction of HAFFEN-MEHR (Map 14). 10 HLI then concentrated in OVERKAMP. The battalion had lost four officers and ten other ranks killed, and four officers and sixty-one other ranks wounded: 120 prisoners had been captured and 92 German dead counted in the battalion area.

2 A & SH had considerable difficulty in getting the LVsT ashore on the Right of their sector owing to sand banks and mud obstructing the exits from the river. On the Left, A and B Coys landed without casualties, but on the Right, D Coy, having lost its Commander wounded, was unable to land in its selected place and one platoon was lost for some time. There was considerable resistance centred on the houses at HUBSCH, but after a sharp encounter this was cleared by D Coy by first light. A patrol along the bund failed to contact 10 HLI as pre-arranged, and in returning had some trouble from LMG (spandau) fire, which had come to life after the artillery concentration lifted.

Meanwhile on the Left A and B Coys had reached their objectives in the WAYERHOF area (Map 14), taking some prisoners against patchy resistance, and encountering a few anti-personnel (schuh) mines. An attempt to capture HOPERHOF however failed and daylight revealed it as a strong point firmly held by the enemy.

Soon after first light D Coy had re-organised and was concentrated with C Coy in the HUBSCH area. It now became apparent that the enemy was recovering from the initial bombardment, and he had re-occupied parts of the bund and the houses to the East of HUBSCH. It was essential that this situation should be cleared up, as the whole ferrying plan in the brigade sector was endangered by it. C Coy was therefore ordered to clear the bund, and at 0615 hours the follow-up battalion, 2 GORDONS, was ordered to send a company across the river in order to assist 2 A & SH.

Crossing of a company of the follow-up battalion

OC 2 GORDONS selected A Coy for this task. As the river bank opposite the stormboat ferry site was still held by the enemy, A Coy had to make a journey of 1,200 yards downstream in the stormboats, running the gauntlet of the enemy posts on the bund. As a result, an officer and three other ranks were killed and ten other ranks wounded by small arms fire, a number of boats being lost. B Coy was also ordered to cross, but was mortared while attempting to embark, and owing to shortage of stormboats, its crossing was postponed.

Capture of LOHR and clearance of the Bund

D Coy 2 A & SH, with under command A Coy 2 GORDONS, attacked in the direction of LOHR at 0815 hours. As the attack progressed considerable resistance was encountered from enemy in houses at HAGENSHOF and RISWICKHOF where C Coy was attacking : artillery support could not then be made available, owing to the safety requirements of the airborne operation, but MMG was laid on, and LOHR was ultimately occupied at 1330 hours (an attack on this area by a company of 7 SEAFORTH supported by a squadron of 44 R Tks was due to start at 1315 hours, but was unnecessary.) Resistance, which had bordered on the fanatical, began to crumble after the arrival of the airborne troops, but the effects were evident less quickly than they had been in 44 (L) Bde sector.

Crossing of the remainder of the follow-up battalion

The platoon of C Coy clearing the bund suffered considerable casualties, but succeeded in carrying out its task, and though the bund was not finally and completely cleared until 1200 hours the remainder of 2 GORDONS was able to start crossing at 1030 hours. The battalion landed, as in the case of its first company, 1200 yards downstream from its place of embarkation and formed up in the area immediately North of the creek at HUBSCH, preparatory to moving up behind A and B Coys, 2 A & SH. While in this area they suffered some casualties from mortar fire.

Relief of 2 A & SH by 2 GORDONS

At 1715 hours B and C Coys 2 GORDONS passed through B Coy 2 A & SH in the direction of HAFFEN (Map 14). Although artillery support for an attack on HAFFEN had to be called off at the last moment, owing to the unexpected appearance of tanks of 44 R Tks from the East, the Western part of the village was successfully occupied, yielding 71 prisoners, mostly from 19 Para Regt. Early on 25 March D Coy 2 GORDONS relieved B Coy 2 A & SH. 2 A & SH then concentrated, less A Coy, which could not be extricated by daylight, and at 0945 hours 25 March the battalion came under command of 46 (H) Bde. The Battalion, less A Coy, then moved by march route to an assembly area near BERGEN, immediately West of the DIERSFORDTER WALD. A Coy 2 A & SH was relieved during the evening of 25 March, "Wasp" flame throwers being used by 2 GORDONS to clear HOPERHOF.

Operations 25 March

During 25 March, 10 HLI remained resting in OVERKAMP. At 2300 hours, the battalion was placed at one hour's notice to assist 46 (H) Bde, and at 2330 hours the Commanding Officer attended an 'O' Group at HQ 46 (H) Bde, where the battalions task was given as taking over positions from 46 (H) Bde in the area HAFFEN-MEHR. During the day, twelve prisoners came in.

2 GORDONS remained in position in the HAFFEN-WAYERHOF area, and contacted 51 (H) Div on the Left, though it was not until next day, 26 March, in the afternoon that complete junction was made one mile East of REES and the bridgehead became continuous over the whole Second Army front. As already stated, the third battalion of 227 (H) Bde (2 A & SH) passed under command 46 (H) Bde at 0945 hours 25 March.

Operations of E RIDING YEO (LVsT)

As has already been mentioned, LVsT of E RIDING YEO in the assault wave experienced difficulty with mud on the far bank exits, while some of those with 10 HLI did not cross until first light. As a result they were not loaded ready to start the ferrying service until 0830 hours D Day (24 March).

Ferrying could not however begin, owing to the enemy posts still holding out on the bund opposite and, apart from one or two special sorties with ammunition, or bridging material, or to bring back wounded, no regular service could be established until 1100 hours. Even then difficulty continued to be experienced with the far bank exits, and ferry sites had to be moved more than once.

By 1820 hours, 180 craft loads, mostly vehicles, had been taken over, and at 2015 hours ferrying was stopped until 0800 hours next day. Between 1430 and 1600 hours 25 March ferrying again closed down, as no serials were available in the Vehicle Waiting Area. The ferries finally closed down at 1950 hours 25 March, after carrying over a total of 345 loads.

46 (H) Bde

Concentration and Plan

Battalions of 46 (H) Bde concentrated in their Assembly Area (Map 4) during the night 21/22 March, and the Brigade Commander briefed all officers on the plan for Operation TORCHLIGHT during the ensuing afternoon.

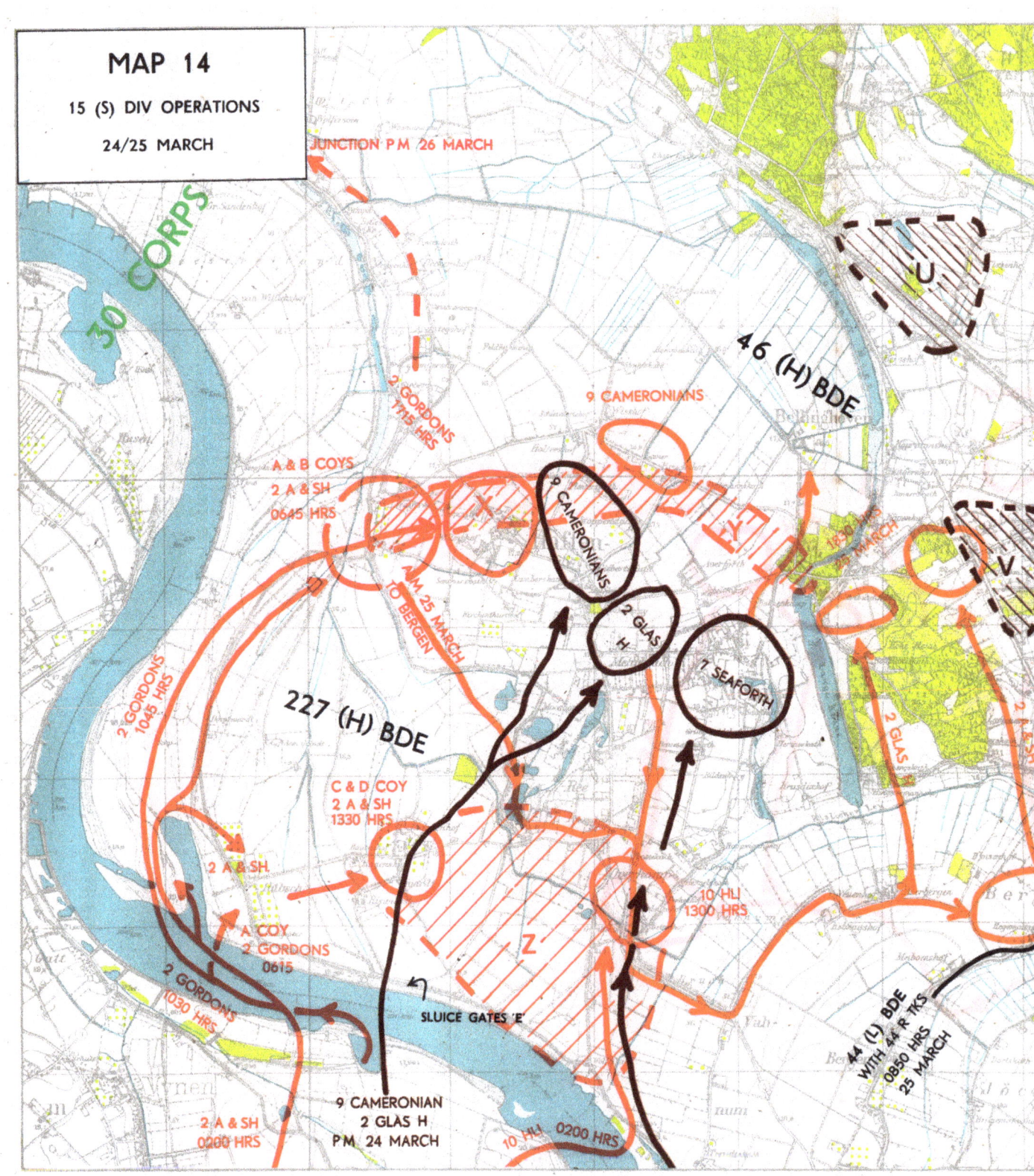

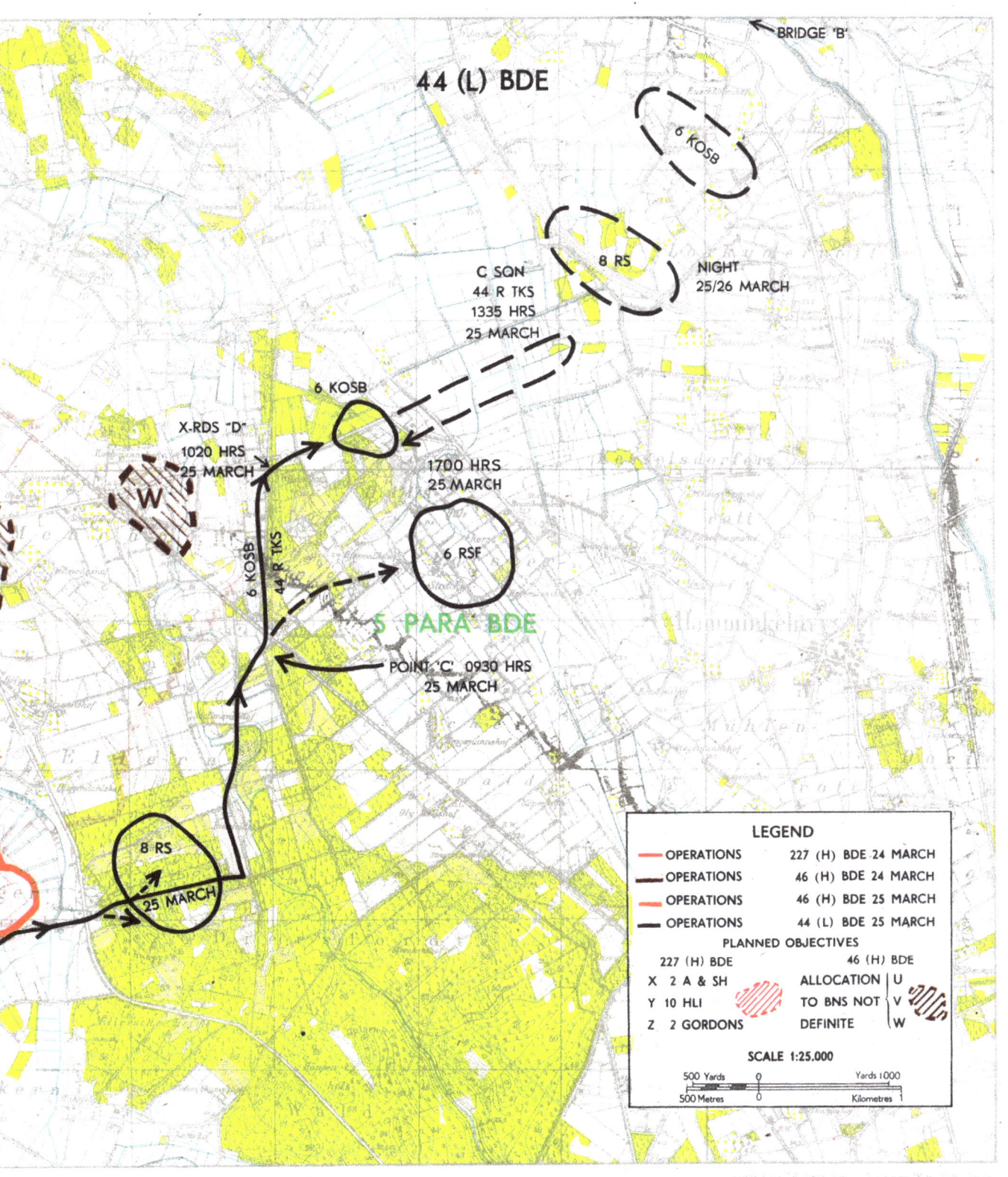

46 (H) Bde was the follow-up brigade of 15 (S) Div, and the Brigade Commander's general intention was to capture and hold the area MEHRHOO–CLASENHO, including the wooded area immediately South East of HALDERN (Map 14). In addition, the brigade had to be prepared to complete the capture of either 44 (L) Bde or 227 (H) Bde bridgeheads, should the efforts of either of these formations fail or only partially succeed.

The plan was therefore a flexible one, and provided for a crossing into either 44 (L) Bde or 227 (H) Bde bridgehead. If all went all, 7 SEAFORTH, with 44 R Tks in support, was to cross in 44 (L) Bde sector, while 9th Battalion Cameronians (Scottish Rifles) (9 CAMERONIANS) and 2nd Battalion Glasgow Highlanders (2 GLAS H) crossed in 227 (H) Bde sector, but the infantry could be switched according to the situation. For the subsequent capture of the MEHRHOO–CLASENHO area, three battalion objectives were laid down (see Map 14), but their allocation to individual battalions depended on developments.

Crossing of the leading battalion

As has already been described, 44 (L) Bde made good progress. At 0600 hours 24 March 7 SEAFORTH was able to cross by stormboat, and was ready in its Assembly Area in the area RONDUIT-GOSSENHOF by 0725 hours. Here it joined up with 44 R Tks.

Crossing of the DD tanks

The DD tanks of 44 R Tks (4 Armd Bde) had started crossing the river at 0545 hours. They had suffered slight shelling and mortaring while waiting in the Inflating Area (Map 6) and three tanks could not cross owing to damaged DD equipment, while one tank went out of control in the river. The remaining fifty-seven tanks were all successfully across the river by 0820 hours.

Advance by 7 SEAFORTH to MEHR (see Map 14)

At 0930 hours A Coy 7 SEAFORTH supported by tanks was sent ahead to clear the bund and capture the area SANDENHOF, and if necessary assist 2 A & SH of 227 (H) Bde into LOHR. 46 prisoners from 1052 GR (84 Div) were captured in the area VISSEL–TREUDEKATH and a further four prisoners from 21 Para Regt (7 Para Div) at WOLFSKATH. The remainder of 7 SEAFORTH followed along the bund to WOLFSKATH. Here the battalion turned North, and at 1300 hours began to pass through 10 HLI, with the object of seizing MEHR, the infantry being carried on the tanks of 44 R Tks.

A Coy consolidated at LOHR, which had just fallen to 2 A & SH and followed the main body to MEHR, which was cleared by 1745 hours yielding 68 prisoners. Opposition to the advance had come from light automatic fire and some SP guns, and some bad going was encountered by the tanks, three tanks becoming bogged. The enemy was now holding the water obstacle of the LANGE RENNE and HAGENER MEER, East and North East of MEHR, and 7 SEAFORTH was unable to advance further. Up to this time casualties in the battalion had been three officers and eighteen other ranks killed and wounded, and in 44 R Tks one officer and five other ranks. 7 SEAFORTH was now holding the Northern and North Eastern outskirts of MEHR, which was under enemy shell fire. A Sqn 44 R Tks was meanwhile moved out towards HAFFEN, which was shortly afterwards attacked from the West by 2 GORDONS of 227 (H) Bde, the retreating enemy presenting A Sqn with some excellent shooting.

Crossing of follow-up battalions and advance to HAFFEN

Meanwhile, owing to the difficulty encountered by 227 (H) Bde in clearing the bund and reaching their objectives, the crossing of the remaining battalions of 46 (H) Bde had been delayed. 9 CAMERONIANS began crossing by 227 (H) Bde stormboat ferry at 1430 hours 24 March and was directed to attack and occupy the HAFFEN area, and by 1750 hours had occupied the South Eastern part of HAFFEN and pushed patrols nearly to the line of the road BRUCKSHOF–HOLTERSHOF where they were held up by light automatic fire across the open ground to the North (Map 14). During this operation 9 CAMERONIANS suffered three officer and forty other rank casualties and took fifty prisoners. 2 GLAS H crossed the RHINE at 1645 hours and moved from the Forward Assembly Area to occupy a position on the Right of 9 CAMERONIANS, which was reached at 2300 hours, without opposition.

Enemy counter-attack on MEHR

During the evening of 24 March, enemy patrols were active in the East and South Eastern sectors of 7 SEAFORTH positions, but were driven off by accurate shooting of C Sqn 44 R Tks and F Bty 4 RHA.

At midnight, a considerable counter-attack developed from the North East, and parties of enemy succeeded in infiltrating into 7 SEAFORTH positions, causing some retirement. Between 0300 and 0330 hours, Defensive Fire was called for in the area previously occupied by C Coy, in the South Eastern corner of the town of MEHR, and mediums engaged the wooded areas to the East and North East of the town. The enemy succeeded in infiltrating to MEHRBRUCH, where earlier in the evening four tanks of C Sqn 44 R Tks had got bogged, while moving to night leaguer. The crews mounted their Brownings in a ground role, but one tank was knocked out by bazooka fire, and the remaining three had to be set on fire by their crews, since, for security reasons, the risk of DD tanks falling into enemy hands could not be accepted.

The Brigade Commander ordered 7 SEAFORTH to hold its positions and 2 GLAS H was warned to assist if required. Between 0430 hours and 0630 hours, the Right of 2 GLAS H positions was also attacked and C Coy 2 GLAS H temporarily pinned down, finally making a successful withdrawal covered by smoke, at 0745 hours.

The position on 7 SEAFORTH's sector was stabilised by 0500 hours, the enemy withdrawing slowly. He was finally ejected from the town by 0700 hours, and companies were able to re-occupy their former positions. One officer and twenty-one other ranks of 7 SEAFORTH had become casualties, and the enemy lost over thirty prisoners and a number of dead and wounded.

Brigade Commander's orders 25 March

At 0630 hours 25 March the Brigade Commander set out to cross the RHINE, but owing to delay at the crossings did not arrive until 0900 hours. At 0945 hours he gave out verbal orders for the future operations of the brigade.

44 R Tks had passed to command of 44 (L) Bde, but 2 A & SH of 227 (H) Bde had been placed under command 46 (H) Bde and was already in the area of BERGEN.

The Brigade Commander's plan was as follows (Map 14):—

2 GLAS H would move by march route round the Southern end of LANGE RENNE. 2 GLAS H would then obtain a footing in the Southern edge of the wood immediately East of LANGE RENNE. 2 A & SH Right and 2 GLAS H Left would then clear the wood Northwards.

When 2 GLAS H reached the East end of the bridge over the Northern outlet of LANGE RENNE, contact was to be made with 7 SEAFORTH which was then to start clearing the small wood West and North of the bridge. 9 CAMERONIANS was to capture the area BRUCKSHOF-WISSHOF as soon as possible after dark.

Operations 25 March

2 GLAS H moved off by march route at 1100 hours, to its forming-up place in the BERGEN area and by 1515 hours was established in the Southern part of the wood and at HOODMANSHOF. From here, the battalion pushed on through the wood, with its Left flank on the LANGE RENNE and by 1830 hours was occupying a position in the Northern edge of the wood immediately South of the road HAFFEN-MEHRHOO. Seventy prisoners were taken during this operation.

2 A & SH moved up through the Eastern part of the wood. (This battalion was short of one company which could not be relieved in its former location in time—this company rejoined the battalion in the early hours of 26 March). By nightfall, the battalion had reached the Northern outskirts of the wood in the KOPENHQF area, taking some forty prisoners. Here they were sharply counter-attacked as they dug in, but the enemy was beaten off at point blank range. During the day the battalion suffered six casualties.

7 SEAFORTH remained in the MEHR area in observation until the evening, when contact was established with 2 GLAS H at the bridge, which was partially demolished and fit only for foot traffic. The wood West of the water obstacle was then cleared, patrols being pushed out towards BELLING-HOVEN. Thirty-five prisoners were taken during the day.

9 CAMERONIANS repulsed a counter-attack on their positions during the afternoon and at last light began the attack on the area BRUCKSHOF-WISSHOFF. By 2130 hours, after a sharp small-arms fire fight, all objectives were taken and consolidated: fifty-seven prisoners had been taken. 9 CAMERONIANS lost, five killed, and fifteen wounded during the day.

At about 2300 hours, 2 GLAS H was counter-attacked by small enemy forces which were beaten off. At approximately the same time, orders were received for the relief, during the night, of 7 SEAFORTH and 9 CAMERONIANS by 10 HLI (227 (H) Bde). 9 CAMERONIANS then concentrated just West of HAFFEN, and the brigade prepared for a further advance North East next day. Brigade HQ crossed the RHINE during the evening and was established immediately South of REE.

C. 4 ARMD BDE

Concentration

4 Armd Bde (less 44 R Tks) concentrated by night South of UDEM on 17 and 18 March. Meanwhile, 44 R Tks was training in DD Tanks in HOLLAND, and did not move to its Assembly Area South of XANTEN until 22 March (see Map 4).

4 RHA came under command CRA 15 (S) Div and moved into 15 (S) Div gun area. In order to reduce movement, with consequent loss of fire power, during its subsequent operations, this regiment was sited as close as possible to the Armour Waiting Area.

The brigade was under command of 15 (S) Div for the operation, with 129 Bty (86 A Tk Regt) (SP) under command and 82 Aslt Sqn RE in support.

Brigade Commander's plan

The Brigade Commander's intention was as follows:—

4 Armd Bde will

(a) Pass 44 Tks over the river at first light D Day with the primary task of supporting 46 (H) Bde in the capture of their objective (Map 14), but prepared also to support 44 (L) or 227 (H) Bdes if ordered.

(b) Form a mobile striking force to operate from the bridgehead with the probable task of seizing and holding WISSMAN — bridge at GREVERSHOF.

(c) Be prepared to support 6 Brit Airborne Div if ordered.

(d) Be prepared to come under command 53 (W) Div when they pass through 15 (S) Div.

The composition of the mobile striking force was as under:—

Royal Scots Greys (2nd Dragoons) (GREYS)
4 RHA
129 SP Bty 86 A Tk Regt RA
82 Aslt Sqn RE
One squadron 49 APC Regt
2nd Battalion Kings Royal Rifle Corps (2 KRRC)
One infantry battalion from 15 (S) Div (to be nominated later in accordance with the situation)

3rd/4th County of London Yeomanry (Sharpshooters) (3/4 CLY) was in reserve.

Operations 24 March

The operations of 44 R Tks have already been covered. On 24 March 4 RHA was in action with 15 (S) Div RA from gun positions West of the RHINE, while the rest of the brigade remained in the concentration areas. During the morning, a troop of Brigade HQ tanks was sent forward to shoot up enemy posts on the far bank from positions on the near bank, in an attempt to assist 227 (H) Bde in clearing the bund.

Operations 25 March

4 RHA was to cross the RHINE under orders of CRA 15 (S) Div on highest priority, but owing to some delays with the class 50/60 rafts due to shelling, was not able to do so until the evening of 25 March. During the day the Regiment was in action from the West bank in support of 46 (H) Bde.

Crossing of the RHINE by the GREYS, next in priority to 4 RHA, was also delayed and the Regiment spent the whole of the day of 25 March in the Armour Waiting Area, and eventually crossed by the class 40 bridge in the early hours of 26 March.

3/4 CLY left the Concentration Area at 1930 hours and crossed the river without passing through the Armour Waiting Area. As a result, it was concentrated on the far side soon after midnight, in advance of the GREYS.

It had originally been intended that 2 KRRC should cross the river carried on the tanks of the GREYS, but owing to the delay imposed on the latter regiment, 2 KRRC crossed independently by ferry during 25 March, and was concentrated in VISSEL by 2100 hours.

The squadron 49 APC Regt was also delayed, and crossed by class 40 bridge at 0200 hours 26 March, with the intention of picking up a battalion of 44 (L) Bde.

Brigade Tac HQ crossed immediately after 4 RHA. (The Brigade Commander had crossed during the morning of 25 March in an amphibious "Weasel" and spent the day with 44 R Tks).

The Brigade, apart from 44 R Tks and 4 RHA, did not therefore go into action until 26 March.

D. 157 BDE (52 (L) DIV)

52 (L) Div had been ordered in the original 12 Corps plan to hold one brigade group (less field regiment) at three hours notice on a jeep and carrier basis from 1200 hours on D Day (24 March) to come under operational command of 15 (S) Div when required. This brigade crossed the RHINE during the evening of 25 March under command of 15 (S) Div, and during the night 25/26 March relieved 6 Airlanding Bde of 6 Brit Airborne Div. The later brigade was thus able to side-step Southwards as foreseen in the original plan (see Map 3).

E. RE OPERATIONS

The 12 Corps Engineeer operation did not experience enemy interference on the scale met on the 30 Corps sector. It was carried out with few mishaps and went from the start almost exactly according to plan. The situation in 227 (H) Bde sector did however delay construction of the class 50/60 rafts, but the rapid advance of 44 (L) Bde enabled the class 40 Bailey bridge to be opened nearly thirty-six hours before the time forecast.

Reconnaissances were completed by D Day on the near bank down to the water's edge. No parties were allowed to cross the river.

By H Hour the approaches to the river for LVsT, which included gapping the bund, were complete. The LVsT entered the water on time.

The stormboats, which had begun to move forward from their hides before midnight, were in the water on the Left by 0200 hours, and on the Right by 0220 hours. There the crews set up their ferry services. They carried across men of the follow-up battalions of the assault brigades, and of the follow-up brigade of 15 (S) Div during 24 March.

Meanwhile, the class 9 rafts had been moved to a Waiting Area near the bank, and the first were called forward at 0230 hours 24 March. On the Right hand site 15 (Kent) GHQ Troops Engineers had rafts down to the water by 0330 hours. By 0630 hours two rafts were operating.

The other two which had been brought down to the river were knocked out by enemy action, but the reserves were called up. A third was operating by 1030 hours 24 March and a fourth later in the day.

On the Left, a far bank reconnaissance party had found the enemy dug in on the flood bank. Although the first raft was completed by 4 GHQ Troops Engineers at 0315 hours, enemy mortar and machine gun fire held up further construction and the start of ferrying.

At 0900 hours work was resumed. Three boats had been damaged, but a rafting service was begun at 1215 hours, although occasional loads had crossed earlier. With an average of three rafts working on each front, the total of vehicles carried over was, on the Right, 611 vehicles by 2100 hours 26 March and on the Left, 435 vehicles by 1200 hours 26 March. The ferries were not however, used to capacity.

The DUKW ferry opened at 1500 hours 24 March.

Owing to its size it was quite impossible to conceal class 50/60 Raft equipment in the forward area, and this was therefore held back on its sledges and trailers, to be drawn forward by AVsRE when required. The site selected for construction was still under observed enemy fire at dawn on 24 March, and CRE 42 Aslt Regt was unable to start the detailed reconnaissance necessary until mid-morning. The equipment was then called forward, and began to arrive at the site at 1300 hours. Rafting began that evening, and continued for 45 hours.

With an average of three rafts working, a total of 311 tanks and SP guns were taken across after which the ferry was closed. One raft was damaged by low-level bombing on the night 24/25 March.

Construction of the class 9 folding boat equipment bridge started at 1300 hours on 24 March and was opened at 2300 hours. Unfortunately, at 0200 hours 25 March, the trestles collapsed, owing to traffic congestion on the bridge, and 22 floating bays broke away, some sinking, some dragging away moorings. The bridge was re-opened at 1515 hours 25 March.

The next bridge to open was the class 40 (low level) Bailey pontoon bridge at 1630 hours 25 March. The class 12 Bailey pontoon bridge did not open till 0900 hours 26 March, having been delayed by earlier shelling of the bridge site and minor mishaps during the construction.

The all weather class 40 Bailey pontoon bridge, which entailed considerable high level flood spans, opened to traffic at 1010 hours 3 April with temporary approaches.

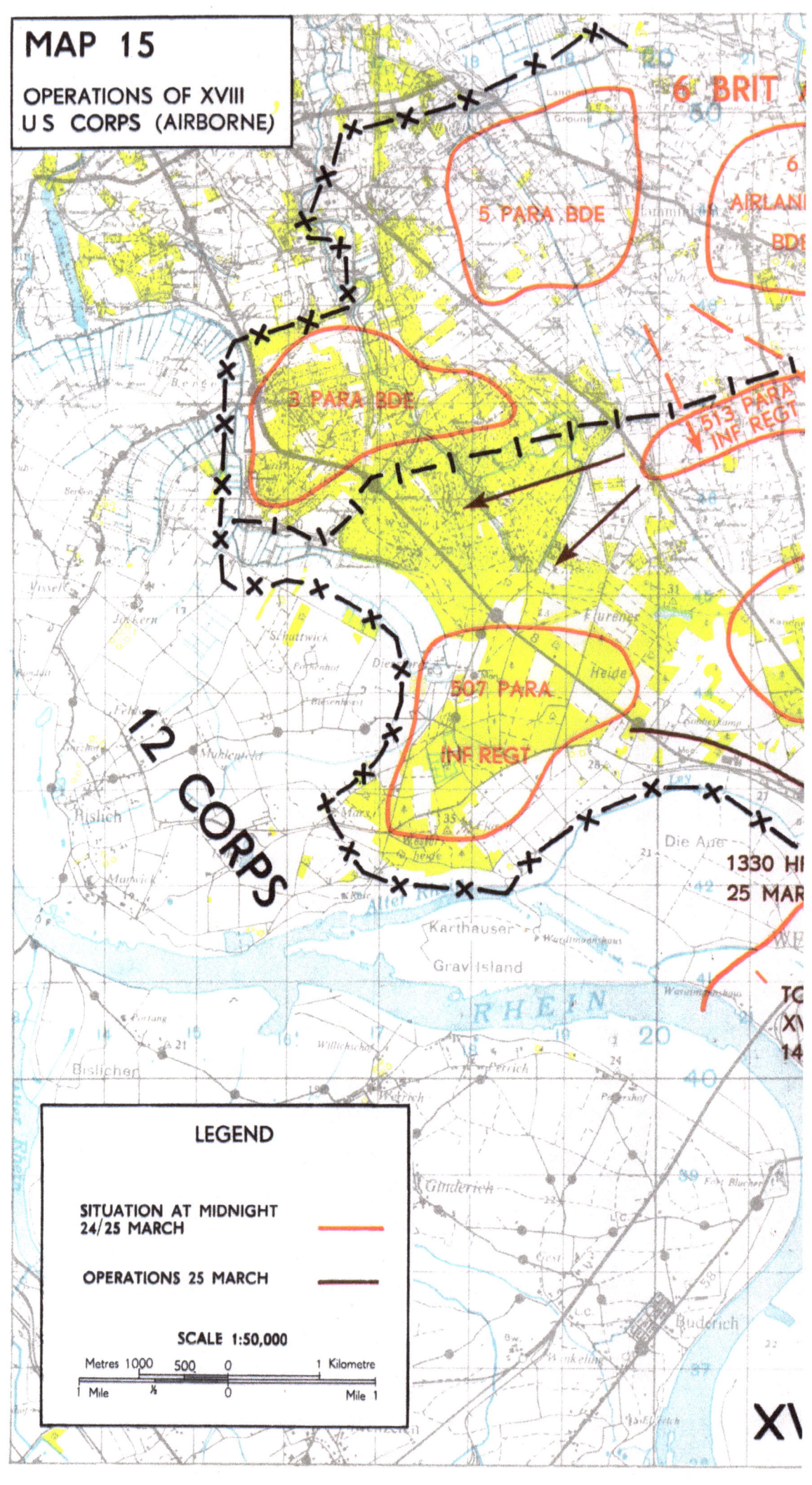

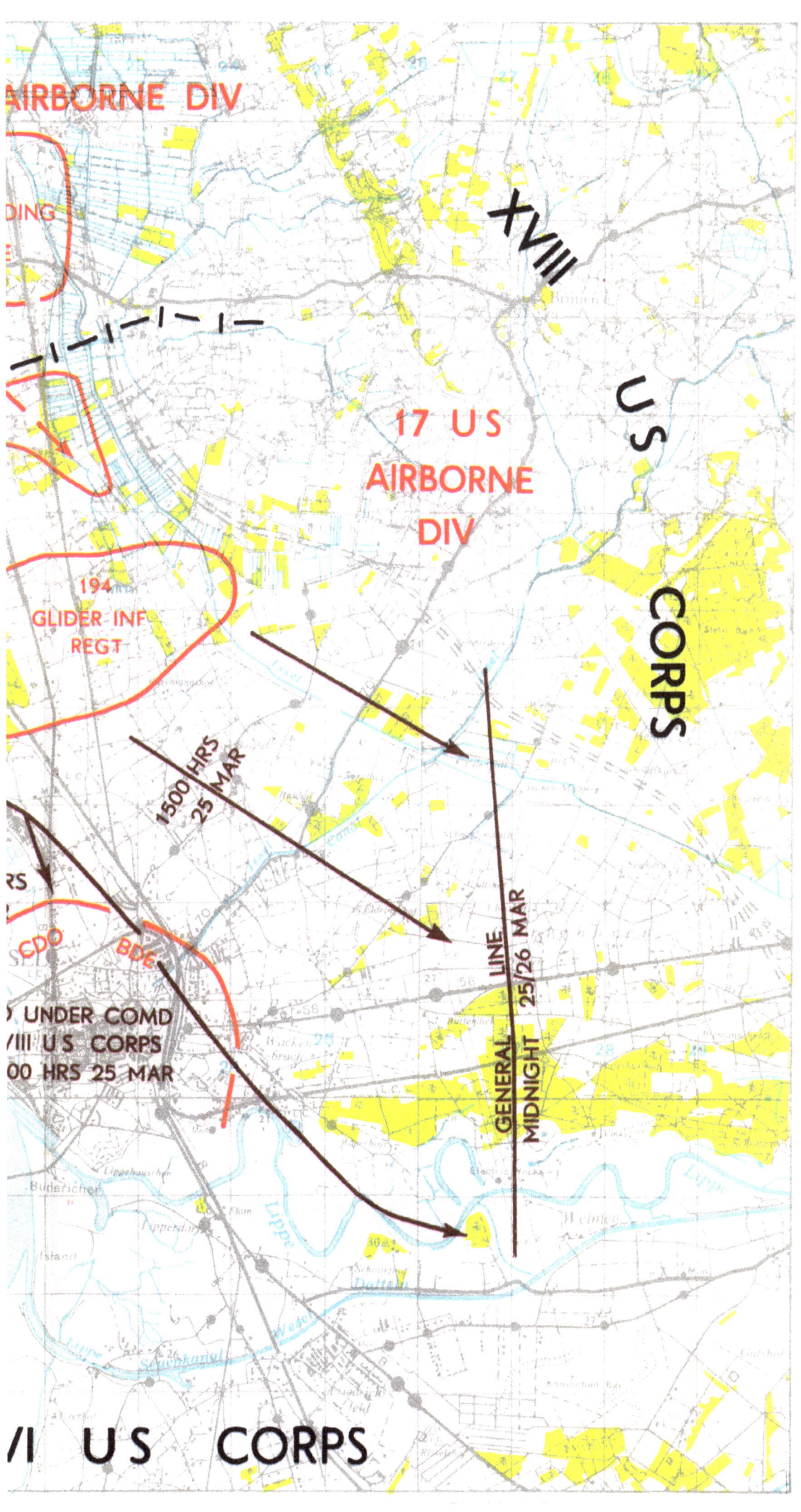

SECTION II

OPERATIONS BY OTHER CORPS OF SECOND ARMY
24/25 MARCH 1945

A. XVIII US Corps (AIRBORNE) (see Map 15)

Operations on 24 March

The airborne drop started at 1000 hours on 24 March in fine clear weather and from a cloudless sky. The aircraft had flown from bases not only in the UNITED KINGDOM but in FRANCE. They converged at a point between BRUSSELS and NAMUR, flying on thence in an impressive procession. Once over the RHINE they encountered moderate to intense anti-aircraft fire.

In the earlier stages casualties were very light but later, and particularly when the gliders began to arrive at about P plus 30 minutes, the enemy flak came to life and caused some trouble till overrun. The drop concluded at noon without interference from enemy aircraft, which proved how successful had been the air attacks on the German airfields.

Immediately after the initial phase there followed a re-supply mission in which 240 heavy bombers dropped 540 tons of petrol, food and ammunition. This comprised one day's re-supply for each of the airborne divisions.

By midday it was apparent that the operation had been carried out successfully. Preliminary reports put 194 Glider Inf Regt and 507 Para Inf Regt of 17 US Airborne Div in areas immediately East of DIERSFORDT and of ISSELROT respectively. 513 Para Inf Regt dropped North of their area and was moving South. 6 Brit Airborne Div was in the area of all its objectives. 6 Airlanding Bde reached the area immediately North East of HAMMINKELN and cleared HAMMINKELN. 5 Para Bde was in the area North West of HAMMINKELN and 3 Para Bde astride the main road WESEL–HALDERN in the North Western corner of the DIERSFORDTER WALD.

By midnight the position was quite clear. In the South 194 Glider Inf Regt had captured intact the two bridges over the ISSEL East of ISSELROT. 513 Para Inf Regt had moved South out of the area of 6 Brit Airborne Div and was preparing to attack the wooded ridge to the East of DIERSFORDT. 507 Para Inf Regt was on its objectives at the South end of the DIERSFORDTER WALD.

6 Brit Airborne Div, by midnight, was on all its divisional objectives. 6 Airlanding Bde was holding HAMMINKELN firmly with 12th Battalion The Devonshire Regiment (12 DEVONS). 1st Battalion the Royal Ulster Rifles (1 RUR) and 2nd Battalion the Oxfordshire and Buckinghamshire Light Infantry (2 OXF BUCKS) were on the ISSEL holding the bridges East of HAMMINKELN, which were intact. 3 Para Bde and 5 Para Bde were holding their objectives at the North end of the DIERSFORDTER WALD. Firm contact having been established with 12 Corps, air re-supply for 25 March was cancelled. During the night 24/25 March, 2 OXF BUCKS was attacked by tanks and infantry, and the Northern of the two road bridges, which had been prepared for demolition immediately on capture, had to be blown at 0200 hours. The attack was successfully held, though there was some infantry infiltration into 2 OXF BUCKS positions.

The impact of the airborne attack during 24 March completly overwhelmed the enemy in the area of the dominating DIERSFORDT ridge. The attack was of sufficient depth to disrupt artillery and rear defence positions. The result is shown in the prisoner totals for the first fourteen hours of the operation. 6 Brit Airborne Div took 1,500 prisoners and 17 US Airborne Div took 2,000. Most of these were from 84 Inf Div, including the anti-air-landing battle group KARST, with a few contributions from 7 Para Div.

Operations on 25 March

On the Right, XVIII US Corps (Airborne) spent the morning clearing and securing the divisional objectives and allowing for a further build-up of supporting arms.

507 Para Inf Regt of 17 US Airborne Div moved forward from the area of DIERSFORDT to come into line for the second phase of the attack.

As has been already mentioned 507 Para Inf Regt of 17 US Airborne Div was ordered to make firm contact with 1 Cdo Bde North West of WESEL. This link up took place at 1330 hours.

At 1500 hours 17 US Airborne Div attacked East across the ISSEL and ISSEL canal with Right 507 Para Inf Regt, Left 194 Glider Inf Regt. 507 Para Inf Regt attacked through the firm base held by 1 Cdo Bde and crossed the WESEL—DORSTEN railway one mile East of the town. On the Left 194 Glider Inf Regt was soon on its objectives beyond the ISSEL canal. 507 Para Inf Regt continued the advance throughout the day and shortly after midnight was firmly on its objectives with its Left flank in contact with 194 Glider Inf Regt and its Right flank on the River LIPPE approximately three miles East of WESEL. Opposition to both regiments was light throughout the day.

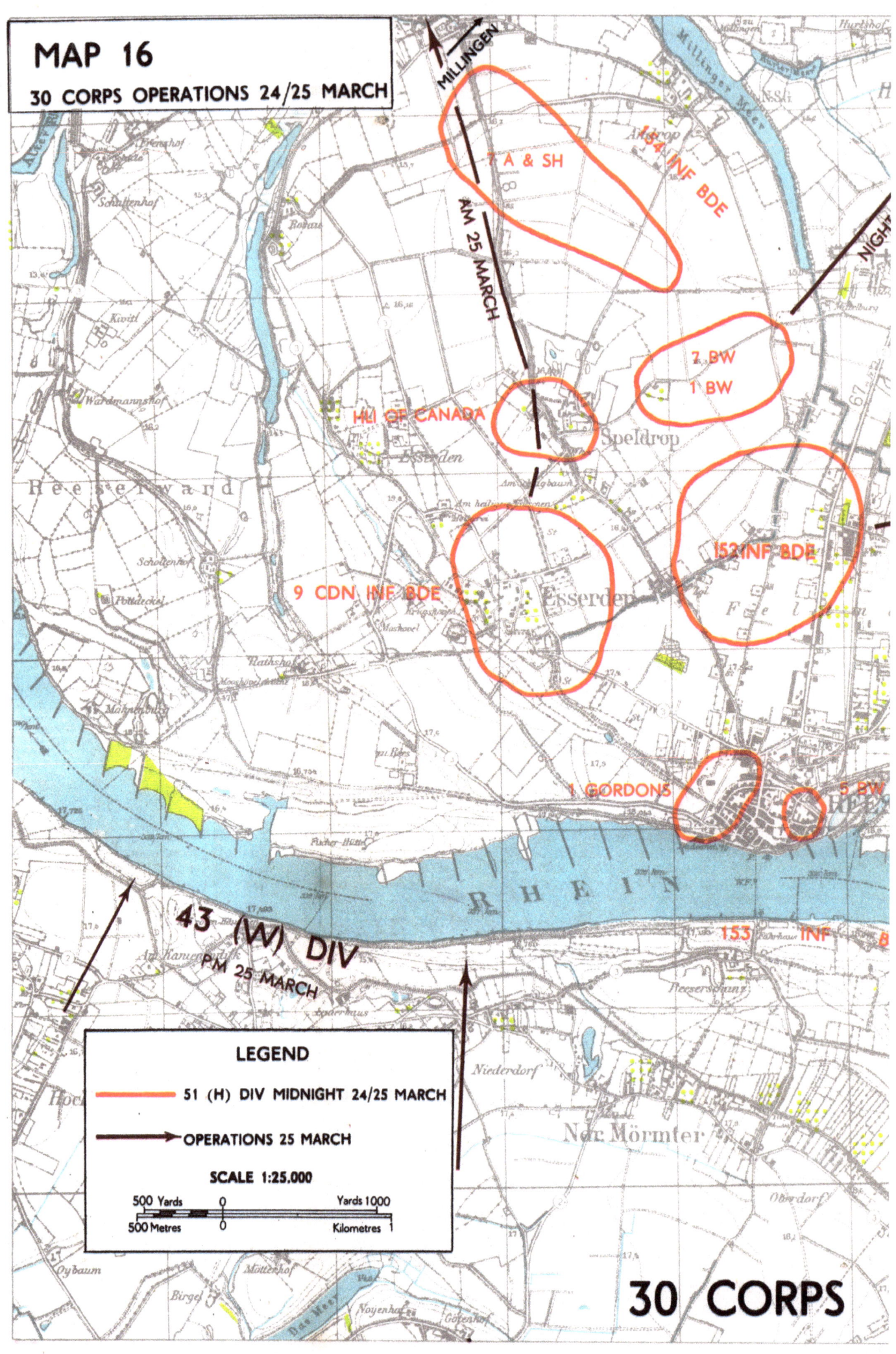

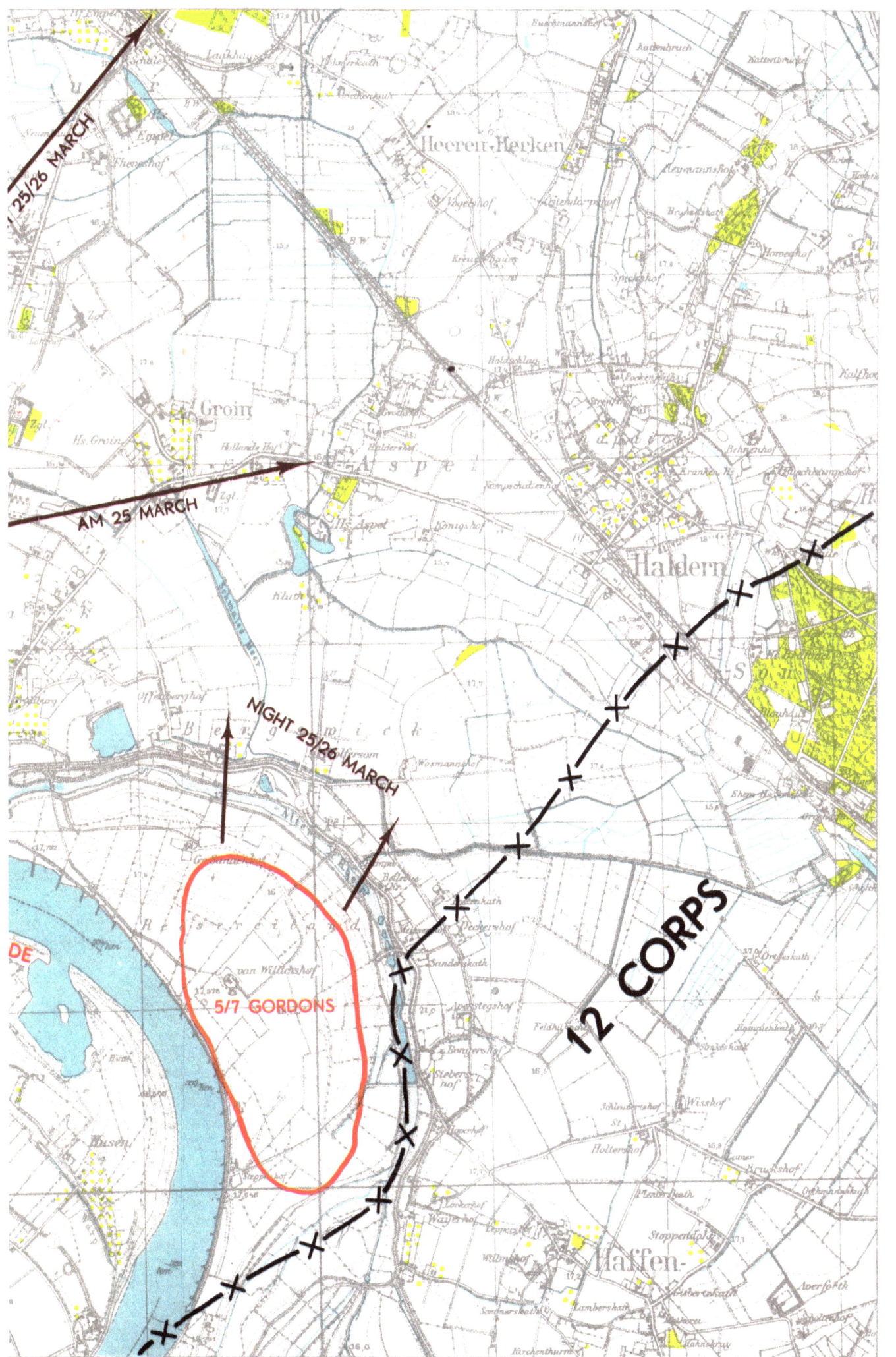

6 Brit Airborne Div did not attack on 25 March but continued to hold the two remaining HAMMINKELN bridges over the River ISSEL East of HAMMINKELN. Towards evening some enemy tanks approached the forward positions of 6 Airlanding Bde. These were engaged by 2 OXF BUCKS and later withdrew. During the night 25/26 March 6 Airlanding Bde was relieved by 157 Inf Bde of 52 (L) Div operating under command 15 (S) Div. 6 Airlanding Bde was thus able to side step Southwards before continuing its advance under XVIII US Corps (Airborne) on 26 March, as had been foreseen in the original Second Army plan.

B. 30 BRITISH CORPS

(See Map 16)

Operations on 23/24 March

51 (Highland) Division began the assault over the RHINE at 2100 hours on D—1, 23 March. The division attacked with two brigades up—Right 153 Inf Bde with 5th/7th Battalion Gordon Highlanders (5/7 GORDONS) and 5th Battalion Black Watch (The Royal Highland Regiment) (5 BW): and Left, 154 Inf Bde with 7th Battalion Argyll and Sutherland Highlanders (Princess Louise's) (7 A & SH) and 7th Battalion Black Watch (7 BW). 152 Inf Bde was initially in reserve.

7 A and SH landed on the East bank of the river at 2107 hours. By midnight all battalions of 153 Inf Bde were across the RHINE as were two battalions of 154 Inf Bde. ESSERDEN was reported clear.

Following the leading infantry came the first squadron of the STAFFORDSHIRE YEOMANRY (STAFFS YEO) (DD Tanks). These found the banks difficult to climb but by 0600 hours two troops were across.

Enemy resistance was not strong at first, but with the morning of 24 March sniping increased and there was considerable shelling and mortaring of the near bank. By midday 5/7 GORDONS had completely cleared REESEREILAND, the island immediately East of REES, but 1 GORDONS (the follow-up battalion of 153 Inf Bde) which was then halfway through REES, met the usual stiff opposition from paratroops. On the Left the forward position of 154 Inf Bde was obscure, but a company of the follow-up battalion, 1 BW, was known to have entered SPELDROP.

Till then enemy artillery fire had not been heavy but towards the evening it increased. It became apparent that there were in REES enemy artillery observers who could direct fire on the ferry and bridge sites and largely prevent their operating in this area. 9 Canadian Brigade (9 Cdn Bde) crossed the river and under command of 51 (H) Div cleared up the situation in SPELDROP.

By midnight on 24 March there was little change in REES where opposition was extremely fierce and 5/7 GORDONS found that heavy mortar and artillery fire made any crossing of the ALTER RHINE impossible. 152 Inf Bde was established to the North of REES. 154 Inf Bde had attacked north and established a footing in BIENEN. 9 Cdn Bde which had assumed responsibility for the Left of the bridgehead, prepared to advance from SPELDROP to MILLINGEN.

By this time twelve infantry battalions and approximately thirty DD tanks were across the river. 30 Corps laid strong emphasis on the capture of REES and during the night 5 BW attacked the town from the East.

Operations on 25 March

In the morning 25 March, 152 Inf Bde attacked East and cut the road REES—HALDERN.

9 Cdn Bde passed through 154 Inf Bde and cleared BIENEN. During the day a decrease of shelling made the work of the ferries at REES easier. The class 9 Rafts had all been concentrated opposite HONNEPEL. The class 50/60 Rafts, between REES and HONNEPEL, had started at 1015 hours on 24 March and the DUKW ferries started at 1015 hours 25 March.

REES was being steadily cleared by 1 GORONS but snipers remained persistent and a small pocket was still holding out at nightfall. It was considered that the decrease in shelling on the 30 Corps front was largely brought about by a method of air support previously untried during the operations of Second Army.

A "cab-rank" of six medium bombers operated every thirty minutes over the Corps area from 1300 to 1800 hours. This enabled the Corps to put upon enemy batteries the weight of a medium attack with the speed usually known only in a fighter-bomber attack on an opportunity target.

43 (Wessex) Division began to cross the river during the afternoon 25 March and assumed control of the Left sector of the bridgehead, taking 9 Cdn Bde under command for this purpose.

The night of 25/26 March saw the continuance of fierce fighting to extend the bridgehead North and East. 5/7 GORDONS made a successful crossing of the ALTER RHINE. 7 BW crossed the road/railway bridge three miles North of REES but confused fighting which took place there lasted all night. On the Left 130 Inf Bde of 43 (H) Div cleared ANDROP.

SECTION III

ENEMY OPERATIONS

As was expected, opposition to 12 Corps came largely from 7 Para Div and to a lesser extent from 84 Inf Div.

The enemy parachutists fought with their usual fanaticism, but resistance from the infantry formation was not so stubborn. The air landing by XVIII US Corps (Airborne) contributed very materially to the collapse of 84 Inf Div's resistance, by its wholesale disruption of the division's gun and rear defence areas.

This effect was less marked in the case of 7 Para Div whose rear areas escaped the initial impact of the airborne landings. Nevertheless as the airborne troops developed their build-up and subsequent operations, resistance even in the 7 Para Div area began to slacken, and the effect on morale of the great air armada passing over had undoubtedly been considerable.

Contrary to expectations, 116 Panzer Div was not committed against Second Army. Owing to the progress made by Ninth US Army, and the failure of 180 Div to impose any real delay on it, the enemy was forced to split 47 Panzer Corps. 116 Panzer Div was moved during the night 24/25 March to positions astride the LIPPE, with the bulk of the troops South of the River.

In general the German Armies opposing the crossing proved quite unable to cope with the great weight of the attack, the speed with which it developed and the rapid build-up of an overwhelming strength. Estimates gave enemy losses as in the neighbourhood of 30,000 men, whereas during the week 24–31 March Second Army losses amounted only to the comparatively small total of 233 officers and 2,941 other ranks.

SECTION IV

BUILD-UP

A. ADMINISTRATIVE

Prior to D Day

As was the case in the preparation for the break-out from the NORMANDY bridgehead, the main administrative problem which confronted Second Army in the preparation for the RHINE crossing was the rapid establishment of stocks in an area which had only recently been captured.

During the preparations for Operation PLUNDER, as the area between the MAAS and RHINE was cleared, it was possible by 12 March to speed the build-up of commodities into 10 Army Roadhead located in the area GOCH—KEVELAER. By 23 March the tonnage lift available to Second Army, excluding corps transport and bridging companies, but including troop-carrying vehicles, was 10,470 tons.

The routes available for the build-up by road transport were, however, limited by the bridge capacity on the MAAS which, in Second Army area, consisted of only three one-way and one two-way class 40. Furthermore, the routes available had to carry operational and maintenance traffic, as well as the transport engaged in this build-up.

It was estimated, therefore, that the routes over the MASS in Second Army area alone would be inadequate to deal with the volume of traffic required and arrangements were made with First Canadian Army and Ninth US Army for the partial use by Second Army of the class 70 bridges at GRAVE and VENLO respectively.

The amount of movement by road necessitated the most careful co-ordination, as both road and rail capacities were strictly limited. All road movement was controlled by HQ Second Army and in the period 8 to 23 March over 70,000 vehicles were under movement co-ordination.

Rail development proceeded apace, the MOOK—GENNEP line being laid at the rate of half a mile a day and the GENNEP bridge was completed within 30 days. The first trains of RE stores for the RHINE crossing were, as a result, discharged in the GOCH area on 21 March.

The railways worked extremely well during this vital period. 284 trains carrying commodities for 10 Army Roadhead were run between 8 and 23 March. At BOXMEER station alone 65 ammunition trains were cleared in these 16 days, although the station was served only by a single line of limited capacity. As much as 3,200 tons was cleared from this railhead in one day, an average of 2,000 tons per day being achieved.

During the Assault

During the early stages of the operation maintenance traffic was carried in DUKWs. The first lift was already loaded before H Hour, and was carried across and dumped as soon as the DUKW ferry sites were ready. Returning DUKWs were used to evacuate casualties, providing a smoother ride than the LVsT which had to be employed in the earlier stages.

The number of DUKWs available was strictly limited, and their mechanical condition, after prolonged use during the winter floods, was in many cases precarious. 12 Corps disposed of 84 DUKWs manned by RASC, and a further 50 from Ninth US Army resources.

B. TACTICAL

The Build-Up of 12 Corps

The tentative initial build-up planned for 12 Corps was as under:—

	Across river by	
	hours	*day*
15 (S) Div on Jeep and Carrier basis (less Artillery)	1930	D Day
53 (W) Div on Jeep and Carrier basis	1400	D + 1 day
Mobile Striking Force	1700	D + 1 day

As has been seen, this planned rate was not fully achieved. 53 (W) Div did not in fact cross the river until 26 March (D + 2); it had however been preceded by 157 Inf Bde of 52 (L) Div.

Estimated Vehicle Totals

It was estimated that for units and formations under corps alone, some 22,000 vehicles would pass through 12 Corps sector and 18,000 through 30 Corps sector, during the first seven days. There would then remain to cross a further 17,000 vehicles of other fighting formations, to which had to be added 17,000 vehicles engaged during the period on maintenance of the formations across the RHINE.

Overall Build-up of Second Army

Within one week of the start of the assault there were across the RHINE under command of Second Army, no less than eight infantry divisions, four armoured divisions, two airborne divisions and four independent armoured brigades, and an advance of 40 miles had been made.

Operation PLUNDER was the prelude to the pursuit of the German armed forces in the West which was soon to lead to final collapse.

SECTION V

CLOSE AIR SUPPORT

24 March, 1945

Air Support for Operation PLUNDER was very much restricted during D Day as the ground troops crossing the RHINE were within range of their own artillery support for the major part of the day. It was obvious, therefore, that the main effort in close support as supplied by 83 and 84 Groups should be devoted to the immediate area beyond the artillery support, namely the area of the drop of 6 Airborne Div. As this support had some direct bearing on the operations of the forward troops, it is worthy of mention.

During the day, 162 sorties were flown on pre-arranged support, 279 sorties on immediate support and 37 on armed reconnaissance. The main task was the attacking of enemy gun positions. The area of the assault and dropping area contained a mass of AA and dual purpose guns. Up to the general line North-South of the partially constructed autobahn these could be and were engaged by 83 and 84 Groups; beyond the autobahn, the area was heavily attacked by 2 Group and IX US Bomber Command before the airborne assault. During the drop, however, the RHINE crossings and the tugs and gliders of the airborne stream were open to attack from the guns that were still capable of firing. A comprehensive cab-rank system was worked out to deal with this period and the pilots who took part in it had no lack of targets. Most of the guns were firing at the incoming stream of troop carrier aircraft, and they had the pleasure of wiping out the flak gunners who had caused so many casualties to allied aircraft in the past. The efficiency of this operation can be gauged from the fact that out of 1500 aircraft which took part in the airborne operation, only 70 were missing at the end of the day.

After the drop had been completed, other gun positions, called for as targets by the ground troops or through Air Contact Teams, were also engaged. In addition to these, HQs and villages judged to be concentration areas for reserves, were also attacked.

Roads leading to the battle area were kept covered all day. The movement sighted and attacked was relatively slight.

25 March, 1945

It was evident that the enemy was beginning to deploy reserves, and as a result an increased number of enemy vehicles and tanks were seen in the forward areas although no free movement along the roads was seen by any but the first light sorties. Nevertheless practically all the armed reconnaissances found either tanks or other vehicles, and they were assisted in this by Tac R information relayed to them while in the air by the forward GCC. The fighter patrols, at the end of their usually uneventful watches, also went down to attack any targets of opportunity. In addition to this a cab-rank of four aircraft, which was maintained all day at 15 minute intervals from 0830 hours, was frequently given targets by the three Air Contact Teams. The most common targets were enemy tanks and transport lying up in the woods, and SP guns which were darting out to harass our forward troops. An unusually large number of targets was engaged by this quick method of close support and a satisfactory feature was the result of attacks on woods and houses where the pilots themselves could see nothing but which produced explosions and fires when hit by rocket projectiles.

The main means of assistance to the Army, however, lay in the silencing of enemy guns behind REES, which were making the supply and exploitation of the bridgehead extremely difficult. Certain batteries had been plotted on photographs the evening before and were attacked on this day. Other wider areas, where identification was less certain, were heavily attacked by carpets of bombs by 2 Group. Later on, as various batteries opened up, they were taken on by Fighter ground attack aircraft controlled by Air Contact Teams, and reinforced by further aircraft from 2 Group operating in sixes. Results on the whole were claimed to be good and were best shown by the Army's report in the evening that only two batteries were still giving trouble and firing into the REES area.

During the day 83 and 84 Groups flew 251 sorties on armed reconnaissance, 24 on pre-arranged support and 258 on immediate support.

PART III

(Directing Staff Edition)

Personal Accounts of Actions for Study

SECTION I

INTRODUCTORY LECTURES

A. GENERAL

Notes prepared by Brigadier G. M. Elliott, CBE, DSO, MC, Chief of Staff,
12 Corps, during Operation PLUNDER, March 1945.

Provision of Planning HQ

"The Commander-in-Chief's action in pulling out Second Army and 12 Corps HQ to plan this operation made a tremendous difference. It would have been very difficult to do with other operational commitments in hand and it seems, to me at any rate, a most desirable first step when undertaking an operation of this magnitude.

Assault Equipment

"Rightly or wrongly, we determined from the outset that we were going to do something better for the assaulting infantry than present them with stormboats. Even if one can marry up each individual outboard engine with the man who will use it on the operation for at least seven days before D Day, there still remains the unpleasant and expensive business of hanging about, embarking and starting up in the midlde of the enemy's defensive fire on the near bank.

The Buffalo enabled us to get away from all this, but it necessitated a completely new drill for the assaulting infantry, and secondly, a certain amount of training and rehearsal before the assault.

Bank Group

"It very soon became obvious that the control of the mass of vehicles, ferries, bridges, etc. was going to be a task which would require something outside Divisional and Corps resources, and, as the operation closely resembled a landing, a battalion from the Beach Group was asked for and called a Bank Group instead.

This Bank Group and the new drill for crossing a river meant the production of a complete new technique and this was tackled.

The Time Factor

"Time was, as always, a vital factor. It was essential to cross the River as soon as possible after the near bank had been cleared by Operation VERITABLE. The Commander-in-Chief, therefore, gave us a fortnight, and in this time divisions had to be pulled out, rested, trained in a new technique and concentrated for the operation. It might appear to be on the short side, but it worked.

This pressure of time meant that we had to present divisions with a complete drill and loading tables and that we had to give it to them in palatable form which they would accept at once, for there was no time for argument. It seemed vital to me that this drill and these loading tables should be flexible to a certain extent. If they were too flexible, we would not be helping divisions enough, but if they were too rigid, formation and unit commanders might very well say that they could not accept them, so what we had to do was to give them suggested loading tables with some spare room and some possibility of making small changes which the individual commander must want to effect. It meant a hard fight with specialised advice, but we won that fight and, in fact, the whole thing was swallowed by both assaulting divisions and by the other Corps HQ without any objections being raised.

This necessity for flexibility of course affects all planning, but I do think that it is particularly important when a completely new technique has to be absorbed in a very short time.

Experiment and Rehearsal

"We were given an infantry brigade and some tanks during the early planning stage and this helped enormously. However much one tries to keep one's feet on the ground and look at the problem from the point of view of the fighting soldiers, one cannot do it with the same success as those who actually have to assault. Added to this, of course, they provided the actual bodies and equipment for experiments and loading and helped enormously in every way. I suppose that one cannot expect to get this help always, but I do think it is most desirable.

Our training programme for the assault divisions included one model demonstration to explain the general picture and two full dress rehearsals, the first by day and the second by night. We thought it essential to include two rehearsals because the first one is practically always a bit of a "mess-up" and a bit of a disappointment, whereas the second one usually goes pretty well and leaves all concerned with a feeling of confidence. In actual fact, on this occasion neither went nearly as well as the actual operation.

We tried desperately hard to have films ready for assaulting divisions by the beginning of their training, but the cinema people could not produce anything in time. I think they would have been extremely valuable if we could have had them.

Concentration

"The concentration of the assault division and of the specialised armour, etc., was a most difficult problem, some details of which are available in the book. It in fact went very well. But the point about the concentration which I would like to make is that we held our follow-up divisions right back in the neighbourhood of BRUSSELS and DIEST until after the assault had gone in. The building of the bridges and the turn-round of ferries involved considerable delay in the crossing of the assault division and so the follow-up divisions had plenty of time to move forward into staging areas and get a rest there before they were required to cross.

Here again, my Commander insisted on flexibility. Follow-up divisions were positioned in Staging Areas according to their most probable task, i.e. 7th Armd Div on the Right opposite XANTEN and 53 (W) Div on the Left, but all arrangements were made so that they could be switched on to the other route if the development of the situation demanded it. These arrangements were very simple and did not actually have to be used.

Priorities

"Another matter in which flexibility was essential was in the priority of crossing of units within the assault division. All units of that division were placed in order of priority for crossing the River according to the most probable development of the situation, but arrangements had to be made beforehand by which this order could be changed by the Divisonal Commander if he wished to do so. Actually, we have since been told that too much use was made of this latter type of flexibility in the case of 15 (S) Div and that this actually resulted in some delay in getting vehicles across the river, but it is quite certain, in my mind at any rate, that it must be allowed for.

Traffic Routes

"A point which had to be watched very early was Army traffic routes. The Staging Areas for follow-up divisions had to be in localities where there was considerable Army traffic and it is a practical point which keeps on recurring that the very closest watch has got to be kept on routes. The closest liaison between Army and Corps traffic staffs is necessary to smooth this difficulty out, with reference, if need be, to the Chief of Staff, Army. Otherwise, you find that your only narrow UP route has become overnight a DOWN route, enforced as such by Army Provost.

Ferries and Bridges

"One of the most striking lessons of this operation, to us at any rate, was the appallingly slow turn-round of ferries. We were also struck by the slowness of bridge building compared to American and German standards. It is, of course, only a question of power and equipment.

Underwater Obstacles

"One point, which caused serious concern to the Corps Commander, but which in the end amounted to nothing, was that of underwater obstacles. I still think we got away with this one very lightly and if the enemy had cared to use even the simplest types as late as the night of D—1, there might have been a very different story in the actual operation.

Co-operation with Airborne Troops

"I have not yet touched on the Air-drop. It is very fully covered elsewhere. The fact that it came down on enemy batteries and close to our own troops gave us a tremendous advantage at the cost of considerable casualties to 6 Airborne Div.

We did out best to "applepie" the flak but we had to stop as soon as the leading aircraft appeared over the gun line and this gave the enemy ample time in which to get out of his slit trenches and man his guns.

The fact that our infantry of 15 (S) Div accepted without question and without a murmur the fact that they could have no artillery support whatever for the 3¼ hours of the fly-in made a great inpression on the Airborne Corps and that is merely one example of the spirit of co-operation which is required in such a complicated operation as this one was. The surprising thing is that it all went off like clockwork."

B. OVERALL AIR PLANNING

Notes prepared by Wing Commander D. G. SMALLWOOD, DSO, DFC, RAF.

Introduction

"When considering the overall air planning for Operation PLUNDER, it is important to remember that planning had to be undertaken not for PLUNDER alone, but to cover every aspect of the RHINE crossing. Only one main air plan was written by Headquarters 2nd Tactical Air Force, for the three main operations PLUNDER, VARSITY and FLASHPOINT. The details of air support for the three main operations were all so closely related that they had, from the outset, to be considered as one main air plan.

Preliminary Air Operations

"Air Operations in connection with the RHINE crossing began some two months before the date of the actual operation, the object being to create a favourable air situation for the assault. The two main types of attack considered most suitable to achieve this object were:—

(a) Attacks against the enemy airforces with intent to destroy as many aircraft as possible. Not only were these attacks to be carried out against enemy aircraft in the air, but also on the airfields and in the factories, and production plants allied to the production of aircraft. In addition, heavy bombardments were to be made on the oil producing and distributing plants.

(b) Attacks on enemy lines of communication carried out in three phases:—

   (i) The first phase, beginning on 9 February and finishing at the end of February, consisted of attacks designed to isolate the RUHR by the severing of its main communications.

   (ii) The second phase beginning in early March, comprised attacks concentrated closer to the projected battlefield area, the main object being to isolate this area from the RUHR.

   (iii) The final phase beginning on D—3 intended to crumble the enemy defensive positions and to disrupt completely the communications system on the East bank of the RHINE.

When considering these phases, it must be borne in mind, that throughout the preliminary period the main consideration in the minds of the planners was to maintain air superiority throughout the general area East of the RHINE and to gain complete local air superiority in the battle area for the period around D Day. The battle for air superiority in general was a continuous affair, and had been going on throughout the whole war, but as D day approached the main effort was gradually concentrated so as directly to affect the actual area selected for the assault crossing.

The Main Air Plan

"The Main Air Plan was issued by Headquarters, 2 TAF in mid-March. It was issued in the form of an outline directive detailing broadly the division of tasks and areas of responsibility of the various Air Forces participating. These tasks had been decided at various conferences held at all levels from SHAEF down to HQ 83 Group, and at these conferences the various Armies and Air Forces concerned were able to select from a multitude of tasks those most likely to assist the land battle.

Detailed Planning

"The detailed planning for Operation PLUNDER was delegated by Headquarters 2 TAF to Headquarters 83 Group. The broad divisions of responsibility given to the AOC 83 Group were:—

(a) The maintenance of air superiority over the assault area.
(b) The neutralisation of flak.
(c) The provision of fighter cover over the assault area.
(d) The provision of close support.
(e) The prevention of enemy movement into and within the battlefield area."

C. DETAILED AIR PLANNING

Notes prepared by Wing Commander P. E. ROSIER, DSO, OBE, RAF

Introduction

"The detailed air planning for Operation PLUNDER was carried out by 83 Group, the tactical group allied to Second British Army. At an early stage in planning, it was necessary to determine how the air forces could provide the maximum support for this operation. Headquarters 2 TAF sent air staff representatives to these preliminary conferences and an indication was given as to what support would be made available from resources outside 2 TAF.

It was appreciated at the time that strategic air operations designed to isolate the RUHR would have an appreciable effect on the conduct of Operation PLUNDER, but it was also necessary to plan a further interdiction programme with the ultimate effect of isolating the battlefield. A great part of this interdiction programme was carried out by strategical and medium bombers. A large scale programme of photographic and tactical reconnaissance was required not only for the provision of basic cover for briefing purposes, but also to provide information from which defence overprints could be maintained up-to-date.

A further phase in the air operations before PLUNDER was due to start would necessarily be:—

   (i) to disrupt communications within the battle area.
   (ii) demoralise the enemy in his billeting areas.
   (iii) hinder the enemy's defensive preparations.
   (iv) destroy enemy supply dumps.

It was further appreciated that additional forces to those within 83 Group would be required for this phase, and these forces were later detailed in 2 TAF outline air plan.

The final phase in the air operations was to support the detailed execution of Operation PLUNDER which would include air operations in support of Operation VARSITY.

The magnitude of this operation was such that 83 Group was given the operational control of forces from 84 Group and 29 USTAC for its task.

The Role of 83 Group

"As a result of these preliminary conferences, at both 2 TAF and 83 Group level, Headquarters 2 TAF produced an outline air plan detailing the responsibilities of various air forces taking part in this operation.

83 Group in addition to playing its part in the preliminary air operations for Operation PLUNDER was given the following tasks :—

    (i) Fighter protection for the assaulting troops of Ninth US Army and Second British Army, including airborne troops on the ground.

    (ii) Fighter protection of the airborne forces, aircraft and gliders, and re-supply aircraft while East of the RHINE.

    (iii) Anti-flak fighter patrols during the period of the airborne landings.

    (iv) Close support of associated ground forces.

    (v) Armed reconnaissance.

Both 84 Group and 29 USTAC were required to implement the fighter cover, anti-flak and armed reconnaissance operations and AOC 83 Group was given the responsibility of co-ordinating these tasks.

Formulation of the Detailed Plan

Deployment

"To make the most efficient use of the air resources within 83 Group, it was necessary to decide on the re-deployment of :—

    (i) Wings.

    (ii) Controlling centres — including Group Control Centre, Forward Control Post, Radar Units, and Control Cars.

    (iii) Tactical Group Headquarters.

It was decided to re-deploy part of the Group Control Centre, alongside the Forward Control Post so that a greater degree of decentralised control could be achieved, and sufficient channels of communication made available.

Role of Wings

"Each Wing within 83 Group and certain units within 84 Group and 29 USTAC were allotted definite tasks for this operation. These tasks included :—

    (i) Fighter sweeps.

    (ii) Fighter cover.

    (iii) Anti-flak.

    (iv) Armed reconnaissance.

    (v) Tactical reconnaissance and photo reconnaissance.

    (vi) Pre-arranged support.

    (vii) Impromptu support to be provided by aircraft kept at readiness on the ground and in the air.

Provision of Impromptu Air Support

"It was decided that a large measure of decentralisation should be adopted and that great use should be made of contact cars and aircraft on "cab-rank".

Administrative Arrangements

"The expected rate of effort of units within the Group was calculated so that the necessary provisions could be made for the supply of POL and ammunition.

Communications

"The re-deployment of various units and the use of additional air forces necessitated the provision of additional wireless channels and ground telephonic communications."

D. 15 (S) DIV PLANNING

In addition to the foregoing lectures, production of the play given in Section V provides a convenient means of putting all Spectators "in the picture."

SECTION II

ITINERARY

NOTE :
- (i) It is recommended that a period of approximately one hour be spent indoors on the planning aspects of 15 (S) Div operation and on the air operations. For this a large scale wall map and/or model are necessary. Alternatively, these accounts might be given and discussed at *STAND* 1, but there is no suitable stand from which the whole divisional sector can be seen at one time.
- (ii) It is assumed that spectators are accommodated in camp at the site suggested in Section IV (065454).
- (iii) Time for debussing and embussing has been allowed for.
- (iv) In the case of *STAND* 5, if means of crossing the river are not available, deduct *forty minutes* from all subsequent timings.

1. INDOORS
(Total time—one hour)

Time	Event	Personal Account
0830—0930 hours	A. 15 (S) Div Plan	Comd 46 (H) Bde
	B. 12 Corps RA Plan	GSO II HQ RA 12 Corps
	C. Medium Bomber Operations	WingComd(Flying) "Mosquito" Wing, 2 Group
	D. RE Plan	Comd 11 AGRE
0945 hours	*Depart Camp*	

2. ON GROUND

Time	Event	Personal Account
1000 hours	*Arrive STAND* 1 (122407)	
	Description of ground	Conducting Officer
1015 hours	*Depart STAND* 1	
1020 hours	*Arrive STAND* 2 (132415)	
	A. Description of ground	Conducting Officer
	B. Assault crossing by 44 (L) Bde	Comd 44 (L) Bde
	C. RE work on right sector of 15 (S) Div	Comd 11 AGRE
	Questions	
	D. Description of route to *STAND* 3	Conducting Officer
1045 hours	*Depart STAND* 2	
1055 hours	*Arrive debussing point* (116432)	
1115 hours	*Arrive STAND* 3 (123439)	
	A. Assault crossing by 8 RS	Adj, 8 RS
	B. Crossing by 44 R Tks	CO 44 R Tks
	Questions	
1140 hours	*Depart STAND* 3	
1200 hours	*Depart embussing point* (116432)	
1210 hours	*Arrive STAND* 4 (110448)	
	A. Issue Problem	Conducting Officer
	B. Study Problem (incl time for lunch)	
	C. Discuss Problem	do
	D. 227 (H) Bde Plan and Operations	do
1350 hours	*Depart STAND* 4	
1410 hours	*Arrive STAND* 5 (119461)	
	(if it is not possible to cross river, this *STAND* may be taken at 118453, see note (iv))	
	A. Assault crossing by 10 HLI	2 IC 10 HLI
	B. Action of C Coy 10 HLI	OC C Coy 10 HLI
	C. 46 (H) Bde operations	Comd 46 (H) Bde
	D. RE work in left sector of 15 (S) Div	Comd 11 AGRE
	Questions	
1500 hours	*Depart STAND* 5	
1530 hours	*Arrive STAND* 6 (086466)	
	Assault crossing by 2 A & SH	CO 2 A & SH
	Questions	
	Summing up	
1545 hours	*Depart STAND* 6	
1600 hours	*Arrive Camp*	

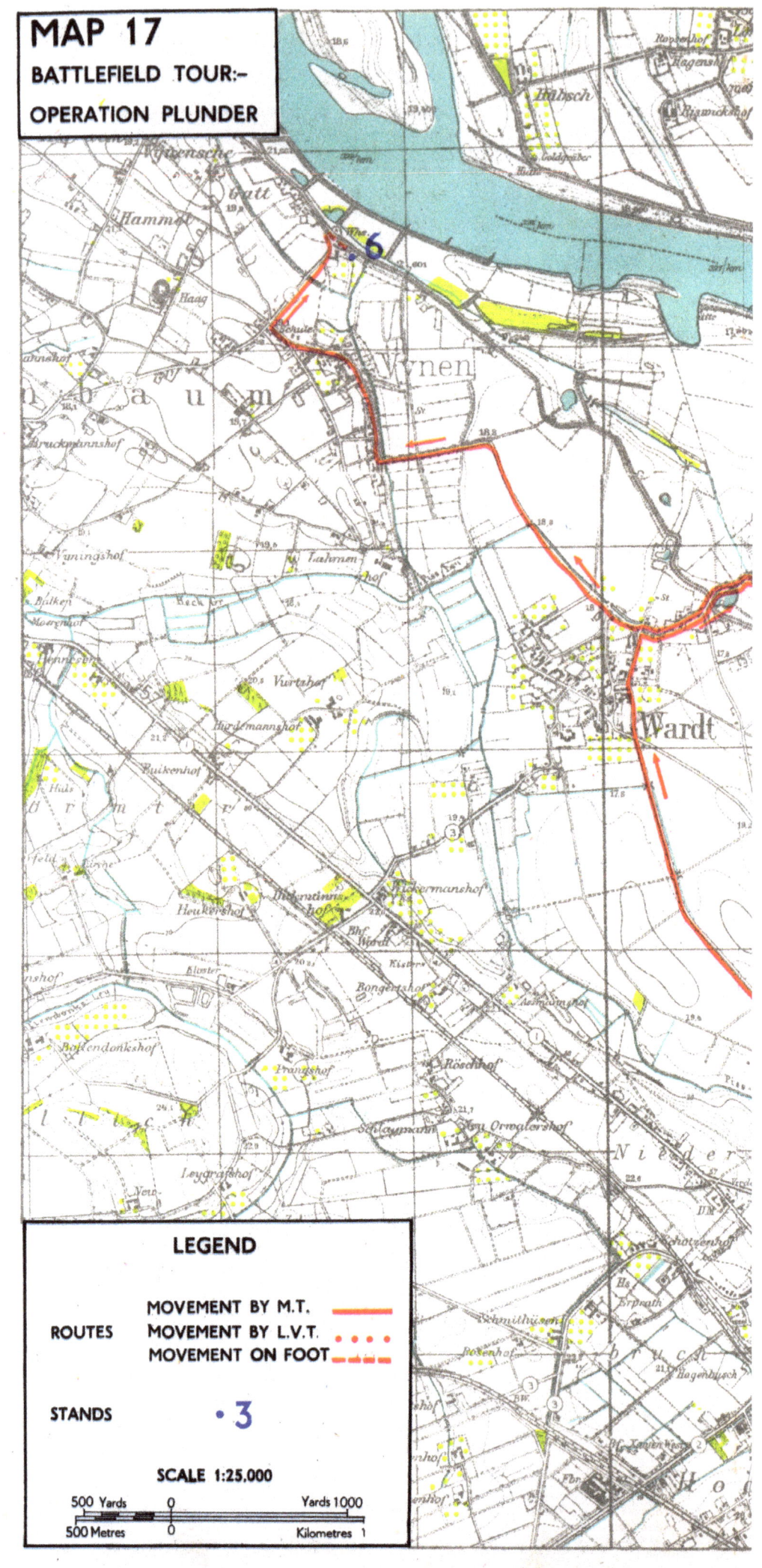

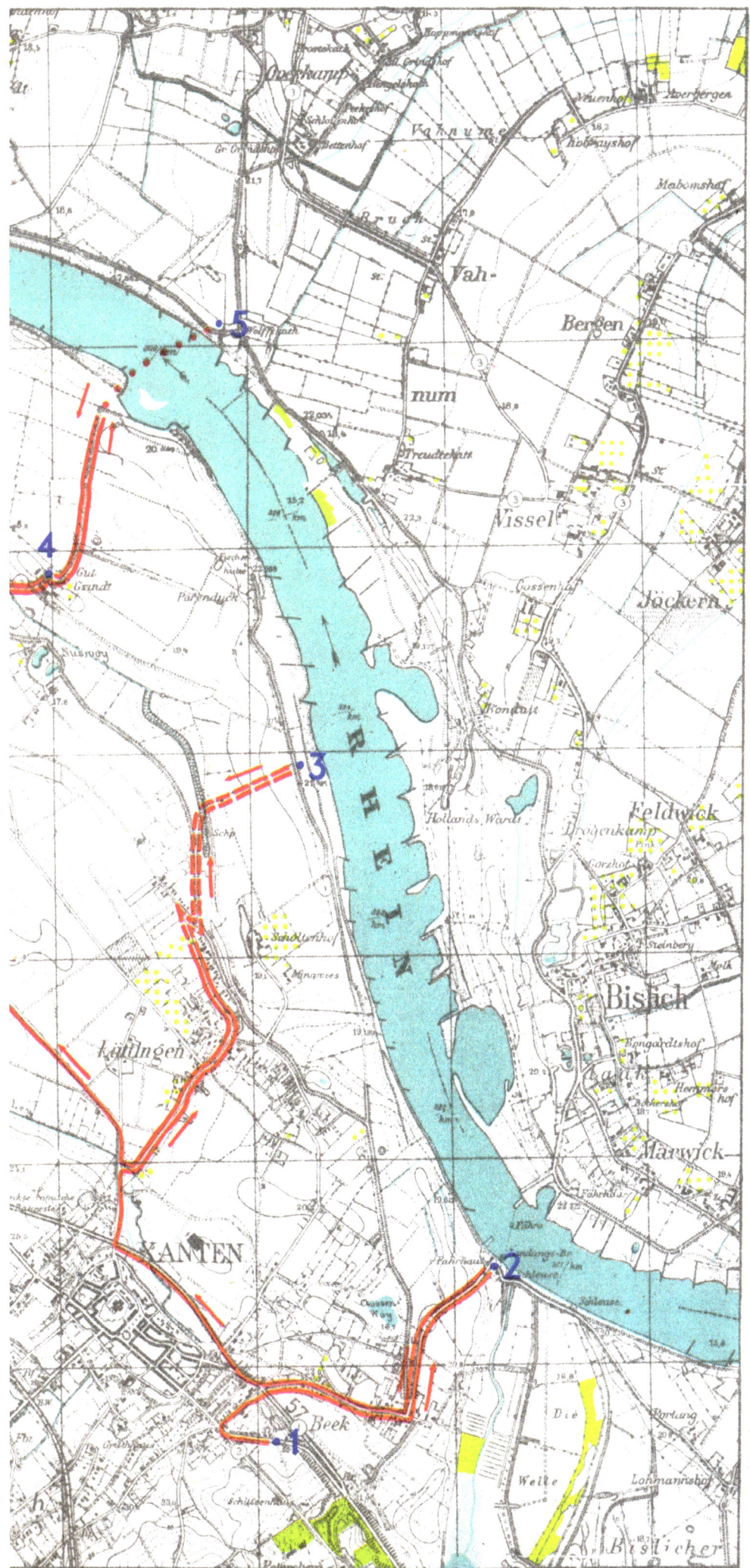

Indoors

SECTION III

PERSONAL ACCOUNTS

(Note :—Officers' ranks and decorations are given as at December 1947.
Appointments shewn are those held during operation PLUNDER in March 1945).

INDOORS

(The following accounts (A to D) are best given on a model or large scale map.
If required they could however be given at *STAND* 1).

Object :

To study :
- (i) Some factors affecting 15 (S) Div Plan and Operations.
- (ii) Artillery planning.
- (iii) Medium bomber operations.
- (iv) RE planning.

A. Brigadier R. M. VILLIERS, DSO, Comd 46 (H) Bde

15 (S) DIV PLAN

Preliminary Planning

"Operations to clear the West bank of the RHINE were not completed till 11 March 1945, and D Day for the assault crossing was fixed for 24 March, only 13 days later. This was only possible as a result of considerable forethought by the Higher Command. Intelligence data re river, banks, approaches etc were being collected in Oct 44, and in Jan 45 HQ 12 Corps were pulled out of the battle and located in BELGIUM to prepare technique instructions for the assault crossing. The excellent brochure they produced was the complete answer to the organisation necessary to get the assaulting troops to the river banks, and to ensure a quick build-up on the far bank. All the division had to do was to adapt the technique to the particular part of the river allotted to it. Without this technique instruction it would have not been possible to launch the crossing successfully at such short notice.

15 (S) Div tasks

"The frontage given to the division by 12 Corps was about 9,000 yards, and the two bridgehead areas where the division was told to establish itself were widely separated, thus making the assault on a two-brigade front necessary. There was little choice, too, in the actual crossing places, as these were determined by the bridge sites, and places suitable for LVsT to enter and leave the river. The technique instruction laid down that each assaulting division must have two bridges, of which one must be Class 40. There were three possible sites for these bridges, largely determined by the approaches to and exits from the river. Thus it was determined that one brigade must cross opposite XANTEN to BISLICH, and the other brigade opposite VYNEN to HAFFEN-MEHR. It was appreciated that there was a gap of about 4,000 yards between brigades, and that the left hand brigade bridgehead would be on somewhat of an "island" from which there was only one good exit—the bridge 1,000 yards North East of MEHR.

"One of the major difficulties facing the divisional commander was that only sufficient LVsT were available to lift the two assaulting battalions of each forward brigade. Thus the reserve battalions of forward brigades and the whole of the reserve brigade would have to cross by stormboats; this would only be possible when opposition on the far bank had been neutralised. In the event, the lack of LVsT for the reserve battalion of the left hand brigade was to be felt, as the two assaulting battalions of this brigade were not able to clear the far bank till about mid-day 24 March.

Reconnaissance

"Facilities for ground reconnaissance of the far bank by junior leaders of assaulting units were very limited. The smoke screen prevented any view of the far bank except on the two occasions when it was interrupted for this very purpose. For security reasons battalion commanders were not in general allowed to take their subordinates closer than about 1,000 yards from the river, except on the extreme Left where good cover was available. Company commanders therefore only had one or two distant glimpses of their crossing places and objectives. This difficulty was largely overcome by the air photos which were issued and by the issue to each brigade of an excellent ground model, constructed by some higher formation. All ranks were briefed on these models so that every man knew not only his own task but also what flanking units were to do. It was this detailed briefing which contributed considerably to the high morale, which was evident in all units, in spite of the obvious magnitude of the tasks ahead.

Indoors

"Another form of preparation which paid good dividends was that every single driver "walked the course" from the marshalling area to as near the river as it was safe to go ; and every officer of those units which were to approach the river on foot also walked the course.

Move forward to river

"In order that the move forward to the river should proceed smoothly it was necessary to have available the following for each assaulting brigade :—

>Two LVT tracks (one for each battalion)
>One vehicle track
>One infantry track.

One of the LVT tracks was later to be used as an AFV track. In addition to these, roads were necessary for the use of bridging lorries. Most of these tracks had to be made or improved, marked and lighted, and maintained. Care had to be taken in the original allotment in the marshalling areas to ensure that no vehicles had to cross the path of others in reaching their appropriate track.

Control of Movement

"All moves forward of marshalling areas were controlled by the Bank Group. This organisation was based on an infantry battalion, supplemented by two squadrons ROYALS, R SIGS and REME detachments, and by 50 officers sent up from RHUs. They had officer representatives at every installation and at every ferry and bridge site, all joined by wireless and line communications. Their task was to ensure that there was never a crowd of vehicles in the vulnerable forward area, and yet that no raft or LVT was kept waiting for a load.

"Every vehicle due to cross within 48 hours was allotted a serial number in the divisional priority tables, and it was a unit responsibility to see that vehicles left the marshalling area in the right order. If the tactical situation demanded a vehicle or group of vehicles to alter its priority, word was passed back and little difficulty was in fact encountered in making any necessary alterations after H Hour.

"One of the biggest problems for the "G" Staff at Div HQ, was deciding on priorities. A very large number of non-divisional vehicles had to be included on the priority list—these included Corps and Army Troops, recce parties of all arms, and the land-tail of the 17 US and 6 British Airborne Divisions. The number of divisional vehicles had to be correspondingly reduced, or rather put further down the list of priorities."

B. Major G.S. HEATHCOTE, MBE, GSO II, HQ RA, 12 Corps

12 CORPS FIRE PLAN

Resources and Command

"The CCRA commanded all the artillery for this operation. It consisted in all of 706 guns, not counting a battery of 12×30 barrelled rocket projectors and groups of minor weapons known as "PEPPERPOTS" which were used by RA 15 (S) Div.

Deployment

"In order to give guns maximum range East of the RHINE and to avoid having to move them during the critical stages of the operation, they were deployed very far forward.

"The problems of concealment, deployment, dumping and movement in this area were considerable. On the day, a number of guns opened on their initial targets at little over 1,000 yards range, which meant the use of reduced charges and possible loss of accuracy.

Fire Plan

"This is described in detail in Part I of the book. The fire plans were made almost entirely from information obtained from air photographs and defence overprint maps, though the counter bombardment programme also included guns located by sound-ranging and to some extent by flash spotting. It is of interest that attempts were made prior to the operation by field and medium guns to destroy certain buildings on the far bank overlooking the RHINE. These attempts were a failure and go to prove that the destruction of well built structures by any but very heavy artillery is a lengthy and uncertain process.

"The Fire Plan for WIDGEON (the Commando attack) consisted of a softening bombardment followed by covering fire in the form of a barrage and concentrations. For TORCHLIGHT (15 (S) Div) the plan was similar except that covering fire took the form of a very elaborate programme of concentrations. In addition six salvoes from the Rocket projector battery were fired in support of 15 (S) Div, each salvo being equivalent to a salvo from something of the order of thirty medium regiments.

Smoke

" "At call" smoke screens were planned in order to be able to blind the high ground around the DIERSFORDTER WALD. 600 rounds per gun of smoke for three field regiments were dumped for this purpose. It was never fired and was left behind on the gun positions. Corps Q Staff, who then had to arrange to collect the ammunition from 72 separate gun positions, were not best pleased.

Staff Duties

"The large number of separate fire plans in Operation PLUNDER coupled with the extensive distribution required made it essential to use a printing press to reproduce the traces, overprint maps, task tables etc. The press was located near HQ RA 12 Corps and formations originating fire plans prepared them for the press on the advice of an officer from HQ RA 12 Corps who then delivered them to the press. Completed work already bundled into the correct quantities by the press was collected by LOs by 1200 hours on D—1. I am sure that the normal methods of duplication are quite inadequate in an operation on this scale.

AA Defence

"Commander 100 AA Bde was responsible for the AA defence of the Corps area and in particular of the bridge sites. Certain LAA guns were ferried across the river early in the operations on 15 (S) Div's front. The two HAA regiments, having taken part in the fire plan in the ground role, then reverted to their primary role and 90 HAA regiment was deployed on the East bank soon after the class 40 bridge was completed.

"In addition to AA defence, Commander 100 AA Bde was also responsible for the ground and water defences of the bridges. This latter task led to frequent fusilades against all floating objects suspected of being mines. CDL tanks and 17-pr A tk guns were placed under command of Commander 100 AA Bde to strengthen the ground and water defences.

Movement Light (Artificial Moonlight)

"This was used on a large scale. Some days prior to the operation, lights were deployed and exposed along the front to accustom the enemy to their use. On the night 23/24 March two batteries of lights were used in banks at varying distances from the river. "Moonlight OPs" were used in order to control the intensity of light from the river bank in accordance with the requirements of the commanders concerned.

Planning

"Most of the planning for this operation was carried out when HQ 12 Corps was at EYSDEN, which is 70 miles from the scene of the operation. While suitable for training formations on the MAAS, the location of 12 Corps HQ made planning very difficult. The distances to formations which were to be under our command for the operation were great and we had satisfactory telephone communication only with RA 15 (S) Div. The planning was coordinated at the Corps level by two conferences, one on 12 March at Second Army HQ and one on 22 March in the forward area in a room lent by HQ RA 8 Corps.

Movement to Deployment Areas

"Traffic control was a major problem during the concentration and deployment stage. The necessity for surprise made it essential to deploy late in the forward areas and in fact few guns were deployed before the night D—2/D—1. On the other hand the wide dispersion of formations prior to the operation together with the limited routes over the MAAS forced Q Movements into implementing a fairly rigid movement plan spread over several days before D Day. It was therefore necessary to stage most artillery formations in the area ISSUM-KAPELLEN about 10 miles from the RHINE before they deployed. The subsequent move from "staging area" to deployment areas combined with the other movements in progress, including a very heavy dumping programme, was only solved, I think, by very close liaison between 12 Corps traffic staff and HQ RA, whose offices were located side by side."

C. **Wing Commander D. MITCHELL, DFC, AFC, RAF,** Wing Commander Flying of a "Mosquito" Wing in 2 Group

OPERATIONS OF MEDIUM BOMBERS

"2 Group RAF was the tactical bomber element of 2 TAF and was charged with the dual role of :
  (i) Providing tactical bomber support to ground forces by day and carrying out offensive bombing attacks in the semi-strategic area.
  (ii) Offensive operations by night attack fighter bomber aircraft, ranging from the tactical to the strategic areas, thereby enabling the interdiction and harassing programme to be carried out by night as well as by day.

"The varied characteristics of these two roles dictated that the Group should be divided, and it therefore consisted of two daylight medium bomber wings and three night attack wings. The latter also carried out various special low level bombing attacks on special strategic targets by day.

"The medium bomber wings were equipped with Mitchell aircraft and carried out their attacks at medium altitude from 8—14,000 feet in formations, usually of six aircraft.

"The night wings employed the fighter bomber version of the Mosquito and attacked singly by night, using bombs, cannons and machine guns.

"In order to ensure that the bomber offensive might be pressed home successfully in adverse weather conditions by day and night, certain radar aids to bombing and navigation were essential. Those used were—GEE for navigation, GH for daylight bombing attacks and the Mobile Radar Control Post for both day and night attacks. Whilst on this subject the value of MRCP should be stressed ; its particular merits being the ability to change targets at very short notice and the control of medium bomber formations at readiness in the air awaiting a target of opportunity, including the run-up and instructions for the formation's bomb release.

Indoors

"Having examined briefly the roles of a tactical bomber force, it will be of interest to see what strength and rate of effort 2 Group was able to supply. The normal daylight operational strength of the medium bomber wings amounted to 72 aircraft, attacking in formations of six, normally operating twice a day. The three night attack wings could provide an effort of approximately 120 aircraft and in certain circumstances could carry out two sorties a night.

"During the preliminary interdiction plan, leading up to the operations to cross the river, 2 Group took no part. This plan, which aimed at the isolation of the RUHR, was carried out by various heavy bomber forces. At this time the daylight element of 2 Group was engaged in support of operation VERITABLE.

"The second phase interdiction plan was designed to isolate the tactical area to the North of the RUHR and East of the RHINE and prevent supplies and reinforcements moving into it. The daylight wings undertook a number of attacks on various targets at the following places with this aim in view: DORSTEN, HALTERN, DULMEN, COESFELD, AHAUS, BURGSTEINFURT, BORKEN, STADTLOHN, WINTERSWIJK.

"During this period, the night attack Squadrons concentrated on preventing movement into this area by night and covered all roads and railways leading into it from the East, going back to the East of HANNOVER and OSNABRUCK. In addition, they had the commitment of disrupting supply movement into the V2 rocket firing area of NORTH HOLLAND.

"This programme was concluded considerably earlier than was expected, due to good results and the excellent weather. The weight of attacks until D Day was therefore turned on to the immediate battle area, with the object of destroying communications, billets and defensive systems. 2 Group took part in this, attacking targets at :—BRUNEN, DINGDEN, RAESFELD, RHEDE, BOCHOLT, HALDERN and AALTEN.

"During the night that Operation PLUNDER began, the night attack force prevented the movement of supplies into the battle area and harassed the towns of ISSELBURG, DINGDEN, BRUNEN, RAESFELD.

"The main opposition to Operation VARSITY was clearly likely to be from light flak in the neighbourhood of the DZs and LZs. An anti-flak plan was drawn up, covering operations by fighter and medium bombers and heavy and medium artillery. Areas were allotted to each force and 72 medium bomber aircraft carried out attacks, using fragmentation bombs dropped in clusters. In view of the short time available for the attack and the necessity of using MRCP, it was decided to employ the mediums in formations of eighteen aircraft, all bombing together.

"The reason why these attacks were not as effective as was hoped may be attributed to three factors :—

(a) Selection of areas for flak neutralisation as between artillery and air forces.

(b) The necessity for fragmentation bombing aircraft to be out of the area one hour before the airborne drop.

(c) The execution of the attack in formations of eighteen aircraft on MRCP which may have reduced the accuracy.

"Further operations in support of the RHINE crossing were undertaken on subsequent days, the most noteworthy being the destruction of a gun area near EMMERICH of 39 guns, which were preventing the completion of bridges across the RHINE.

"In conclusion, it should be pointed out that none of these operations were other than normal routine work as carried out by the tactical bomber element throughout the campaign. Throughout, the principal limiting factor to tactical bomber support was the small size of the force, which was partially overcome by the high intensity of operational effort and the ability to operate in adverse weather conditions."

D. Lieutenant Colonel R. N. FOSTER, DSO, OBE, Commander 11 AGRE

THE RE PLAN

Necessity for an AGRE

"The execution of the RE plan was the responsibility of the Assaulting Divisional Commander. The Divisional Engineers, however, had not the resources to execute the tasks themselves nor to control the number of additional sappers required. Consequently, an AGRE was put under command 15 (S) Div together with the additional engineer units required for the task, including attached RN, Aslt RE, RASC and R Pnr Corps units. The total came to nearly 9,000 Sappers. Provision of two such forces, one each for 12 and 30 Corps, practically skinned Second Army of RE units and American assistance had to be sought in the rear areas.

Factors influencing the Plan

"Bridging sites are limited by possible approaches, which may easily take far longer to construct than the bridges themselves. On this score, our sector had only three possible sites, and one of these involved 1,000 yards of approach-road construction—this had to be a class 9 site.

We therefore chose sites as follows for our bridges :—

(a) Class 40 on the only good route, XANTEN—BISLICH.

(b) Class 9 opposite WARDT (where approaches had to be constructed).

(c) Class 12 at VYNEN.

The far bank of the river had a retaining wall in places up which LVsT could not climb. This limited the choice of site for LVT work. Unfortunately, sites suitable for bridges are also wanted for DD Tks, LVsT, rafts and ferries since all require approximately the same conditions of stream and bank, i.e., the most favourable. This brings us to inevitable conflict, which has to be settled by the Commander.

Decisions by Commander

"The question to be decided is one of priority. Who is to have priority of choice of sites and for how long? Once the really essential F Echelon vehicles and anti-tank guns are over on the far bank, it is better to give way to bridging, which later will pay a dividend in rate of build-up of vehicles. Ferrying is inevitably a slow and unreliable process. LVsT were therefore given complete carte blanche for their first flights and first choice for their ferry sites, though two out of four LVT ferries were to be stopped when bridging began.

River Defence

"The extensive plan for floating patrols, booms, and artillery defence against swimmers, debris, floating mines or craft (enemy or our own) was based on experience at NIJMEGEN where the conditions were not really similar.

"There the enemy was established and undisturbed on the river upstream whereas on the RHINE, upstream of 12 Corps Sector, he was being subjected to a full scale assault. It is doubtful if the full effort was necessary in this operation, and though more than 50 "mines" were claimed, nobody in fact ever produced a mine or even a part of one for inspection. However none got through—perhaps a somewhat remarkable fact!

Planning Difficulties

"Some of our difficulties were the following:
 (a) The AGRE staff was inadequate and we had to co-opt officers from elsewhere.
 (b) CsRE under command were fully engaged on MAAS bridging or roadwork, and briefing was therefore none too easy.
 (c) The executive orders for stores for preparatory work had to be given at the same time as a colossal list of stores was being prepared for the main operation.

Site of the RE Stores Dump

"This was originally chosen off the map in an area South-West of the HOCHWALD which at the time was still held by the enemy, but which appeared to offer cover from the air and reasonable access. When the time came it could not be used as it was mined and too restricted, and the roads were useless.

"A new site was chosen near KEVELAER, which was a good centre of communication. This is an essential requisite though it may conflict with security from enemy air bombing.

LVT and DD Tk units

"It proved difficult to obtain, early, firm decisions on the exact routes LVsT wanted. It must be remembered that LVsT cannot disregard country if they are to travel with certainty in line ahead by night. Sappers had to do a lot of preparation of crossings over ditches and roads, and the necessary orders had to be transmitted to a CRE 60 miles away. We also had to produce twelve gaps in flood banks for the LVsT, but were not allowed to start this work until after dark on the night D—1/D day. It was the subject of considerable experiment, both with explosives and otherwise, but in the event the gaps were cut by bulldozers.

Security

"Crossings of streams, made for LVsT, had to be camouflaged from air observation, a matter of some difficulty. For security reasons, the time for dumping of stormboats and class 9 raft equipment was very restricted, and these also had to be camouflaged. This took place during the three nights prior to D—1 and involved 140 lorry-loads, comprising 80 stormboat loads and 60 loads for class 9 rafts.

"For 52 (L) Div, this meant producing working parties each of the three nights.

Movement of Stormboats and Class 9 Raft Equipment to the River

"50 half-tracks were laid on to tow the sledges with raft gear or stormboats to the river bank from the hides. In case this did not work it was necessary to keep no less than 980 men of the holding division standing by to carry the equipment.

Communications

"Neither AGRE nor GHQ Tps Engineers were equipped with wireless. In consequence sets and operators had to be borrowed from a variety of units and it was a great relief when the improvised net of 13 outstations worked. Owing to previous wireless silence, no practice had been possible between the assorted operators, few of whom were known to each other.

Bridging Troops kept fresh

"Sappers due to work on bridges were not moved into the forward area until they could begin work. This saved casualties and kept the men fresh for their tasks as they arose.

Indoors

Movement of RE Vehicles

"The Divisional Staff was staggered when we produced our first intimation that 3,000 Sappers and 1,000 lorry loads of equipment must be moved down to the river for bridging. In practice, however, once a limited bridgehead has been established there is little movement on the roads, except for RE vehicles, until bridges are open, and Bank Control, Divisional Staff and AGRE found no difficulty in working out the necessary traffic arrangements.

Conclusion

"The planning period with the AGRE living at Divisional HQ paid useful dividends. The proof of the value of team training was brought out at the subsequent crossing of the ELBE, where briefing was almost unnecessary. CsRE, AGRE, HQ Div and LVsT had all worked together on the RHINE and knew and appreciated each other's problems."

Stand 1

STAND 1 (122407)

(Spectators stand facing North-East towards RHINE)

Object of Stand

(a) To give spectators a general idea of the ground leading down to the river bank.

(b) To give spectators a general view of 15 (S) Div sector, with particular reference to 44 (L) Inf Bde.

Conducting Officer

Description of Ground

"We are now standing just under a mile from the river RHINE, in the sector in which 44 (L) Bde assaulted. The line of the river is clearly visible. In front of you, you can see the two churches (one with a small spire and the other with a tower), of the village of BISLICH, which was one of 44 (L) Bde's objectives on the far bank. Immediately on your left, with the big church, is XANTEN. Two miles beyond XANTEN, just off the main road to CLEVE, Commander 15 (S) Div set up his Tactical HQ. Half left, beyond the trees, there is a small church with a tower ornamented by a squat spire. That is LUTTINGEN, which was virtually the hub of 44 (L) Bde's sector, and contained the Bde Commander's Tactical HQ, crossing control, and the stormboat and class 9 raft hides, while vehicle waiting areas and LVT loading areas were located either side of the village. Over the roofs of LUTTINGEN, you can see with glasses some big farm buildings. Those are RISWICKHOF, on the far bank, which together with LOHR proved a tough nut for 2 A & SH in the left brigade sector of 15 (S) Div. The extreme left of the divisional crossing area is not visible from here but you can get some idea of the frontage covered by the division. The wooded high ground visible beyond BISLICH is the DIERSFORDTER WALD, and the ridge you can see was one of the objectives of 17 US (Airborne) Div. Running diagonally across our front is the road which led down to the class 40 bridge, which was built at the end of the line of trees in the distance. We shall pass down this road on our way to our next stand.

"We have no speakers to give accounts here and our object in bringing you to this stand was to give you a general idea of the ground which 15 (S) Div had to traverse on its way to the assault of the river. It may also serve to show the very wide frontage on which the assault had to be made, nearly 9,000 yards from the ferry site in front of us to the farm buildings at HUBSCH which are well to the left of RISWICKHOF. With the exception of the church tower at XANTEN, there is no observation point from which the whole divisional front can be observed at one time."

Stand 2

STAND 2

River Bank at Ferry House XANTEN—BISLICH Ferry (132415)

Object of Stand

(a) To study the assault crossing by 44 (L) Inf Bde.

(b) To study RE work on the river.

A. Conducting Officer

Description of Ground

"Across the RHINE in front of you, you will see the houses of MARWICK, just to the right of the ferry. As you follow the bund on the far bank round to the left, you will see it goes away from the river bank, skirting the village of BISLICH. It reaches a maximum distance of about six or seven hundred yards from the river and then turns back to approach the bank again near RONDUIT, on the left of 44 Bde's sector of assault. The left boundary of 44 (L) Bde is about 3,000 yards downstream from here."

B. Lieutenant Colonel Hon. H. C. H. T. CUMMING-BRUCE, DSO, Comd 44 (L) Inf Bde

The Assault Crossing by 44 (L) Bde

"44 (L) Bde was to assault with two battalions, crossing in buffaloes, and one battalion (follow-up), in stormboats.

"We are now standing at the site of the right crossing of the right battalion, 6 RSF.

"Before the crossing, all platoon commanders had been able to see the far bank, either from the XANTEN Church Tower or from the bund on the bank. Tremendous value was also got from the oblique air photos.

"I anticipated that the enemy would be occupying trenches behind the bund. We therefore arranged for part of the "PEPPERPOT" to be fired from the right flank round the bend of the river, from where these positions could be enfiladed. A considerable weight of LAA, MMG and other weapons was thus directed right into his weapon pits, and I believe was more directly effective for our purpose than the main artillery concentrations.

"The initial bridgehead included the line of the bund and part of BISLICH. In my orders I particularly stressed the importance of clearing all the ground between the river and the bund from inclusive the ferry at MARWICK to RONDUIT (indicated on ground), before any further advance was made so that no aimed fire could be brought on the sector of river in the brigade bridgehead.

"The assault waves entered the water punctually at 0200 hours, and landed all troops safely. In some cases Buffaloes carried their parties right up to the bund and the enemy were overwhelmed in their slit trenches. A few mines were met on the ferry jetty and the track running North-East from it. The left bn (8 RS) was equally successful. The follow-up battalion got its orders to cross at 0310 hours, and embarked at 0330 hours. The stormboats were not popular owing to frequent difficulty in starting the engines. At the later ELBE assault, a second lift by LVsT was arranged. The remaining phases proceeded according to plan—a plan which aimed at speed, using all three battalions at once, but having a proportion of each battalion firm, when the remainder pushed on. Speed was essential, in order to capture as much ground as possible before all artillery was "turned off" for the airborne landings.

"Contact was made with the airborne troops first by 6 KOSB at 1400 hours, then by 6 RSF at 1510 hours, and 8 RS at 1515 hours.

"The enemy opposition was patchy and never very determined."

C. Lieutenant Colonel R. N. FOSTER, DSO, OBE, Comd 11 AGRE

RE Work

RE Work in the area

"In this area in addition to the LVT crossing of 44 (L) Bde were established the following:—

(a)	DUKW crossing	— from the inlet just to your right to the small bay in front of the large grey house opposite.
(b)	Class 40 (tactical) Bailey Bridge	— just to the left of the civilian ferry site.
(c)	Class 40 (all weather) Bailey Bridge	— from bund level by the grey house opposite, back 100 yards inland on this side to join the road from XANTEN we have just come down.
(d)	DD crossing	— some hundred yards downstream.
(e)	Class 9 rafts and stormboats	— just downstream of the lagoon which you can see on the far side half left from here.
(f)	Anti-mine booms and naval net	— some hundred yards upstream.

Stand 2

Points to Note

"The principal points worth noting are the following :—

"The DUKW crossing was too close upstream from an important bridge. It was selected as the entry and exits were suitable and this saved some work, but it was very worrying to the CRE engaged on bridge construction, as he had always to guard against the possibility of a DUKW fouling his anchor cables, or getting out of control and ramming his bridge. As a matter of fact, we originally underestimated the number of DUKWs in use, and although we made them a special approach track parallel to the road, it was not entirely adequate. They require something considerably better than what is suitable for normal 3-tonners.

"The Class 40 (tactical) Bailey pontoon bridge was built in record time and was in fact the first Class 40 bridge on Second Army front. Ninth US Army with their "Treadway" equipment, however, beat us to it, in spite of starting later. It is perhaps worth noting that in an operation of this kind, one is invariably and naturally asked by one's commander, "When will such and such a bridge be open," in relation to H Hour. This is of course exceedingly difficult to estimate, as the time of opening depends on when the sappers can start building, which in its turn depends on tactical rather than technical considerations. It is virtually impossible to erect heavy bridges under aimed small arms fire.

"The CRE responsible for this bridge found an enormous crater in the approach road, which was filled in before H Hour with stone and material brought down in tip-trucks which had been specially loaded earlier on for this particular purpose. He took a certain risk in doing this, but the noise of the work was drowned by the bombardment, and there was no enemy reaction. One result of the early completion of the bridge was that traffic control was caught napping, and it was some time before the necessary provost could be got up from corps and proper traffic control instituted. The necessity for full liaison between RE and Provost is emphasised.

"The Class 40 (all weather) Bailey bridge was designed to compete with a rise and fall of 20 feet of level in the river. Thus it had to start further inland on this side and was at bund level on the far side, so as to keep its ends above anticipated flood level. The centre part was of course floating and would rise and fall with the water level.

"We used the crane on the old jetty here to launch our LCV (P)s, which were manned by RN personnel and used to patrol the river and as tugs.

"The Class 9 raft ferries for 44 (L) Bde were set up just downstream of the large lagoon you can see to your left. Two rafts were knocked out by shell fire here, but spare ones were brought up and successfully constructed. Returning passengers, in the form of German prisoners, were made to pay for their trip by being put to work on approaches while awaiting evacuation to the rear. One of them, an officer, was pleased to compliment the raft crews on the excellence of their watermanship. Had he seen our first attempts during training on the River MAAS he might have been even more complimentary."

D. Conducting Officer

Description of Route to Stand 3

"From here to *STAND* 3 we shall go back along the Corps class 40 route as far as the main class 40 lateral which ran along the main road RHEINBERG—XANTEN—CLEVE, where we shall turn right. The road then by-passes the town of XANTEN, and on the right as we pass the town, you will see a concrete road running off at right angles. This was constructed subsequently to the operations we are studying, to provide access to a semi-permanent pile bridge built at the site. The bridge itself has since been removed.

"We then turn off right handed to the village of LUTTINGEN, which was mentioned at *STAND* 1 as being the centre of 44(L) Bde's area, and containing the Bde commander's Tactical HQ, stormboat hides etc.

"After debussing at LUTTINGEN, we shall walk along the bund and then turn off to the river bank, following approximately the route taken by LVsT carrying 8 RS."

STAND 3

Object of Stand

(a) To study the crossing and subsequent action of the left assaulting battalion of 44(L) Bde, 8 RS.

(b) To study crossing of the river by amphibious tanks, 44 R Tks.

A. **Major B. A. FARGUS**, Adjutant, 8 RS.

Action of 8 RS.

Assembly

"8 RS moved up from HAELEN in BELGIUM during the night 22/23 March 1945 into its concentration area around BIESENHOF, which is about 3½ miles from here as the crow flies on the other side of the main road XANTEN—CLEVE.

"The day was spent mainly in resting by the troops. Officers and senior NCOs did not however get much time to sleep, as there were reconnaissances, final conferences and preparations to make. The Brigade Commander spoke to all troops by companies in this area.

"The Commanding Officer held a final co-ordinating conference at Bn HQ at 1800 hours, just as a battery of heavy guns by the next farm began the bombardment. This did not make for easy hearing.

The Assault

"The troops got into their LVsT at about midnight and shortly afterwards moved forward in line ahead across country by the LVT track through ROSCHHOF to the prepared gaps in the bund North of LUTTINGEN where the single column fanned out into three. The places where the gaps were made in the bund can still be seen, where the bank has been made good (indicated on ground if still visible). The LVsT entered the water where we are now standing.

"Spasmodic mortar and shellfire was directed at the LVsT as they approached the river and during the crossing some very inaccurate Spandau fire was opened. This caused no casualties and the crossing was accomplished without incident. The empty LVsT returned across the river and went to an LVT Collecting Area at SCHOLTENHOF (indicated on ground).

"The remainder of the battalion vehicles were gradually being called forward from the Marshalling Area, according to the prearranged priorities, into the vehicle waiting area in LUTTINGEN, whence they were called out either to the LVT Loading Area or to the class 9 Rafts which were functioning by 0700 hours.

"8 RS completed Phase I of this operation without great difficulty. No mines were met in the flood bed as had been feared and the initial objectives of RONDUIT — bridge 137439 and track junction 135434 were taken. (These latter are South of RONDUIT and not visible behind the bund).

Enemy encountered

"Isolated Spandau posts gave some trouble dug in on the slopes of the bund, but the whole battalion area had been cleared by first light. As anticipated all PW came from 84 Inf Div except for one soldier whose *soldbuch* showed a formation unknown to the IO. The mystery was solved when he stated that he was on leave from the Eastern front, and had no intention of fighting on the RHINE.

"It was interesting to see that since 84 Div's recent setback on the Siegfried Line it had apparently become a Mountain division. The battalion opposing 8 RS had been issued with the *Edelweiss* sign the previous day and all the troops had the signs still in their pockets not yet having had time to sew them on to their sleeves.

Further Advance

"Phase II of the operation consisted of an advance to GOSSENHOF and X tracks (131448) to the West of it. This operation was carried out shortly after first light. B Coy had a sharp fight for GOSSENHOF, but the objectives were soon captured. Patrols sent forward established the fact that there were enemy in JOCKERN and VISSEL.

"The operation to clear these two villages began at 0945 hours. Two companies were used. The left hand company, attacking VISSEL, was supported by one squadron 44 R Tks.

"The operation was soon completed and VISSEL produced 28 PW.

"Bn HQ then moved forward to GOSSENHOF.

"The next and final tasks of 8 RS were :—

(a) to link up with 6 Airborne Div and patrol up to and if necessary capture and hold, the bridge 155469 North-East of BERGEN and

(b) to patrol to the high ground in the DIERSFORDTER WALD just beyond the road WESEL–HALDERN (indicated on ground).

"The battalion had been given an American wireless set on 23 March which was said to be netted in with sets in possession of all Airborne units. No codes were issued or link signs, and instructions were that normal security precautions could be relaxed within reason.

"After the Airborne drop, the set was opened up but initially nothing was heard. After the move to GOSSENHOF the set was erected in the upstairs of the farm with a 'bottle' aerial, and the following conversation took place :—

8 RS :— 'Hullo, hullo, can anyone hear me, Over.'

Voice ;— 'Hullo, hear you OK. Over.'

8 RS :— 'We are ground troops, are you Airborne? Over.'

Voice :— 'Yes, we are Airborne. Over.'

8 RS :— 'What is your location ? Over.'

Voice :— 'Wait one. I will put it into SLIDEX. Over.'

8 RS :— 'That is no good. We haven't got your SLIDEX. Over.'

Voice :— 'That is OK. We have yours. Out.'

(After a pause) Voice :— A message in SLIDEX, which being decoded read :

'We are HQ 3 Para Bde located at 147469.'

"Thus the final task of 8 RS was rendered unnecessary as the bridge and high ground were firmly in the hands of 6 Airborne Div.

"A carrier patrol was sent out along the road from VISSEL to contact HQ 3 Para Bde. This patrol flushed a party of Germans on the way, and provided some good shooting for the Airborne troops. In Bn HQ we were able to talk to our own patrol by wireless, and at the same time talk to the Airborne troops on the special set, so that we could follow and direct the patrol's progress in detail until the link up was made at 1515 hours.

The enemy

"Enemy reaction throughout the day had been extraordinarily slight, and the battalion incurred only about 30 casualties, mainly on the bund in the initial assault.

"There had been very little shelling throughout the day, and even the spasmodic shells and mortar bombs which had fallen in the battalion area during the early hours of the morning practically entirely ceased when the Airborne troops landed.

Effect of our Artillery bombardment

"A good testimony to the efficacy of our counter-battery fire was seen in an orchard in the village of BERGEN when two enemy 150 mm howitzers were dug in. One of these had received a direct hit in the gun pit and there were 3 large shell holes within 30 yards of the other. Both of these guns had clean barrels, and neither had fired a single round.

Concentration prior to further advance

"By evening the entire area up to the 6 Airborne Div had been cleared of enemy, and the whole battalion spent the night in farmhouses in the VISSEL—GOSSENHOF area, ready to move on through 6 Airborne Div next day."

B. Lieutenant Colonel C. G. HOPKINSON, DSO, MC, CO 44 R Tks

Crossing and Action of 44 R Tks

"The battle of the RHINE crossing, so far as 44 R Tks was concerned, started on 7 March, when we were suddenly pulled out of the HOCHWALD battle.

"Mystified tank commanders and first drivers were piled into lorries and despatched for an unknown destination, whilst second drivers were left to hand in the tanks at NIJMEGEN.

"The road party climbed out of its lorries next morning and learned that it was on 79 Armd Div's *Top Secret* island on the MAAS, surrounded by a permanent smoke screen. Then, and only then, did we learn that we were to be the DD Regiment for the RHINE Crossing, none of us ever having seen a DD, let alone travel in one.

"The next ten days were spent in intensive training lasting from morning to night. Drivers and commanders had to be trained in working the DD whilst afloat, and at the same time the tanks themselves had to be serviced and prepared for the land battle after the crossing.

"Meantime Regimental HQ was studying large numbers of airphotos and trying to fix entry and exit points. Early on it was decided, though not after a struggle, that we couldn't be expected to make a night crossing in view of the limited time available for training. So all final crossing practices and dress rehearsals were carried out at first light. All squadrons did one of these final schemes and timings for *"The Day"* were worked out from them.

"On 21 March the tanks made their final crossing of the MAAS and lined up ready to be loaded on to transporters. Concentration was completed by midnight on 22 March in the STAATSFORST DIE HEES XANTEN, and by first light, thanks to the enthusiastic efforts of an American camouflage company, no signs of our arrival were noticeable.

"By some curious error it was only at 1100 hours on 23 March that we were told that the crossing was to take place next morning, all planning had heretofore been worked on the assumption that it was to be at dawn on 25th. All briefing of crews and reconnaissance had therefore to be completed on 23rd; this left little or no time for operations on the far bank to be discussed with the infantry.

Stand 3

"The plan as far as we were concerned was split into two phases.

Phase I
   To cross the river and assemble on the far side.

Phase II
   (a) Having assembled, join up with 7 SEAFORTH and operate as part of the Reserve Bde, 46 (H) Bde) of 15 (S) Div.
   (b) Be prepared to support 44 (L) Bde or 227 (H) Bde on the far side of the river.
   (c) Be prepared to support 6 Airborne Div if ordered.

"This multiplicity of probable tasks on the far bank was necessary because we would be the only tanks for some time to come. In fact we operated with all these formations.

Phase I—The crossing of the River

"It was planned to cross the river between 132422 and 126437 (pointed out on ground), starting the actual crossing at 0600 hours on 24th; on reaching the far side the Regiment was to assemble in the area South East of RONDUIT. It had to be accepted, owing to the suitability of exits from the river, that both the crossing places and the assembly area were in fact outside the probable initial 44 (L) Bde bridgehead, and might therefore be held by the enemy. The regiment would cross the river on a two squadron front, preceded by a reconnaissance party who would go over with the assaulting infantry. The sequence of events on the afternoon and night 23/24 March was therefore as follows.

"During the afternoon tank crews were briefed by using a scale model of the river and large scale airphotos. At the same time reconnaissance parties marked the inflation area and routes from it to the water's edge, all this being done under cover of the smoke screen. The timing over the route through XANTEN was carefully worked out, as it was necessary for certain guns to cease fire whilst the tanks were passing.

"As soon as darkness fell, the near bank recce party completed their task by laying tape and lighting routes to the river. At 0230 hours on 24th the far bank recce parties crossed, carried in Buffaloes of 11 R Tks and E RIDING YEO. These parties, drawn from the Recce Troop and Provost, were each responsible for establishing one exit; for this purpose they had with them their landing mats and "airborne" bulldozers. By 0515 hours exits had been completed at 130426 and 128427, the left hand one after a fair amount of enemy opposition from RONDUIT which caused them several casualties (pointed out on ground).

"Meantime at 0400 hours the Regiment moved off from leaguer and wended its way down through XANTEN, moving into the inflation area at 0515 hours. There was a moderate amount of shelling, chiefly directed at the CDL lights which were shining on the river. However we were fortunate in only having three tanks rendered unfit, and at 0545 hours we entered the river.

"Initially all went well, and all except the last two tanks of A Sqn on the Right got across before the enemy brought down his mortars on the entry point. One of these tanks received a direct hit and sank immediately, the crew managing to escape; the last tank was able to reverse back on shore and retired for repairs. On the Left the exit from the river collapsed after the passage of seven tanks, so the remainder were directed to use the Right hand exit until a substitute was found. The remainder of the crossing passed off with only one further incident; a tank of B Sqn was hit in midstream, three of the crew being wounded. These were evacuated on to a Buffalo. It speaks well for the equipment that it was a good fifteen minutes before the operator, who had remained with the tank, announced on the wireless that he was abandoning ship.

"By 0800 hours the Regiment was across the river and concentrated at 135435 (pointed out on ground); we had lost a further five tanks bogged in the bad going on the far bank. These remained bogged for the next few days as our recovery vehicles were not amphibious. However we had successfully accomplished Phase I and were now ready to carry on with Phase II.

Phase II—Actions East of the RHINE 24 March

"The ground situation at this stage was somewhat obscure; on the Right 44 (L) Bde were firm in MARWICK—BISLICH—FELDWICK. The enemy were very definitely in JOCKERN and VISSEL, and between us and 227 (H) Bde, who reported slow progress some three miles North of us.

"7 SEAFORTH had not yet completed their concentration and, as 46 (H) Bde had no orders for us yet, A Sqn joined up with 44 (L) Bde in their attack on JOCKERN and VISSEL; both these places were cleared by 1000 hours, without much trouble.

"Whilst this attack was going on we decided to clear the bank in a Northerly direction. B Sqn were ordered forward to clear RONDUIT and GOSSENHOF (South East of VISSEL), and by 1200 hours had established themselves in WOLFFSKATH and VAH. Enemy opposition was light, consisting of small parties of infantry with machine guns. They evinced their usual dislike of surrendering to tanks.

"227 (H) Bde now reported that they were being held up by enemy in LOHR (pointed out on ground); B Sqn and a company of 7 SEAFORTH were therefore directed to attack this place from the rear, whilst C Sqn pushed on with our advance on OVERKAMP. By this time we were definitely operating in support of 46 (H) Bde and were transporting 7 SEAFORTH on the backs of the tanks. The advance commenced at 1430 hours and except for bad going, which limited manoeuvre, all went well until we reached the Southern outskirts of MEHR. Here several pockets of enemy infantry were met with and we were also severely shelled by our own artillery. The going was now very bad and it was impossible to deploy off tracks; however, the village of MEHR was occupied by 1600 hours with the capture of some 100 PW.

Stand 3

"Having secured MEHR, A Sqn were now directed on HAFFEN. As 227 (H) Bde were in the process of launching an attack on the village proper, the Sqn was stopped in the area of the Cross-roads to the South East (119492). From here they were able to catch the enemy in the flank and rear as he was driven out of HAFFEN by 227 (H) Bde's attack; several excellent targets were engaged with good results. Meantime, C Sqn in pushing out Northwards from MEHR had encountered several mined roads blocks; these were circumnavigated with difficulty and eventually the Squadron flushed and engaged some enemy SPs in the woods to the North of the LANGE RENNE.

"At about 1700 hours Commander 46 (H) Bde ordered the brigade to go firm on the line HAFFEN—cross-roads 119492; whilst this was taking place the enemy launched a counter-attack in company strength, supported by artillery, down the track into MEHR, from SCHOLTENHOF 127493. This was beaten off by the combined fire of C Sqn and F Bty 4 RHA.

"The Regiment was now ordered to withdraw back to a central area ready for the next day's operations. The Commander of 46 (H) Bde put in a strong bid for some tanks to stay with his Brigade during the night, so eventually B Sqn remained in the area South of MEHR. During the withdrawal four of C Sqn's tanks became bogged just North West of MEHR. At about 2300 hours the enemy put in a strong counter-attack in this area which overran the infantry company and the bogged troop. The latter had dismounted their Brownings and were attempting to hold a perimeter round the tanks; however a lucky shot from a Panzerfaust set one of the tanks on fire and owing to the resultant illumination the position became untenable. The troop therefore withdraw, setting fire to the other tanks before going; this had some effect as the enemy did not continue with his attack, either because he was satisfied with the result or because he, in turn, found light from the burning tanks too much for him. This small incident serves once more to show the need for an amphibious recovery vehicle in this type of operation.

Operations on 25 March

"Orders for 25 March were as follows: —

"The Regiment, less B Sqn, was to operate with 44 (L) Bde with the object of seizing the bridge at GERVERSHOF over the ISSEL West of DINGDEN. B Sqn was to operate in support of 3 Para Bde of 6 Airborne Div. Accordingly the Regiment RV'd with 44 (L) Bde on the track North East of JOCKERN and headed East into the DIERSFORDTER WALD at 0830 hours, 25 March.

"The country was thickly wooded and very marshy off the tracks; it was therefore necessary to advance at infantry pace. The first brush with the enemy occurred at 1000 hours in the area of the WESEL—EMMERICH railway at 168490.

"After a sharp action in which some 30 PW were taken the advance North was resumed. It was soon obvious from the amount of armour piercing that was flying about that we had run into an enemy anti-tank gun screen. The main core of enemy resistance appeared to be in the area of the main cross-roads 146495, to the West of our axis, this was also, unfortunately, the only direction in which the tanks could deploy owing to the density of the forest to the East.

"A fairly brisk battle ensued for the next two hours, before we managed to break through and cut the main East-West road and start our advance to the East. At this stage A Sqn were covering to the North and West and were engaging a variety of targets which were being presented by a very active enemy; C Sqn had passed through and began to push East. They, too, were soon in trouble. As they deployed from the cover of the woods, they were heavily attacked from the North by enemy SPs, losing four tanks including their OP.

"At this stage the Regiment was being engaged from three sides and this somewhat unpleasant situation continued for the rest of the day. By 1600 hours it was obvious that no progress was going to be made, so it was agreed by the Comd 44 (L) Bde that the advance would be resumed that night.

"During this day's operation we had lost a further eight tanks, but had the satisfaction of knocking out some four enemy anti-tank guns. Meantime B Sqn, who were now with 6 Airlanding Bde, had had a fairly peaceful day in counter-attack reserve.

"During the night 25/26 March the advance was resumed by 44 (L) Bde and at first light we joined up with the infantry on the high ground overlooking the ISSEL.

Stand 4

STAND 4

Gut GRINDT (110448)

Object of Stand:

To study plan of 227 (H) Bde

A. Conducting Officer

PROBLEM

"It is 20 March 1945, and you are Comd 227 (H) Bde. You have just attended a final co-ordinating conference at 15 (S) Div HQ at which the Div Comd issued his final orders, from which the following are extracts :—

The Div will assault with two Bdes up.

(i) *Right* — Codeword "POKER"

44 (L) Bde supported by 11 R Tks will capture and hold area SCHUTTWICK—LOH—BISLICH.

(ii) *Left* — Codeword "NAP"

227 (H) Bde with in support E RIDING YEO will capture and hold area HAFFEN—MEHR.

(iii) The clearance of the area between 44 (L) and 227 (H) Bde's objectives will be carried out by them, dividing line being inclusive 44 (L) Bde road from road junction 1546 — road and track junction 142464 — track to road junction 136453 — cross tracks 130453 — thence track to river at 125453.

(iv) *Reserve* — Codeword "WHIST"

46 (H) Bde with in support 44 R Tks will capture and hold the area CLASENHO—MEHRHOO. They will firmly establish themselves on the high ground 1452—1351 and will ensure clearance of woods 1252—1352 overlooking HALDERN 1153.

They will cross one battalion through 44 (L) Bde LVT and stormboats ferries to assemble with 44 R Tks in area North of VISSEL 1345. The remaining battalions will cross through 227 (H) Bde and assemble in area OVERKAMP 1247 and SANDENHOF 1047. The initial advance will be carried out by a battalion carried on 44 R Tks but should blown bridges or going preclude use of tanks the brigade will carry out a normal advance through positions held by 227 (H) Bde.

"After the conference the divisional commander calls you on one side and says :—

" "I am afraid this means a very wide frontage for your brigade but we must have room for all our various ferries and bridges. We must get the enemy away from the bank area as soon as we can, so the sappers can get on with their jobs. I am a bit worried about your routes on the far side. You have two bridges due for construction in your area, and once they are ready we don't want to get congestion at either. As you know, one is due to be built near WOLFFSKATH and we want to get the road leading North from there through OVERKAMP clear early. The other bridge by HUBSCH leads up to WAYERHOF and we must certainly get hold of that bridge South West of WAYERHOF (103495).

" "At the same time I must impress on you the need to push on quickly. It looks from the map and air photos as though you may find yourself in an island in your brigade area, and we must therefore try and bounce the bridge North East of MEHR (134494) intact and as early as possible : otherwise we may never get 46 (H) Bde through you, and the whole party will be in danger of congealing.

" "You have the outline of the main Corps fire plan, and I hope the PEPPERPOT will be of help to you. The CRA will put it on to any target you particularly want dealt with, so just let him know.

" "I am giving you a company of 1 MX (MG), as I am not too happy about your fire support when Corps have to turn off the guns to let the airborne landings go in. I don't expect 4.2" mortars to get over before mid-day D + 1, but get on the blower if you need them earlier when the time comes and we will try and push them over to you.

" "As regards anti-tank, you will have to rely very much on your own resources, as I see no possibility of the 17 pounders of 99/102 (NH) A Tk Bty getting over until late on D Day, if then. But I don't want any anti-tank mines laid, except Hawkins' Necklaces for temporary road blocks and so on.

" " I am giving you an Air Support tentacle, and this has been rigged up in a jeep, so you can get it across in an LVT when you want it.

" "I can't get you any more LVsT, and I do not wish the stormboats used in an assault role so I am afraid this will limit you to a two battalion assault.

" "I think we shall find the enemy pretty thin on the ground, though I have no doubt the 7 Para Div will give a good account of itself as usual. I am inclined to believe it will go for a series of strong points holding such places as the farm houses at LOHR and SANDENHOF.

Stand 4

" "I do not think we shall find it lining the bund in great strength, and I shall be surprised to meet any armour until we are over the LANGE RENNE water obstacle".

PROBLEM

"What, in outline, is your brigade plan ? (details of loading of LVsT are NOT required)"

Notes :

(i) E RIDING YEO is equipped with sufficient LVsT (72) to carry in one lift two battalions at "assault scales", plus one platoon MMG per battalion. The "assault scale" includes minimum fighting vehicles e.g.: four 6 pounders and towers, three jeeps and two or three carriers for FOOs and reserve ammunition—any increase in vehicles of course means less troops. One LVT carries one platoon or one vehicle.

(ii) For planning purposes, you may assume remaining F-ech vehicles cross by LVT ferry (carriers and jeeps) and Class 9 raft (other F-ech vehicles). The establishment of these depends on the progress of operations, as neither can be operated under observed fire. Class 9 rafts in addition take about 3—4 hours to construct, once the equipment and sappers can be got down to the water.

(iii) Divisional orders do not allow recce forward of the bund which runs just behind this farm. From here it goes diagonally forward towards the river and reaches the bank near the bend at the extreme Left of the position. In point of fact the smoke screen has been in operation for three days and and will continue until D — 1, with occasional short breaks. You are taking advantage of one of these breaks at this moment to try and get a view of your brigade assaulting area.

B. Conducting Officer

Plan and action of 227 (H) Bde

(Based on accounts by Brigadier R. M. Villiers, DSO, Comd 46 (H) Bde and Colonel D. R. Morgan, DSO, MC, CO 2 A & SH).

Task

"227 (H) Bde was the Left assaulting brigade of 15 (S) Div. The divisional commander gave the brigade the task of securing the area HAFFEN—MEHR, and then extending the initial bridgehead so gained to link up with 44 (L) Bde on the Right. The inter-brigade boundary ran from a point about 1500 yards upstream from WOLFFSKATH (pointed on the ground), West of VISSEL and then North East along the road through BERGEN. On the Left, 30 Corps were due to assault into the REESER EILAND, so that 227 (H) Bde was on a frontage of nearly 6000 yards.

Considerations

"The area allotted to the assault of 227 (H) Bde was an island bounded by the two lakes beyond MEHR and the streams running from them to the RHINE. We had to try and get the bridge (134494) North East of MEHR early, so that the follow-up brigade (46 (H) Bde) could pass through. At the same time, we had to clear the routes from our own bridge sites at WOLFFSKATH and HUBSCH, leading up to MEHR and WAYERHOF respectively. Lastly, until the bund and the area up to and including LOHR were clear, work could not begin on the various ferries and bridges at all, as the river could be kept under observation from this area.

"Unfortunately there were not enough Buffaloes to lift more than two battalions in the assault wave, and the follow-up battalion had to follow by stormboat. We could not be certain when this crossing would be possible. We were impressed by the need for speed, so as to overwhelm the enemy before he could recover from the hammering he was to get in the initial bombardment. Above all, it was important to be at least well on our way to our objectives before the artillery support had to stop altogether on account of the airborne landings.

"It was therefore decided that the assaulting battalions should push right on to the brigade objective and the follow-up battalion would come in behind them, taking over the ground they had won and mopping up.

Plan

"10 HLI was to assault on the Right—in the area WOLFFSKATH—and push on through OVERKAMP to MEHR. 2 A & SH was to assault on the Left crossing at the creek by HUBSCH, and directed on WAYERHOF. The latter battalion was responsible for clearing LOHR and each battalion was to clear the bund in its sector, junction being at the sluice gates.

"The final objective of these two battalions was the general line of the road from the bridge 134494, through BRUCKSHOF and WAYERHOF to the bridge 103495.

"2 GORDONS was to cross by storm boat and take over the area OVERKAMP—REE—LOHR, when ordered by the Brigade Commander.

Stand 4

The Action

"In the event, 10 HLI had to fight hard for WOLFFSKATH and again for OVERKAMP, where a battalion from the follow-up brigade (46 (H) Bde) supported by tanks passed through during the afternoon of D-day to capture MEHR.

"On the Left, 2 A & SH managed to get two companies on to the Left of the objective in the WAYERHOF area before dawn, but they were pinned down there as daylight came. The remaining companies had difficulty in landing and got involved in the orchards and houses in HUBSCH, which were strongly held.

"In consequence, the bund and the LOHR area were not clear by daylight.

"The Brigade Commander directed 2 A & SH to press on with the clearing of LOHR and the bund, and ordered 2 GORDONS across to assist them. One company got across but its losses in the stormboats were heavy, and the remainder of 2 GORDONS was held back until later in the day. 2 GORDONS then moved up on the Left with the object of extending the area of the objective held by 2 A & SH Eastward towards HAFFEN, occupying the Western parts of that village shortly before dusk."

STAND 5

River Bank at WOLFFSKATH (119461)

Object of Stand

(i) To study the action of the Right assault battalion of 227 (H) Bde, 10 HLI.

(ii) To study RE work on the river.

(iii) To study the action of the follow-up brigade, 46 (H) Bde.

A. Lieutenant Colonel F. B. NOBLE, MBE, 2 IC 10 HLI

Action by 10 HLI

"10 HLI was the Right assaulting battalion of 227 (H) Bde which was the Left assaulting brigade of 15 (S) Div.

"After this account, Captain MURRAY will give an account of the action taken by "C" Coy which was the Right assaulting company of the battalion. He commanded this company and was wounded during the action.

Preliminary Training

"Prior to the crossing, the battalion was given three weeks in which to train and plan at MAASTRICHT on the banks of the MAAS. This period was naturally invaluable as we had with us there our squadron of Buffaloes and all the supporting arms, and the MAAS on which to practice the crossing technique.

"There were two set-piece rehearsals carried out; one by day and one by night. As far as our battalion was concerned, they were failures. The main reason was that the MAAS, over which we rehearsed, had too fast a current—about 7 knots—for the Buffaloes to get out of the river on the far side. We had been already practising in ones and twos, but the whole lot together in this quick form of current proved unworkable. There were many casualties particularly during the night rehearsal, and on each occasion on the far bank we had only about two-thirds of the battalion safely over. These rehearsals did, however, produce many lessons from which we benefited regarding control and organisation, but it was somewhat depressing for the CO to have at the back of his mind, the thought of arriving on the far bank minus a large percentage of his battalion.

The Battalion's Task

"As the Right battalion of 227 (H) Bde, our task was to cross the RHINE and capture the village of MEHR and also to capture intact the bridge at the North end of LANGE RENNE which was 2¼ miles from the river bank; 2 A & SH were to capture HAFFEN on our Left and on our Right there was a gap of about two miles between us and 44 (L) Bde.

Reconnaissance

"Previous to the Operation, the CO was able to go up and make two reconnaissances of our crossing places. On the second occasion, he was able to take his company commanders. Very little value was gained from this reconnaissance because nobody was allowed to go very far forward. In any case the bunds along the river bank precluded one seeing very much. Permission for the CO to carry out the reconnaissance in an Auster aircraft was refused. In consequence, planning had to be carried out from maps and air photographs.

Enemy Dispositions

"No patrols were allowed to be sent across the river and in consequence very little was known concerning enemy positions. We knew, however, that they had some posts along the bank itself as they opened up occasionally with spandaus on fixed lines. Personally, we thought that the enemy would be holding in strength about half a mile inland with the object of allowing us to get ashore and then having the intermediate ground as their killing area.

Loading Plan

"The loading plan as regards our Buffaloes was extremely complicated. Not only did we have to take our own troops, but we also had certain attached personnel as well, such as a platoon of RE, a detachment of the bank control unit, a section of MMGs, some Provost and a casualty evacuation point. There were really only two alternatives as regards formations, namely, to go over in two flights, i.e. 18 Buffaloes in the first and 18 in the second, or in three flights of twelve each. Six Buffaloes would take approximately a company plus odds and ends, and we finally decided that the best method was to go in three flights with two rifle companies leading, C on the Right and A on the Left. The second flight to consist of two rifle companies, plus Battalion HQ, D Coy on the Right, B Coy on the Left and the last flight to contain 12 vehicles of various sorts. It was most difficult to decide exactly what vehicles would go across with us. Everybody wanted something. However we eventually came to an agreed solution.

Stand 5

"It was as follows

Composition of the third flight

Commanding Officer's carrier
Battery Commander's carrier
Medium Regiment FOO—one Jeep
Two 6-pounders
Two towers
Pioneer Platoon Jeep
Spare ammunition carrier
Medical carrier
Two medical jeeps.

This made a total of 12 vehicles.

"The reasons for crossing in three flights rather than two, were :—

(i) If three companies were to cross in the first flight, it would interfere with the plan we had arranged for exploitation on the far side.

(ii) Moreover it seemed, with so many unknown facts regarding the enemy and his defence on the far bank, that it was unwise to commit so much of the battalion in one go, because, once they were set in the water, there was no calling back. By sending only two companies in the first flight, it gave us a reserve which really consisted of half a battalion in the second flight and it could be switched if necessary to another part of the far bank for assaulting if the first two companies got into difficulties.

(iii) The Commander of the Buffalo Squadron favoured the three flight policy as it was easier to control.

(iv) Although we knew the current of the RHINE was a good deal slower, from our experiences in the MAAS, we did not want to have too many Buffaloes in the water and scrambling out on the far side at the same time.

Plan in detail

"The battalion's plan was greatly influenced by the Brigade Commander impressing on the CO the vital importance of two things. The capture of the bridge at the North end of the LANGE RENNE, and, once landed, and the bund clear of the enemy, to get away from the river and to get inland with everyone. The reason for this was to make room for the Sappers to start bridging operations. The plan in detail was in two phases :—

Phase 1 — The approach march. There was nothing very much in this, other than getting into our Buffaloes near the HOCHWALD FOREST and then a long and slow ride down to the river which the leading company had to enter at 0200 hours.

Phase 2 — Capture of the far bank and the exploitation on to the final objective.

"In Phase 2 there were three objectives. The first was to cross the RHINE, and capture the river bank and bund from WOLFFSKATH to the sluice gate. The second objective was the villages of OVERKAMP and REE. The leading companies were responsible for both the first and second objectives, C on the Right and A on the Left. They were particularly told to clear the river bank and to secure the way for the second and third flights of the Buffaloes. At OVERKAMP and REE, the two leading companies were to halt, consolidate and form a firm base for B and D companies to go through to capture the third objective, the village of MEHR and the bridge.

"B and D companies were also told to be ready to exploit if the situation warranted it to the SCHLOSS at BELLINGHOVEN and the large farm area of AVERFORTH.

Battalion Headquarters and firm base

"We decided that, as early as possible, Battalion HQ should move inland some two or three hundred yards from WOLFFSKATH, but that we must have some form of firm base on the river bank close to the bund, and this we decided to carry out with S Coy which was chiefly in the last flight.

D—2 and D—1 Days

"The battalion moved up to the HOCHWALD in MT by daylight arriving soon after dark on the 22 March and they had a really good night's rest in the forest. Early on the 23 March the CO explained the operation to all ranks.

The Approach and Crossing

"There is very little to say as all went smoothly. At 2300 hours, companies paraded and loaded into their Buffaloes. We then had a long 2½ miles drive down the river. The route to the river had been excellently marked with lights. At about seven minutes before H Hour the leading two companies started to move forward in their Buffaloes and some 300 yards before the river they fanned out. Exactly at 0200 hours the leading Buffaloes then nosed their way into the RHINE. Six minutes later, through the Buffaloes' wireless net, we heard that the two leading companies had landed on the far side with little opposition and that the empty Buffaloes had already started to return. The CO gave the order for the second flight, including Battalion HQ, to cross the river and they all arrived safely on the far bank at 0217 hours.

Stand. 5

The Assault by leading companies

"It was planned for C Coy on the Right to land at WOLFFSKATH and for A Coy about 200 yards to their Left (i.e. downstream). In actual fact, both companies were landed upstream from WOLFFSKATH; reasons for this seemed to have been as follow:—

(a) No navigation lights were allowed

(b) Darkness and very thick mist.

(c) The Buffaloes did not drift downstream nearly as far as was expected.

"On landing, both companies rushed the bund and took 60 prisoners with hardly a shot being fired. Both companies then attacked WOLFFSKATH which was strongly held and was only taken after a fierce fight. Both company Commanders were wounded.

The leading companies start inland

"A and C Coys were definitely disorganised and it took a little time to get things going again. Our artillery programme had now moved inland and the Germans were beginning to come to life and were not prepared to surrender like the original party. A and C Coys moved forward towards OVERKAMP but were unable to make much progress.

Rear companies cross the River

"By this time the two rear companies, B and D, with Battalion HQ, had safely crossed the river in the second flight of Buffaloes and were landed at the same spot as the first flight. The CO was unable to contact the leading companies by wireless. He therefore ordered D Coy to form a firm base on the bund where it had landed and for B Coy to ensure that the bund down to the sluice gates was clear of enemy. B Coy found twelve posts to eliminate before its task was done. These posts were skilfully dug into the reverse slope of the bund and had not been touched by our artillery bombardment. D Coy on the bund were twice counter-attacked from the Right, both of which attacks they beat off after hand to hand fighting. A good deal of enemy shelling and mortaring now started in the WOLFFSKATH area.

Battalion HQ

"Battalion HQ now came in for a bad time. They attempted to move forward as planned but were counter-attacked and suffered a good many casualties including the whole of the Battery Commander's party killed.

Dawn D Day

"At dawn, it was a cheering sight to see A and C Coys charging into the farm houses of OVERKAMP and to hear from B Coy that they had successfully cleared the bund down to the sluice gates. The third flight of Buffaloes was then ordered to cross the river.

Planning for further advance

"The battalion was by now far behindhand in its timed programme for the advance and a long way from its final objectives. The CO went forward to A and C Coys taking with him D Coy and leaving B and S Coys as a firm base at WOLFFSKATH. He found A and C Coys very mixed, somewhat disorganised and a little shaken with only one officer left between the two companies. They were not in a fit state to take part in a further advance. An attack on REE by D Coy was then laid on preceded by a Victor Stonk. This attack petered out fairly soon as every house and farm was held and the battalion had no tank support. The battalion had about "had it" by then, but it had at least got a bridgehead of about 300 yards in depth fairly well established.

The arrival of Reserves and the attack on MEHR

"At 1200 hours, the SEAFORTHS of 46 Bde, with a squadron of DD tanks, came to our assistance. At about 1500 hours they launched an attack on MEHR.

Some lessons

"The vital importance in an operation of this nature of having plenty of time beforehand to plan and train especially with the Buffalo personnel with whom one is going to operate.

"The battalion Commander must be allowed to make a personal reconnaissance with his Buffalo Commander of the crossing places and come to an agreed plan, otherwise companies may be landed in the wrong place and, in the dark, confusion becomes inevitable.

"In such an operation, it is not advisable to give an assaulting battalion too ambitious an objective on the far bank. It is suggested that only a very limited objective should be given, such as forming a close bridgehead which should then be enlarged by follow-up units passing through. In the action just described, the battalion did not, in effect, take its objectives and a follow-up formation came through to do so. The opposed crossing of a river and the forming of a close bridgehead is a major operation for a battalion, and it is doubtful whether the same battalion is really capable of further exploitation."

Stand 5

B. Capt I. H. MURRAY, MC, OC C Coy, 10 HLI

Action of C Coy 10 HLI

"Before speaking in detail of our landing I would like to make a few additional points about the preparatory training, as it affected my company.

"As you have already heard, our practice crossings were somewhat abortive, and when companies found later on that their loading plans had to be drastically altered, we felt we might just as well never have practised. I had been allocated six Buffaloes for a low strength company with a few additional personnel, when I was suddenly told I was to have the major part of a platoon of GORDON HIGHLANDERS to carry as well. This completely upset my plan and made most of my preparatory training in loading and unloading nugatory.

"My second point is, although many excellent photos were produced, it was only possible at a very late time for company commanders to see the best enlargements of their landing places. Platoon commanders never saw them at all. For reasons which you have already heard, our reconnaissances were not very satisfactory. I myself had the best available view of my landing place, but that was from a church over a mile away. The assaulting companies were therefore faced with an opposed assault crossing onto a shore which to all intents and purposes they had never seen. The fact that we were told that there were very few enemy on the bank and that they were low quality troops did not reassure us, as we had heard this story before!

"The only point I have to make with reference to our rest area is that being, as nearly always, short of officers in the company, those officers who were present had so much to do that they had very little rest. This meant that though the men were reasonably fresh at H Hour, the officers were not.

"The detailed loading of our Buffaloes is of no special significance, and it will suffice to say that we went over in two flights of three. The first contained two platoons and a small company HQ party. The second contained the remainder of the company and the attached personnel.

"Our landing plan for the capture of the bank was in two parts. We were the Right leading company of the battalion, with A Coy on our Left. Part I was the securing of the bund and the clearing of WOLFFSKATH Farm.

"I intended at first to form a horseshoe shaped perimeter with all three platoons. Having cleared the bund I intended to leave only an observation section on the far side of the bund and withdraw the remainder to the river, or safer, side. The GORDONS platoon would then relieve my Right hand platoon who would pass through to the Left and clear the farm. Thereafter we had extensive plans for exploitation to a depth of a mile and a half.

"We entered the water at 0200 hours after a perfect loading and advance to the river. We landed at 0204 hours after an uneventful though somewhat agitated crossing. It had been decided that if we could land in silence we should. As the enemy had apparently not seen us we landed in a mine-free area in almost complete silence. We had not been able to see the far bank when we entered the water and when we landed we had no idea where we were. Just before we landed I saw A Coy about fifty yards to my left and I was then under the impression that my company was much too far downstream.

"The first part of my plan went perfectly and to our surprise we found no mines. As a matter of fact the only mine casualties on the bund occurred among German prisoners. As we were getting established I recognised the bushes on my Right and realised that I was in fact slightly *upstream* of my objective and that A Coy was *between* me and WOLFFSKATH. The mist and smoke were very thick but they eddied, and as I went over to A Coy I saw the farm beyond them.

"About this time some Spandau fire opened up from the farm area. I told A Coy Comd that he must now clear the farm instead of me and he prepared an impromptu attack. I returned to my company where I interrogated a prisoner and finding that he was not of the expected unit and obtaining some other useful information from him I tried frantically to get this information back. None of our wireless worked, although the circuits were duplicated.

"Shortly afterwards I heard A Coy attack go in and led off my company to follow them. As we moved across, B Coy did a spirited landing and assault through us, and at right angles to our line of advance. Chaos ensued for several minutes.

"Eventually A Coy told us that the farm was clear and that they were moving on. B Coy extricated itself from us, and we had a few casualties from the first mortar or shell fire that had come down. The GORDONS Platoon commander was hit.

"I did not altogether trust A Coy's clearing of the farm so I made Lieutenant McVEAN carry out the original clearance I had planned. He came back and reported the farm clear and that his platoon was holding the bund a few yards beyond it. The rest of the company followed McVEAN and myself as we went forward. As the pair of us went round the building a German appeared from a doorway and with one burst killed McVEAN and laid me out. There was a short delay while my 2 i/c, who was a few yards behind me, found out what had happened; two abortive attempts were made to rescue me and at last I heard my 2 i/c say: "We shall have to leave them and get on." He was the only surviving officer of my company and had a very difficult task.

"At this stage of the battle, personal matters became of some importance and I am afraid I lost interest in matters of greater military value. I would like to say that once I got into the hands of my regimental stretcher bearers my evacuation was extremely efficiently carried out. I had an extremely unpleasant period of some length when I lay unable to move, but fully conscious, while the enemy shelled the bank. I was hit about 0245 hours, and by 1230 hours I was in the CCS at KAPELLEN, had had a major operation and had regained consciousness.

"In conclusion I would like to say from a company angle that much fuller reconnaissance, practice with exact Buffalo loads, signal communication and above all a *much* more limited objective would have helped a great deal. All of us were thinking of operations half a mile to a mile inland whereas all our initial fighting occurred much closer to the river bank."

C. Brigadier R. M. VILLIERS, DSO, Comd 46 (H) Bde

Action of 46 (H) Bde

"46 (H) Bde was the reserve or follow-up brigade of 15 (S) Div. We were to cross by stormboats into the bridgeheads already established by the assaulting brigades, and pass through them to capture the high ground South East of HALDERN.

"You can see from the map that the area of 227 (H) Bde's bridgehead which provided the shortest route to our objectives, was virtually an island formed by the lakes East and North East of MEHR and the streams running into and out of them. It was obviously essential to seize the bridge North East of MEHR between these lakes, early and if possible intact.

"44 R Tks was in support of my brigade on 24 March, and, together with 7 SEAFORTH, was to cross in 44 (L) Bde area, while my remaining battalions were to cross in 227 (H) Bde area.

Action by 7 SEAFORTH

"7 SEAFORTH crossed into 44 (L) Bde bridgehead in the early morning of D-day and after receiving their essential F-Echelon transport, married up with 44 R Tks. The group was then ordered by wireless to make their way West to assist 10 HLI clear the bund near WOLFFSKATH. It was midday before they found their way there, and 10 HLI reported that the bund was then clear of enemy.

"Another order was sent by wireless to 7 SEAFORTH to assist 2 A & SH clear SANDENHOF and LOHR (indicated on ground). They despatched one company and two troops of 44 R Tks to this place, but found that the enemy had withdrawn just before their arrival.

"At about 1500 hours 24 March I issued verbal orders to CO 7 SEAFORTH to push on to MEHR and to try to capture the all-important bridge 1,000 yards North East of the village. MEHR was occupied by 1730 hours, but all efforts to reach the bridge that night failed.

Action by 9 CAMERONIANS

"9 CAMERONIANS crossed at 1430 hours 24 March in stormboats, and I then issued verbal orders to the CO to move to HAFFEN. This was reached just before dark, and companies were established at the cross-roads in the Eastern part of the village and at STOPPENDAHL and PLENTERSKATH. Attempts to move forward to the line WISSHOF—BRUCKSHOF were frustrated by the Germans.

2 GLAS H

"2 GLAS H crossed during the early evening of 24 March and concentrated South East of HAFFEN in 9 CAMERONIANS area by 2330 hours.

Action by 46 (H) Bde on 25 March

"After a most unpleasant night during which the enemy in the MEHR area had shown himself to be aggressive and full of fight, I decided that a frontal attack on the bridge would be suicidal particularly as 44 R Tks had by then been withdrawn.

"2 GLAS H therefore did an approach march round the Southern end of LANGE RENNE, via VAHNUM and BERGEN and we then put in a two battalion attack Northwards, to the East of LANGE RENNE, the other battalion being 2 A & SH (less one company), of 227 (H) Bde, which had been placed under my command that morning.

"This took a long time, but undoubtedly saved many lives.

"The bridge was found to be impassable to vehicles, and as no bridging equipment could be made available, transport of 2 A & SH had to follow units round by the South. The bridge was however usable on foot."

D. Lieutenant Colonel R. N. FOSTER, DSO, OBE, Commander 11 AGRE

RE WORK in left sector of 15 (S) Div

"Upstream from WOLFFSKATH on the WEST bank is a lone cottage called PARENDYK. There the 50/60 Rafts were constructed and operated. You will see that this area is opposite the gap between 44 (L) Bde and 227 (H) Bde and, as a result, accurate shelling and small arms fire prevented the CRE beginning his recce until 1100 hrs D day. His equipment was got down to the river by 1300 hours. It had been concentrated South of the HOCHWALD and in the woods South-West of XANTEN. Each of the two columns consisted of 28 tanks (AVsRE) towing either a sledge or a trailer and they were a tremendous encumbrance on the routes. The effort was worth while, however, as in the first 30 hours of operation 190 Tks and SP guns were ferried over.

Stand 5

"This party was responsible for the capture of a German post on the far bank. The unit APTC Sergeant, acting as guide to three light airborne-type bulldozers, which had been taken over by Buffalo, bumped into an unexpected German post. He ordered the baby-bulldozers to raise their blades, and led them into action in a spirited charge, so unnerving the Germans that they surrendered on the spot.

Class 9 FBE bridge

"The Class 9 FBE Bridge, which was constructed just upstream of the lagoon opposite WOLFFS-KATH, was also delayed by shelling, but was completed in eleven hours work. The 1,000 yards of approaches which we had to make were not used until rain started. Two other cross-country approaches (one for wheels and the other for tracks) were marked out and used as long as possible.

"The original exit was constructed left-handed so as to let vehicles clear into 227 (H) Bde sector. Owing to enemy resistance on this sector, traffic had to be diverted along the bund to the right. Negotiation of the resultant hairpin in the dark caused a traffic block on the far end of the bridge during the night D/D+1, and a lot of boats sank, fortunately without loss of any vehicles. It was thirteen hours, however, before the bridge could be reopened, incidentally a longer period than had been taken in its original construction.

Stormboats and Class 9 Rafts

"The stormboats and class 9 rafts of 227 (H) Bde sited a few hundred yards away downstream from here were caught at dawn by enemy still on the far bank. They sustained damage and casualties.

Class 12 Bailey Bridge

"You will see at *STAND* 6 the site of the class 12 Bailey Bridge. This was built in two sections to make use of existing approaches. The start of construction was delayed due to shelling from the REES area, where 30 Corps had not made the progress expected. Difficulties were met in sandbanks and awkward currents at the mouth of the creek, which you will see, and which also caused much trouble to the LVsT landing 2 A & SH. LCV(P)s in this sector were unceremoniously tipped off their trailers and pushed into the water by bulldozers, as we had no crane large enough to deal with them."

STAND 6

Bund at VYNEN (086466)

Object of Stand

To study the action of the Left assault battalion of 227 (H) Bde, 2 A & SH.

Colonel D. R. MORGAN, DSO, MC, CO 2 A & SH

Action of 2 A & SH

"2 A & SH was the Left assault battalion of 227 (H) Bde, the Left assault brigade of 15 (S) Div.

Reconnaissances

"These were very much easier and more beneficial than for the other battalions, as it was possible for us to view the far bank, and country beyond, from behind the bund near here which is directly opposite the point where the battalion was put ashore. As you see, the bund on this sector runs quite close to the river. Each company and platoon commander plus the various commanders and drivers of the Buffaloes (E RIDING YEO) were able to make this reconnaissance at least once.

Plan

"The battalion objective was HAFFEN, but the Brigade Commander stressed that we had to capture both the area around LOHR and the bridge over the stream South-West of WAYERHOF—the latter intact if possible.

"This meant that the battalion would have to be split and companies separated by some 2,500 yards, which was most untidy but, through lack of Buffaloes, it was not possible to make available any further troops.

"It was decided to land and assault with three companies up.

    Right — D Coy
    Centre — B Coy
    Left — A Coy

followed by Battalion HQ and C Coy.

The Crossing

"The trip in the water took 12 minutes and the Buffaloes carrying the assault companies entered the river punctually at 0200 hours, the appointed H Hour.

Company Tasks

"D Coy was to land on the East (Right) bank of the inlet which you can see opposite, and immediately attack HUBSCH, at the same time it was to send a platoon down to clear the bund as far as the sluice gates where it was to contact a similar patrol from the 10 HLI, which was the Right assault battalion of the brigade.

"A and B Coys with an FOO party were to be put ashore on the main bank to the West (Left) of the inlet. Their task was to advance to the bridge, with B Coy on the Right and A on the Left divided by the bund which was inclusive to B Coy.

Capture of A and B Coys' Objectives

"B Coy was ordered to clear en route the houses of AUF DEM GRINDT and DORNEWARDT, whilst A Coy was to deal with a suspicious looking piece of raised ground just West of DORNEWARDT. The bridge and adjacent track-crossing over the bund were secured intact and B Coy reorganised in that area, inclusive WAYERHOF. A Coy pushed on up the bund towards HOPERHOF but got held up there by a strongpoint and dawn found the company in very close contact. An enemy counter-attack against B Coy from HAFFEN was successfully engaged by artillery and SA fire. A number of enemy were killed and many others were made prisoners.

Action of D Coy at HUBSCH

"On the Right things were not going so well. D Coy Commander had been hit soon after entering the river. Only one of D Coy's Buffaloes was able to get into the inlet, and then it was forced to land its platoon on the West (Left) bank. The platoon was completely confused by this and it was not until some time later that I was able to find it and direct it on to its objective.

"The remainder of D Coy was put ashore where A and B Coys had landed. This meant that the platoons had to walk round the Northern tip of the inlet and all surprise was lost.

"With one of the platoons lost, and one detached clearing the bund, D Coy was left with only one platoon to assault HUBSCH. Lieutenant STEWART was killed during this attack. Fighting was fierce and the situation was somewhat confused for the next hour.

"The situation improved when the second platoon rejoined and the patrol returned from clearing the bund. The latter encountered no opposition on the way out nor did it make contact with the HLI patrol. On the return journey however it was engaged by an enemy post well dug-in and the

Stand 6

platoon suffered some casualties before the post was silenced. By dawn HUBSCH was completely cleared up but it had been a long process winkling the enemy out of his buildings and cellars, and his positions in the orchard. Casualties were fairly heavy on both sides and about 15 prisoners were taken.

Battalion HQ

"Battalion HQ, which had halted close to HUBSCH at the tip of the inlet, were now out of touch with the advancing A and B Coys and so it was decided to move to DORNEWARDT and set up Battalion HQ there—midway between the companies.

"As the buildings were approached a few enemy came rushing out—one firing his automatic, but he was quickly and effectively overcome by one of the Battalion HQ signallers. The others ran round the buildings and were rounded up later on in the morning.

Attack on LOHR

"I then decided to attack LOHR as soon as possible with available resources under Major GRAHAM, Commander of C Coy.

"He was given the remnants of D Coy and a platoon of MMGs. Before the attack against the buildings around LOHR could be launched it was essential that some posts which had come to light on the bund should be cleared.

"C Coy then carried out this task supported by fire from HUBSCH.

"A Coy of the GORDONS suddenly appeared from out of the blue with orders to assist us and they provided valuable and very necessary additional fire support.

"When the bund-clearing operation was almost completed, D Coy attacked the buildings at HAGENSHOF, whilst C Coy turned their attentions towards RISWICKSHOF.

"As these companies were making satisfactory progress and a firm base seemed no longer necessary, A Coy 2 GORDONS attacked, and this allowed D Coy to pass on to deal with the enemy in buildings beyond, whither a number had withdrawn, and into LOHR itself. By 1300 hours LOHR was clear but it had been very fierce fighting against fanatical paratroopers of 7 Para Div. The attack took place without the assistance of artillery or smoke. Neither was permitted on account of the airborne operation.

"A number of Germans were killed and several finally gave themselves up, amongst whom were a dozen or so women snipers. Various ribald references were made over the blower concerning these women but even the Jocks reckoned that they had few of the attractions normally associated with the fairer sex.

Further Operations

"Early the next morning, 25 March, we were put under command of 46 (H) Bde and we were relieved by 2 GORDONS. A Coy however was too closely committed to be relieved by day. Consequently at noon, when we started our forced march of 5 miles in the smoke and thick dust to join the GLASGOW HIGHLANDERS for a successful wood clearing operation that evening, we did so without A Coy who rejoined us on our objective on the afternoon of 26 March."

SECTION IV

NOTES FOR THE GUIDANCE OF CONDUCTING OFFICERS

Preliminary Reconnaissance

The Conducting Officer should try to have at least three to four days on the ground before the Tour starts (exclusive of days spent briefing the Transport Officer, Provost etc.). This is necessary in order to check up descriptions of the ground appropriate to the time of the year and weather conditions, and to become fully conversant with the whole area. Binoculars and prismatic compasses are necessary.

It should be remembered that operations took place in March, whereas tours are likely to take place in summer. This will of course affect the going across country, visibility through foliage, and the level and consequently width of the RHINE itself.

All speakers whose personal accounts are included in Section III, had an opportunity to refresh their memories of the area before speaking in November 1947, when a brief tour was held without spectators.

During this preliminary reconnaissance, the Conducting Officer should spend at least half a day familiarising himself with the country and landmarks on the East bank of the RHINE up to the DIERSFORDTER WALD.

Stands

It is virtually impossible to select a stand from which the whole of 15 (S) Div sector can be surveyed at one time by upwards of 100 spectators. *STAND* 1 is considered to be the best available for this purpose, but does not satisfactorily cover the left of the sector.

It is therefore recommended that the planning stages are dealt with largely indoors (see below, "Introductory Lectures").

A second difficulty arises from the fact that, from the West bank, observation of the country East of the RHINE is very much restricted, especially in the left sector, by the line of the bund itself.

It is therefore recommended that *STAND* 5 be taken on the East bank, spectators being transported across the river in LVsT if available, or in motor launches. If this is not possible *STAND* 5 may be taken on the West bank, but the Conducting Officer will have to be capable of giving a very detailed description of the ground on the far bank, and to relate it to the 25,000 map.

Introductory Lectures

In addition to the Introductory Lectures to be based on Part III Section I, which are of a general nature, and should be given by high ranking officers of the Army and RAF *the previous evening*, it is recommended that one hour is spent indoors on the planning aspects of 15 (S) Div's assault before going out on the ground. The itinerary in Section II is based on this recommendation and suitable personal accounts will be found in Section III. It is felt that operation PLUNDER from the Corps and divisional aspect was very largely a "planning" battle, and that the planning stages should be studied, as they were in actual fact, from maps and models. A large scale wall map, which need show the topographical details in outline only, must be provided, and a floor model would be an advantage.

It is important that all spectators are given ample opportunity to study Parts I and II of the book before attending the Introductory Lectures.

A useful means of putting all spectators in the picture as regards the planning stages might be by the use of a play, and a synopsis of a suitable play written for this purpose is included at Section V.

Accommodation

(a) It is probable that operation PLUNDER will be studied in conjunction with operations VERITABLE and VARSITY. This should be done in correct chronological order, viz, VERITABLE, PLUNDER, VARSITY.

(b) For this purpose, accommodation might be provided by one or other of the following alternatives:

   (i) Tented Camp (suitable site in MARIENBAUM at 065454).

   (ii) The Police barracks (German) at WESEL.

   Alternative (i) would involve pitching the camp, providing minimum structures, all furniture and staff etc.

   Alternative (ii) would involve provision of staff and possibly some furniture only. Condiderable prior warning to the British police commandant at WESEL would however be essential.

(c) If numbers on the tour are very small, not more than say forty, a possible further solution might be the use of a train of sleeping cars and dining car parked in WESEL or other convenient station for the duration of the tour.

Lunch

The lunch site suggested in the itinerary is a large farm, where under-cover accommodation can be arranged. The owner (1947) is German, but his wife is of French origin, and anxious to be of assistance. It is therefore suggested that a buffet lunch is provided Alternatively all spectators could take a haversack lunch.

Transport

Buses can traverse all roads and lanes on the itinerary. Previous reconnaissance by the Transport officer or NCO is essential to ensure that he knows the route and that turning places are adequate.

Provost

A detachment of Provost is useful to erect any necessary signs, and should be taken on a previous reconnaissance.

Arrangements will also be required to guard the camp, if a tented camp is adopted.

Loudspeaker Equipment

Two complete stations, preferably mounted in jeeps, are required, and should leapfrog from stand to stand. One station should be portable, independent of the jeep, for purposes of *STANDS* 3 and 5. Reconnaissance is necessary to show the operators the route, and exact location of microphone and loudspeaker at each stand

Conduct of the Tour

(a) The conducting officer should be first away from each stand. It is an advantage if he speaks German or has an interpreter in his car, to deal with any traffic problems which may arise with German police, farm carts etc.

(b) He requires the following equipment in his car :—
   Megaphones.
   Wire cutters.
   Barbed wire to mend any fences cut.

(c) Spectators require binoculars. They should not take the books on the ground but the general map found in the end cover, or its equivalent, is essential.

Possible Alternative Speakers

Since all speakers who are shown as giving personal accounts may not be available at the time of the tour, the following alternative speakers are suggested :—

SECTION I

Introductory Lectures	*Name*	*Appointment at time of PLUNDER*
A. GENERAL	Lieutenant General Sir NEIL M. RITCHIE, KBE, CB, DSO, MC	Comd 12 Corps

SECTION III

Personal accounts

Indoors

A. 15 (S) Div Plan	Major General C. M. BARBER, CB, DSO	Comd 15 (S) Div
B. 12 Corps Fire Plan	Brigadier G. W. E. HEATH, CBE, DSO, MC	CCRA 12 Corps
D. RE Plan	Colonel R. K. MILLAR, DSO	CRE 15 (S) Div

Stand 2

B. Assault crossing by 44 (L) Bde	Lieutenant Colonel J. T. BANNATYNE, MBE (Cameron Highlanders)	BM 44 (L) Bde
C. RE Work	Colonel R. K. MILLAR, DSO	CRE 15 (S) Div

Stand 3

A. Action of 8 RS	Lieutenant Colonel B. A. PEARSON, DSO (Argyll and Sutherland Highlanders)	CO 8 RS
B. Crossing and Action of 44 R Tks	Lieutenant Colonel R. M. P. CARVER, CBE, DSO, MC (Royal Tank Regiment)	Comd 4 Armd Bde

Stand 4

    B. Plan and Action of of 227 (H) Bde   { Brigadier E. C. COLVILLE, DSO   Comd 227 (H) Bde
                                                      { Colonel D. R. MORGAN, DSO, MC   CO 2 A & SH

Stand 5

    A. Action by 10 HLI   Lieutenant Colonel R. A. BRAMWELL-DAVIES, DSO (Highland Light Infantry)   CO 10 HLI

    C. Action by 46 (H) Bde   Major W. B. LAWSON (Late Highland Light Infantry—now released)   BM 46 (H) Bde

    D. RE Work   Colonel R. K. MILLAR, DSO   CRE 15 (S) Div

SECTION V

PLANNING PLUNDER

A PLAY
(Reference should be made to MAP 6).

Exercise Director (or Conducting Officer)

The object of the short play you are about to see is to shew in pictorial form how the divisional plan for PLUNDER might have been evolved.

The scene is HQ 15 (S) Div and the date about 10 March 1945. Before beginning I will get the conducting officer to describe the model.

Conducting Officer

The outline of the model is shewn on the maps, here and here. This end of the model corresponds to this line on the map.

The area represented on the model is 12 miles × 9 miles. These vertical marks are 1,000 yards apart.

The North point is shewn here.

Exercise Director

In an operation of this nature I suggest that, broadly speaking, division of responsibility between Army, Corps, and Division, and the sequence of planning are as follows :—

(i) Army must produce their outline plan, which includes the tasks of Corps, the allotment of formations and equipment to Corps, and order the Corps to build a certain number of bridges, specifying classification. In addition, Army, in consultation with Army Group, must produce all requisite information ; particularly about the river, its banks, the approaches to it and the exits from it.

(ii) It is then for Corps to allot Assaulting Formations and give them their tasks, distribute special equipment and to specify exactly where the bridges are to be built ; and which class goes where.

(iii) Then Division decides on the actual Assault places.

This done, one starts from the back; Corps and Divisions together working out the concentration, while Division settles the Marshalling Areas, the routes from them forward and the whole layout in front of them as far forward as the near bank. But throughout, Corps must keep in the closest touch to see that Divisions fit in with the bigger picture. In addition, it is the responsibility of Army so to direct Corps that the routes forward into the concentration fit in with the Army plans of movement. If LVsT are being used, as in this case, it is vital that the area chosen for the assault should suit them, otherwise the whole thing may go wrong from the start. The LVT Commander must, therefore, be brought into the planning at an early stage on a Corps level.

Before we go any further, there are a few topographical points to which I must draw your attention. The importance of the road centres of WESEL, REES, BOCHOLT ; the river ISSEL, which you observe forms a second obstacle roughly parallel to the RHINE and about 6 miles from it; then the high ground on the Western edge of the DIERSFORDTER WALD, which forms "the lip of the saucer" overlooking the bridging sites and all the low lying ground East of the River on the Corps front. Now to turn to bridge sites. There are only three reasonable possibilities. One on the extreme right opposite XANTEN. One on the extreme left at VYNEN. One on the left centre opposite WARDT. The approaches to them on the near bank are good on both flank sites, and indifferent in the centre; on the far bank the exits are not at all good. Opposite XANTEN there is a narrow road on top of the "bund" for the first three-quarters of a mile before it reaches BISLICH and splits into two reasonable roads. In the case of the two Northern bridges the exits are narrow, one way gravel roads of very poor quality, but they will just serve the purpose unless the weather lets us down badly. Over and above these there is only one more place, here, where wheeled vehicles can be got down to and away from the river.

This first-class lateral road from XANTEN is, of course, a great asset and is a feature which is so often met in the valleys of the larger rivers in North-West Europe.

The Commander of 12 Corps has decided to build a Class 40 here, Class 9 FBE here and a Class 12 Bailey here.

Now the river itself. It varies from about 400 yards, opposite XANTEN to about 500 yards in the northern part of our sector. The current is running three to four knots. The suitability of the banks for use by LVsT or stormboats is as shown on the model. It is practicable to make use of these small patches of suitable bank here between the groins for LVsT to cross opposite BISLICH.

These main flood banks or "bunds" here and here present a serious problem. They are ten to fifteen feet high and steep sided and loaded LVsT cannot cross them. The preparation of crossing places for them will need two or three hours' Sapper work, and they are, of course, in full view of the enemy's position.

One more point. By taking up the rails it has been possible to turn this railway into a good one-way road covered from view as far as here.

The Div Comd would have had time to study the problem and the ground and by the time this Conference is held is prepared to state his outline plan, and will have had an opportunity of thinking out previously how the various problems can best be solved.

We will now get down to ACT I.

PLANNING PLUNDER

CAST

COMMANDER	15 (Scottish) Infantry Division.
GSO 1	15 (Scottish) Infantry Division.
A/Q	15 (Scottish) Infantry Division.
COMMANDER	11 Army Group Royal Engineers.
BRIGADIER	Representative 79 Armoured Division.

ACT 1

DIVISIONAL COMMANDER

Now you know that Div has been allotted all the Corps resources except 50 stormboats and a squadron of LVsT which have been given to 1 Commando Bde and you know what the job is, but I will run through it once more and stress certain points.

The Div, with the additional troops and equipment already allotted to us, are to force an assault crossing between incl XANTEN and the Corps boundary here and we are to secure crossings over the river ISSEL East of HAMMINKELN and West of DINGDEN.

7 Armd Div and 53 Welsh Div will later pass through us; the former capturing BORKEN and the latter BOCHOLT.

52 Lowland Div is initially to hold the West bank of the RHINE on the Corps front and then after we have assaulted through it, to pass into Corps reserve as a follow-up formation.

There are certain points the Corps Comd particularly stressed.

The enemy must not be allowed to seal off the bridgehead. It is essential that operations on the far bank should not congeal; speed is, therefore, of the highest importance.

The depth of the bridgehead must be increased as quickly as possible by threats designed to drive the enemy's field gun line out of range of the bridges and ferry sites.

This postulates the need :—

Firstly, to establish a firm base on the far bank in the form of a series of shallow bridgeheads with light reconnaissance ahead, then to fan out laterally and join them up into one bridgehead.

These bridgeheads should be deep enough to prevent the enemy from bringing aimed small arms fire on the crossing places, but should not be out of supporting distance of the full weight of our own field artillery.

And secondly, to establish as large a balanced Mobile Striking Force as possible on the far bank so that strong thrusts, with armour in support, can be made at the earliest time to seize dominating ground, the enemy's field gun line and centres of communication. Wherever possible this will be done from the rear.

It is now almost certain that a large scale airborne operation will take place in conjunction with the assault by our ground forces. This will be under US Command but will include 6 British Airborne Div. Airborne troops will land in the area between (incl) HAMMINKELN and (excl) WESEL, and we shall take over from 6 Airborne Div in the HAMMINKELN area as soon as feasible. This will, of course, be a tremendous assistance to us, particularly in our right assaulting sector.

Before I go any further, there are two more points which I want particularly to stress :—

The first is that the build-up on the far bank must envisage a counter-attack by the enemy with armour three or four hours after daylight.

And the second is that infantry will be required in the greatest possible numbers and the plans to pass troops across the river must keep this in mind.

To continue —

Delay to construct roads cannot be accepted nor can operations be retarded to await the construction of bridges. Therefore, all resources for ferrying are to be developed to the utmost and a high proportion of tracked vehicles will be used in order that we can be independent of roads in the early stages.

It will be a night crossing under movement light.

Assault battalions will be pre-stowed in LVsT in Marshalling Areas far enough back to be out of enemy observation and clear of his defensive fire. Battalions will then be carried in these LVsT down across the river.

It is of the greatest importance to have DD tanks on the far bank as early as possible, first to keep the situation there fluid and, second, to assist in repelling the inevitable enemy counter-attack. But the performance of the DD tanks in negotiating the difficult river bank is such that they cannot be committed to the crossing until their exits have been prepared and the feasibility of their getting out of the river ensured. They will, therefore, cross as soon as they can but will wait until their carpets have been laid for them.

Owing to the magnitude and complexity of the bridging, ferrying and transit problems the following will be placed under my command until such time as these responsibilities should pass to Corps Control :—

One CAGRE with adequate staff and signals to command all the RE formations allotted and to advise on all RE matters.

A Bank Group with adequate staff and signals to run for us, under my direction, all the movement, policing, transit, assembly and dispersal of all personnel and vehicles. You know already the general composition of this Group.

Now I will give you my outline plan. The Assault will be carried out on a two brigade front. Each brigade will attack with two battalions up and I want the right brigade to cross here and here and the left brigade here and here.

That will mean that we will be attacking at or near the bridge sites and will clear the enemy from the far bank in these areas from the beginning.

The first objectives of the Brigades which I have in mind are :—

Right Brigade   —   LOH — MUHLENFELD — FELDWICK
Left Brigade   —   MEHR — HAFFEN.

The latter are a bit far out but I feel that they will be very difficult to take later and should fall much easier in the initial assault, and the CCRA says he can reach with plenty of guns.

In view of the width of the river and the consequent delay in getting the guns across, we must take the risk of putting the guns well forward in their initial deployment. This enables them to cover this task easily and also to support the infantry up to inclusive the main road through the DIERSFORDTER WALD. They will be very exposed but we have got away with it many times already.

The next step is to join up the two bridgeheads, and then get the "lip of the saucer" so as to deny the enemy all observation on the crossings. That means getting MARS, DIERSFORDT and the main road through the woods here.

After that I should bring up my left to here. This should clear the enemy field guns line out of range of the crossings and enable me to clear a good lateral before tackling the ISSEL.

ACT II

Scene 1

DIV COMD

Now that we know where we are going to assault we can start at the back and work forwards.

I will touch briefly on the general lay-out of the Army so that you can see what the CONCENTRATION will involve. We will not touch on it in detail, but I wish to give you all the background so that as the plans develop you can ensure that they fit in.

Right back here round DIEST and BRUSSELS are the two formations for immediate exploitation. And the first point is that the assaulting division takes so much time to cross on the ferries that the main bodies of these two follow-up formations need make no move until after H hour. But these moves must be fitted in to suit the Corps and Army traffic plan.

The second point is the general administrative lay-out in the back areas and I will get the A/Q to give the salient points.

A/Q

The administrative build-up has already started. Army Railheads are in this area (NIJMEGEN, MOOK, GENNEP). The one that interests us chiefly is the Amn Railhead at GENNEP, as we shall draw a proportion of the amn for dumping direct from there and not from Army Roadhead.

Army Roadhead is on the East bank of the MAAS (GOCH, GELDERN, VENLO).

Corps FMC is at KEVELAER. It holds Supplies, but no Amn or POL, which will be drawn direct from Roadhead except for such amn as we get from Railhead.

A large dump of RE Stores is being built up here (GOCH) and there is a forward RE Area for pre-loaded Bridging and Raft material here (WINNEKENDONK).

A forward Div dump of Amn, Sups and POL will be required somewhere in the SONSBECK Area.

The Movement problem is intricate. We have Class 40 bridges over the MAAS at GENNEP (two-way) WELL and LOTTUM and certain running rights over the Class 70 Bridge at VENLO.

Railheads can only handle a portion of the maintenance traffic and a great deal has to be carried over these bridges. During the last week before D Day, operational moves of formations will involve the passage of over 35,000 vehicles, including 600 Tanks.

COMD

The third point is reconnaissance which will, of course, have to be going on throughout the concentration and dumping period.

I have fixed that 52 Div will co-ordinate and exercise the strictest control over all movement in the forward area and all recces will have to report to their headquarters for a pass. They will also carry out all patrolling and reconnaissance of the far bank with the help of the special under water recce teams which I am getting from ENGLAND.

Special measures have been taken to prevent disclosure of the actual front of the assault by this reconnaissance. (This means that similar reconnaissance is going on over the whole Army Group front). It is vital that the situation on the far bank about under water obstacles and mines is cleared up for the LVsT and about under water subsoil and slope for the DDs.

There is one more very important matter—concealment of the concentration and marshalling. There are two aspects; first from enemy air observation, second from ground observation. And the two of them, both in daylight and darkness.

So far as the AIR is concerned the RAF have pretty reasonable air superiority but they cannot prevent the single enemy recce aircraft.

So by day there is to be NO abnormal movement. Concealment and camouflage are very important.

All abnormal movement must take place at night. This means movement light and the lights deployed in great depth. Vehicle lighting is to be severely restricted. At night we are even less sure of keeping enemy aircraft away.

Now against enemy ground observation. Army has arranged a standing smoke screen covering and overlapping the whole Army front. Provided that conditions remain good this should prevent the enemy overlooking us in daylight.

GSO I

But the continuous daylight smoke screen cuts both ways. It means you can't do any daylight observation of the enemy and you'll want to have facilities for this.

COMD

Well, if you are only referring to the officers, they can get in a "whizzer" and have a look over the top of the screen.

GSO I

No. It's not that. It's the junior commanders who must get a look.

COMD

All right. The only solution I can see is that on certain days for certain periods we cut the smoke screen out altogether to allow for this. Can this be arranged?

GSO I

It can, but it must be tackled by Army and Army Group because this screen will have to be co-ordinated over the whole front including even outside the Corps and Army boundaries.

COMD

I have put my divisional Staging Areas back over here, and the Marshalling Areas in this "RAILWAY Wood" here and in the HOCHWALD here. I had to discard XANTEN Wood as the built-up area of XANTEN hinders approach to the river while the development of the 'railway road' made this RAILWAY wood a practicable alternative.

I am not putting in them anything more than is absolutely necessary. I propose to hold everything I can in my Staging Areas further back and move them up into the Marshalling Area as and when vacancies there occur. My plan is to hold in Marshalling Areas initially everything which has to cross before H + 12 hours and nothing more.

GSO I

What do you propose to have in the way of roads and tracks leading forward to the river from our Marshalling Areas?

COMD

From each Marshalling Area two LVT tracks (one for each assaulting battalion), an infantry track and a road for vehicles. One of the LVT tracks can later be turned into a tank track which will, of course, have to branch off to the 50/60 ferry when it gets near the river. I'd like to get a thorough grasp of this. Would you get the Staff to mark the beginning of these tracks from say, the Right Brigade Marshalling Area and we can see what we expect it to look like at last light on 'D' Day.

GSO I

This is a vehicle track in brown. This in an infantry track in black. This an LVT track in red which is used for the assault only and this an LVT track which later becomes a tank track (purple).

Here and here I would have the assault battalions married up to their LVsT which would be placed so that they have direct and easy access to their LVT tracks. Here would be the Reserve Infantry Battalion resting at the end of the infantry track. South of the railway would be the vehicles which are early competitors for the LVT and Class 9 ferries all formed up ready in their serials with direct and easy access to the road.

COMD

It's obvious that these Marshalling Areas will have to be highly organised. How do you propose to control movement within them?

GSO I

First of all, Sir, by placing everybody so that they do not have to cross anyone else either entering or leaving.

Secondly by allotting each group of vehicles or personnel a serial number and by giving each track a reference letter.

And thirdly by having an adequate staff with loud hailers and very good communications in the area. I envisage the Bank Group running all this for me, except that my staff will check on arrival, show them where to go and warn them when to move.

COMD

Yes, I agree. And that leads me to the big point of division of responsibility. G I, what are your suggestions ?

GSO I

That normal formation staffs should be responsible for moving troops into the Marshalling Area and that the Bank Group should run this area and should then take on their transit until they emerge from the sausage machine on the other side of the river.

As I see it the whole organisation must admit of flexibility. We shall have to make out an order of priority for all units and sub-units under your command including Army and Corps units. But battles always produce surprises and we shall be certain to want to change the order and call up a serial out of its turn.

COMD

I agree entirely. Will you arrange that ?

ACT II

Scene 2

THE APPROACH

COMD

Before we go on I will get my G I to explain the colour scheme.

GSO I

Purple denotes tracks and installations for armour and tracked vehicles.
Brown for wheeled vehicles, Class 9 and under.
Black for infantry.
Red for LVsT.
Green for Sappers.

COMD

The next question I am going to consider is the approach to the river and the first major point is the necessary sapper work to enable LVsT to cross the "bunds".

This will take two to three hours and we can do it on the night of the assault but, if we do, it may have a serious effect on our choice of H Hour. So we will make all preparations now so that we can do it, if necessary, on the previous night (D—1) under cover of a "stonk" and have the gaps completely camouflaged by dawn. Really good camouflage screens and the smoke screen which is already operative on the whole Army Group front will, I am sure, eliminate all risk of disclosing the points of attack.

With the exception of the gapping of the bund the advance of the assault waves is, I think, pretty straightforward up to the time they near the river bank and we will consider their deployment, and subsequent action, when we tackle the Assault later.

It is the approach and control of the mixed assortment of troops and vehicles to the various ferries which needs our attention at the moment.

Now, GSO I, I know you have already got my views about routes forward to the bank and have put them on the model. Just explain them.

GSO I

Here are the LVT assault crossing places of the brigades. Here are the bridge sites: Class 40 here, Class 9 FBE here and Class 12 Bailey here. LVT ferries initially at each LVT assault crossing place and later here and here only. Class 50/60 ferries here. Class 9 ferries here. Storm boat ferries here. DUKW ferry here.

The vehicle routes are shown here in brown, the infantry tracks in black, the separate DUKW route is here and the LVT tracks in red. Of these latter, these two become redundant once the assault wave has passed, and this one (marked purple) becomes a tank track and leads to the 50/60 ferries.

This miniature harbour here is an asset, as it enables stormboat engines to be started before entering the current.

COMD

Right. That's clear. Now, so that we can all be working from a common basis, run through the lay-out of the Bank Group on the near bank.

GSO I

We suggest that the CO of the Bank Group and his HQ should establish what we call Bank Control at Tac Div with the Divisional Commander. The CAGRE would be there also. And that a Company of the Bank Group should exercise control in the area of each Assaulting Brigade on the near bank, establishing what we call Crossing Control at the corresponding forward Brigade Headquarters and manning all the installations in its area.

COMD

Will you explain these installations ?

GSO I

Firstly a traffic post at each bridge and ferry site and at all other installations required by the Sappers, the LVsT or anyone else.

Behind them a waiting area for each type of track. These to be far enough back from the banks to be clear as possible of shelling and mortaring at them and in the best available cover. The object of them being to make certain that no ferry ever has to wait for a load and that no ferry site is ever congested with waiting vehicles. We have called them Armour Waiting Areas, Stormboat Waiting Areas and Vehicle Waiting Areas and they are marked on the model. All, as you see, are on their appropriate routes forward.

COMD

What installations do you require for your LVsT ?

BRIG 79

First of all an LVT Collecting Area at the near bank point of exit of each LVT ferry. Here we would 'screen' all LVsT for fitness to continue on the ferry service and put any unfit ones into running condition again at the earliest possible moment.

This Collecting Area should be sufficiently far back to give cover from enemy observation. Immediately behind the bund would be suitable in this case.

As you know, Sir, these LVsT are very susceptible to mechanical damage, particularly the tracks, and I suggest that this small maintenance organisation is absolutely necessary if the required number is to be kept "on the road". If an LVT gets out of control in mid-stream it can also cause serious damage to a floating bridge—though we have taken the precaution to site the LVT ferries as far as possible downstream from any such bridges.

As a last resort LVsT can be "scuttled" if out of control and endangering our bridges.

Secondly we need an LVT Loading Area with easy access to the near bank LVT point of entry for each ferry. The jeeps, carriers, etc., have a direct cross country route to this from the Vehicle Waiting Area and the LVsT come to it in complete troops from the Collecting Area as soon as they have returned and have been screened and re-organised.

As soon as it is clear that enemy shelling or interference has ceased the whole organisation could be moved forward nearer the bank to decrease the "land" part of the turn round.

COMD

And what do you need for your DDs ?

BRIG 79

Merely an Inflation Area with a clear run over open country from it to the chosen point of entry.

COMD

What do the Sappers need ?

COMD AGRE

A Bridge Marshalling Harbour for each Bridge Site for bridging lorries, and forward hides for ferries and stormboats. Class 9 here and here and stormboats at these sites here and here which later become Stormboat Waiting Areas. As the 50/60 rafts with their AVsRE and sledges are so difficult to hide I suggest that they should be held back as far as possible and moved forward as soon as practicable.

COMD

I agree entirely with that last point and have sited them here and here initially. Right. Now, A/Q, what do you require ?

A/Q

I want a DUKW Waiting Area here where batches of pre-loaded DUKWs await calling forward by DUKW Ferry Control.

A "DUKW Area" here where the bulk of the pre-loaded DUKWs harbour and where empty DUKWs come back to re-fill from a dump established by us.

In the early stages, casualties will come back in LVsT and we want a Casualty Disembarkation Point, manned by the specially allotted Fd Amb in each LVT Collecting Area.

Prisoners are going to be a problem in the early stages. They should be brought back in returning LVsT and we have decided to establish a cage in each Assault Bde Area.

COMD

Any other points or difficulties ? Can the CRSigs provide all these communications ?

GSOI

Yes, Sir, but all lines close to the river will have to be buried and that needs time. Even with help from Army and Corps it will take about a fortnight to do and then the lay-out will be rigid; so that locations of HQs and their communication centres must be decided very early and not changed after that.

Bank Control will need a lot of wireless. The squadron of armoured cars will help besides giving protection for detachments near the bank: but Corps resources will have to be pooled to find the remainder.

He doesn't anticipate any difficulty in getting signal lines across early, as they practised hard on the MAAS, which is faster flowing.

I suggest you ask for some Weasels for 15 Div Sigs for laying their forward lines on the mud flats.

Finally, Sir, we will need the usual complete wireless silence for all formations and units involved in the assault and the most careful use of forward telephones during the preparatory period.

COMD AGRE

I have the problem of getting bridging lorries back to refill against the flow of traffic.

COMD

Just explain the problem briefly, will you ?

COMD AGRE

Advance Parties of each br site are held fwd in this area; with them are a minimum number of vehicles to enable the sappers to get busy on initial preparations as soon as they are given the office to start.

The remainder of the equipment is held back here in vicinity RE Dump. Br Vehicles ready loaded with their first loads are organised in Columns for each Br site. These will be called forward behind the main bodies of bridge builders as soon as the situation permits, by previously laid down routes. Having off loaded at their respective br sites, vehicles return to refill at the dump and return with their second loads: similarly for any subsequent loads necessary. Can they be treated as fire engines and have right of way ?

COMD

No, they cannot. Every move in this forward area must be controlled by the Bank Group and you will have to telephone or wireless the Bank or Crossing Control to get an all clear before you send any vehicles back to refill. This applies to all other arms too. But I think that this restriction will not appear so alarming when it is understood that I shall not be using this road through XANTEN here or the main down route here for my forward flow once the battle starts. This gives the sappers a clear run for their main job at XANTEN and there is a return route as far as here for the Northern bridge.

The capacity of the ferries is so small during the difficult period that there are bound to be large gaps in the forward flow into which other requirements like this can be fitted but I will suggest to Corps that it should be laid down in principle that vehicles moving in the main forward flow must have absolute priority over everything else and that bridging lorries come next in priority. Now I want to tackle one last point and that is the degree of control necessary once bridges are open. G I, what are your suggestions on that ?

GSOI

The first step, Sir, is when only the FBE is open for brief periods and then closed again for maintenance. During this time we see all traffic still passing through Marshalling Areas but only using Waiting Areas during those periods when the bridge is closed.

As soon as the other bridges are open we want to work on two main straightforward UP routes—through XANTEN and over the Class 40 for 7 Armd Div and over the Class 12 for 53 (W) Div—with a central return route over the FBE and the ferries. The Marshalling and Waiting Areas will then become redundant but XANTEN WOOD and the HOCHWALD will provide reserve parking space in case anything happens to the bridges. We will also maintain control at both UP bridges so that we can regulate the flow and deal with the many gate crashers who always try to crowd on to a bridge.

ACT II

Scene 3

THE ASSAULT

COMD

We will now consider the assault and the first point is the actual time of H Hour.

We know what the Marshalling Areas look like at last light on the night of the assault. (Turning to GSOI). What have we got to do between that time and H Hour?

GSOI

The Bank Group will have to man all their headquarters and traffic posts which they have not been able to man unseen already.

The marking and lighting of the tracks will have to be continued forward to the river banks from the furthest points which they have been able to reach unseen.

Class 9 rafts and stormboats have to be got out of their hides and prepared for movement to the river. The sappers hope to be able to tow them, but carrying parties from 52 (L) Div will be standing by, in case the half-tracks cannot make it.

The bunds have to be breached to permit the passage of LVsT, unless we do this the night before.

The jeeps, carriers and 6 pounders which are due to cross in the early LVT ferries will move to Vehicle Waiting Areas. The vehicles for other ferries need not move until after H Hour as it will be some time before these ferries become operative.

COMD

How long do you reckon all this will take?

GSOI

Two to three hours, Sir.

COMD

Right. Now the DDs. (Turning to Brig 79). As I have already said, it is vital that we get them across as soon as possible after the infantry. Can they cross under movement light?

BRIG 79

As you know, Sir, the driver is beneath the surface and his periscope only gives him a limited view. Emergence on the far bank is not easy and we should naturally prefer to do it in daylight. But you have given me time to train and I consider that, if you go as early as possible in the night and phase Assault RE over very early, the DD Regt could be operative on the far bank by first light.

COMD

Now when do we want to assault? The sooner we go the better for us, provided we can have movement light and the CRA's help with flare shell to show me my objectives. Did you ask about that?

GSOI

Yes, Sir. The CRA says that if you have movement light far enough forward to give good light for the actual assault, it will be strongly reflected in the water, and there's no doubt that whenever craft get into the reflected light, the enemy will see them well enough to bring aimed fire to bear. Unless you are prepared to accept this risk, he recommends siting it only so as to give good light in the Marshalling Areas, and sufficient light to be some help to the forward move from there, and to the various installations on the near bank. It should be shown on as wide a front as possible so as not to give away the crossing places. We can mark the flanks of the assault with Bofors tracer and the objectives with flare shell.

COMD

I agree to that; we don't want too much light forward, so we will adopt the CRA's recommendation. Q and Signals are not affected. What about the Sappers?

COMD AGRE

The more darkness tempered by movement light or moonlight I can have in the early stages the better for me, Sir.

COMD

Right. It is dark at 2000 hours so I'll tell the Corps Commander we will be ready for H hour by 2300 hours. I think we shall have to accept a later H hour however, as I know he wants 1 Cdo Bde to go for WESEL first, and they will need all the Artillery support they can get. Now let us just run through the salient points about LVsT in the assault.

BRIG 79

Taking the stock formation of two flights each of three troops, the first flight carries three companies and the second Bn HQ, the reserve company and the supporting arms.

The squadron would leave the Marshalling Area in line ahead up the LVT track. Near the river the first flight fans out, checks temporarily on a Start Line about 200 yds from the river to get into formation, and then the leading LVsT enter the river at H hour.

COMD

When would you want the gunners to lift off the far bank ?

BRIG 79

At H hour, when we enter the water, Sir. I wouldn't like to risk leaving it any later. Once committed we cannot paddle about in midstream waiting for fire to lift. I realise this means leaving the far bank un-neutralised while we are actually crossing, i.e., for about 3½ mins before we reach it; but I think we must accept this and use our weapons to fill the gap. The onus is on us to enter the water at H hour exactly if possible, and on no account before it.

COMD

How would you compete with mines on the far bank ?

BRIG 79

Sapper delousing parties could clamber out over the bows and deal with them while the LVsT returned and waited for lanes to be cleared. But under water obstacles would be the devil.

COMD

I take it that you would normally discharge both personnel and vehicles as soon as possible after climbing the far bank. But it might help a lot if the reserve companies could go straight on in their LVsT to their more distant objective inland. Is there any objection to that ?

BRIG 79

Yes, Sir. They should not be used as APCs. They are soft vehicles and are very conspicuous and vulnerable. With a load of 23 men you have a lot of eggs in one basket and they would suffer heavy casualties if the LVsT ran into trouble or hit a minefield. In the initial assault they should put the infantry down on the far bank without emerging ; later flights and the ferry service can discharge their loads further inland when the far bank has been checked for mines.

GSO 1

Now, Sir, about support. During the night we obviously cannot have any close air support but Corps have arranged that the enemy reserves will be taken on heavily in their billets and on their approaches to the river. What about artillery support ? We will have the whole Corps artillery effort allotted to us from about H—2 to H+5 hours. After that we shall be able to call on something like five field and two medium regiments, but I understand that all firing will cease during the airborne fly-in, if the airborne operation takes place. Do you agree about the time fire should lift from the far bank ?

COMD

Yes, and I shall plan for it to move back in two lifts to a line about 400 yards from the river and then dwell there until we have cleared any mines and are ready to go forward. I must say I am not too happy about the loss of fire support during the fly-in, but we shall have to accept it, I suppose. It is an added reason for speed, and we must try and be well up to our objectives by then. I shall also have to pay special attention to the flanks and the CRA thinks that "PEPPERPOT" will be the main thing there. I think he wants to get some extra help for it.

GSO I

Yes, Sir. The CCRA has allotted him all he can spare from the Corps A Tk regt and has arranged for 52 Div to help with their MG bn. You asked for contact cars, and we are getting two, plus two normal tentacles. They are trying to fit these up in Jeeps or a DD tank so that they can be got over in the early stages.

COMD

I think the contact cars had better cross at first light. We shall want to keep one tentacle at div HQ in reserve and the Mobile Striking Force will want one.

Now G I, give me your suggestions about Bank Group responsibility in the very early stages.

GSO I

Although an officer and 17 men of the Bank Group accompany each battalion in the assault wave we suggest, Sir, that the battalions themselves would want to organise their own LVT Unloading Points and Forward Assembly Areas to start with.

Assaulting Brigades would then want to take control using the better of the two Battalion Assembly Areas and leaving the other to die out.

Later, Brigades would want to be shot of this commitment and the Bank Group, which has been building up steadily, would be able to take it over at once.

COMD

That sounds sense. But I have one more point and that is the command of our troops while in the LVsT. (Turning to Brig 79). Any views on that problem ?

BRIG 79

Yes, Sir. I suggest that the commander of an LVT is in just the same position as the commander of a Naval craft as regards command.

COMD

I am happy about that as long as the infantry have the right to demand the LVT to halt and unload at any time.

ACT II

Scene 4

THE BUILD-UP

COMD

Now to consider the build-up. We have to have some basis for calculation but I must make it quite clear that actual events on the day will NOT conform to these calculations. A very great deal depends on the amount of enemy opposition, mortaring and shelling. But certain points do emerge. They are :—

LVsT are least affected by shelling and mortaring and have a considerable total lift. More really than we need after the initial assault. This means that we can count on getting across all the Jeeps, Weasels, carriers and six pounders that we've got and, by fitting superstructures, 17 pounders as well but without their "towers". If we had any 3.7 Howitzers we could get them across in LVsT as well, but they have been given to the Commandoes.

The 200 Weasels allotted to us by Army should be a great asset in the early stages.

Our stormboat capacity is very high and should get across all the men we want despite casualties. They may, however, be delayed by mortaring and shelling on the banks.

The capacity of the Class 9 and 50/60 ferries is the merest dribble.

We hope to be able to get a Class 9 FBE bridge across by about H + 29, a Class 12 Bailey by H + 53 and a Class 40 Tactical Bailey by H + 70 but these timings are very dependent on enemy opposition and shelling, and the FBE will be a very fragile affair on this river.

If we take H hour at 0200 hours on the 24th, the 24th looks like being a difficult day. Some more DDs or a treadway would just make all the difference. We might be able to get some field guns over on the 25th, but we shall probably have to wait until the early morning of the 26th before we can get tanks in any numbers operative on the far bank.

We will now tackle the problem of local defence of the bridges and ferries. The enemy is bound to go for them from the air, on the ground and both on and underneath the water. What are the CRA's suggestions for defence ?

GSO 1

Comd 100 AA Bde which is supporting us, is responsible for the AA defence of the bridges anyhow, and I suggest, Sir, that you make him responsible for their purely local defence against waterborne attack as well. He may be able to use some of his HAA for this as a secondary role, and we can give him some of the SPs from the Corps A-tk regt, and the CDLs which should be ideal for this job. I also suggest that you give him some Lyon Lights, the Asdic equipment, and a couple of LCVPs; the whole lot to be under his comd as a special force. He has his hands pretty full with the AA layout, and if he wants a deputy for this job we can give him the Corps A-tk regt comd.

The AGRE Comd tells me that he is fixing up a boom upstream of XANTEN.

COMD

Yes, I agree. Now, A/Q, run through again, will you, the general administrative arrangements on the far bank in the early stages.

A/Q

We are sending Div HQ recce parties early in the assault to choose a suitable site for a Div Dump somewhere in the BISLICH area. This will be stocked by DUKWs in the first instance until the Class 40 bridge is open for administrative traffic. High priority is being given to ammunition and three days' estimated expenditure for all weapons likely to be across the river within the first 48 hours will be available in the DUKW Area. Sups; Petrol and Medical Supplies will also be ferried over. Units will draw from the BISLICH dump in First Line tpt.

As soon as Div Second Line can be phased across the Class 40 bridge, it will deliver its load to this dump and return by the FBE to replenish.

Maintenance will then become normal and the dump will be taken over by Corps to form the basis of an FMC.

COMD

What about the build-up of the Engineer Stores Organisation on the far bank ?

COMD AGRE

Initially, bridge equipment and other stores required must be phased over with the Divisional Vehicles as part of the Field Park Company equipment.

As soon as possible after bridges are open an advanced party of Corps Field Park Company and a quota of bridge and engineer stores vehicles must be phased over to dump at the advanced Corps Field Park site from which divisional RE can refill their vehicles.

COMD

Now then G I, let's see your build-up Table.

GSO I

With H hour at 0200 hrs on the 24th we expect to have:—

The Assault Bdes across on a Jeep and Carrier basis by first light, on the 24th.

The Reserve Bde across on a Jeep and Carrier basis by 1200 hrs on the 24th.

A Mobile Striking Force of another regiment of tanks, an SP Field Regt, an SP Anti-Tank Battery, and a battalion in Kangaroos across by 1700 hrs on the 25th.

COMD

That will give us a basis but you must all remember that the capacity of the ferries and bridge is not the only factor which governs the speed of build-up on the far bank. An equally important one is the rate at which the bridgehead there expands. You may find that this, by itself, will limit the amount you can accommodate on the far side of the river.

ACT II

Scene 5

THE FAR BANK

COMD

Now, to turn to the far bank and to knit our organisation there into that on the near bank.

We know something about it already. As on the near bank there will be a company of the Bank Unit running each Assault Brigade Area, the only difference being that their HQ will now be called Dispersal Control instead of Crossing Control. We must also have the CO or his 2nd in Command at Tac Div on the far bank and this we have called Forward Control.

Assault battalions start the transit organisation on the far bank with Unit Landing Officers, Assault Brigades improve on this as soon as they can and then hand over to the Bank Group as soon as they want to be rid of the commitment. Besides dealing with casualties and prisoners their main task would be to collect up vehicles and personnel from the various ferries into a Forward Assembly Area where they would be organised into parties under a commander and then sent forward to a rendezvous notified by forward formations and units. The Bank Group must have an area on the far bank over which they have control. Of course when they take over they will find various bits and pieces of the Assaulting Divisions in that area but they must give them 'squatter's rights' until they can move forward. The area I suggest is inclusive BISLICH, exclusive the road thence—VISSEL—VAH—LOHR.

There is another big problem and that is the command and control of the engineers on both banks. I have been given a CAGRE and initially I see him being my sole RE adviser and commanding all the RE, including my own Divisional Engineers. He will be responsible for all RE work within the Corps boundaries. Now I will leave the CAGRE to explain further details.

COMD AGRE

I suggest that 15 Div RE be allotted to tasks on the far bank in the most intimate co-operation with the formations and units of the Div.

They should have no tasks on this bank or on the water. They are then not committed till they get over the other side and are available to move forward with their Div. I will make arrangements to relieve them from work on the immediate exits from the crossing places and from work within the Bank Group area as soon as possible to enable them to work further forward.

The essential thing is that the Sappers working on the ferries and bridges, including approaches and exits on both banks, should be units which can be left behind by the Div and pass to Corps control together with the CAGRE without dislocation of work.

As 15 Div RE get fwd with their Div we shall have to push up further RE units which have finished their tasks on the near bank or on the river.

There may well be 15 Div Sappers living in the Bank Group area at the time when comd of the Bank Group area passes to Corps; but by then, or very soon afterwards, CRE 15 Div will be moving them further forward.

COMD

That raises the whole question of the passing of command. Initially the whole Bank Group and all the RE and the gunners protecting the bridges and ferries must be under my command. But there will come a time when I want to devote all my attention to operations on the far bank and not have to look back over my shoulder and worry about the transit problem. The actual time will have to be decided by the Corps Comd in consultation with me. This will probably be just before 7 Armd and 53 Divs start crossing. It may be necessary to have our sappers relieved first but I see the command of the whole area passing to Corps more or less at one and the same time. The CAGRE and Comd 100 AA Bde will then revert to Corps as well as the Bank Group.

COMD AGRE

There is one further point, Sir, and this is that the CE would like me to command everything afloat on the river if possible but I realise that it may not be practicable for the LVsT.

COMD (Turning to Brig 79)

Any views on that ?

BRIG 79

I suggest that it would be far better, Sir, to limit us to certain sectors of the river and to allow us to exercise command within these sectors.

COMD

Yes, I agree. We will make it then that the CAGRE will assume overall responsibility for river control, but that he will divide the river up into sectors and will delegate his responsibility to Sector Commanders who may be either Sapper Officers in charge of a bridge or ferry or the LVT Commander running an LVT ferry.

Now, A/Q, what about recovery on the far bank ?

A/Q

First essential is to ensure that Ferry and Bridge exits are not obstructed by broken down vehicles.

I think the first vehicle across on any ferry should be a tracked recovery vehicle (D4 or D8).

Recovery at exits should be controlled by the Bank Group Recovery Section.

As usual, there must be no attempt at backloading until the all clear is given by Corps.

COMD

And last, but by no means least, what about the evacuation of casualties ?

A/Q

Initially we shall have to get them back in LVsT. It is not a comfortable ride, but we have made arrangements so that stretchers can be wedged to prevent them being jolted out.

Arrangements have been made to establish Casualty Evacuation Points near the LVT unloading areas and the stock loading of the assault battalions allows for this.

On the near side there will be Casualty Disembarkation Points in the LVT Collecting Areas.

I hope to get Ambulances up to these Points, but if the going is too bad I have got Jeeps and Weasels laid on.

As soon as the DUKW Ferry gets going we shall evacuate in specially fitted Medical DUKWs that will run right back to a Main Dressing Station.

DIRECTOR

That concludes the play. We have tried to cover every possible point of interest in the time available, and to shew you how 15 (S) Div plan might have been evolved. Obviously there are other ways of tackling the problem, but we have tried to keep as nearly as possible to the plan as actually adopted by 15 (S) Div for the assault over the RHINE which the Division undertook on 24 March 1945

Appendices

APPENDIX "A1"

ORDER OF BATTLE

12 CORPS
(Lieutenant General Sir Neil M. RITCHIE, KBE, CB, DSO, MC)

1 ARMD DIV (Major General L. O. Lyne, CB, DSO)

75 (S) INF DIV (Major General C. M. Barber, CB, DSO)
    44 (L) INF BDE (Brigadier Hon H. C. H. T. Cumming-Bruce, DSO)
        8 RS
        6 RSF
        6 KOSB

    46 (H) INF BDE (Brigadier R. M. Villiers, DSO)
        9 CAMERONIANS
        7 SEAFORTH
        2 GLAS H

    227 (H) INF BDE (Brigadier E. C. Colville, DSO)
        10 HLI
        2 GORDONS
        2 A & SH

    15 (S) RECCE REGT

    RA (CRA Brigadier L. Bolton, DSO)
        131 Fd Regt
        181 Fd Regt
        190 Fd Reg
        102 (NH) A Tk Regt
        119 LAA Regt

    RE
        20 Fd Coy
        278 Fd Coy
        279 Fd Coy
        629 Fd Pk Coy

    1 MX (MG)

52 (L) INF DIV (Major General E. Hakewill-Smith, CB, CBE, MC)

53 (W) INF DIV (Major General R. K. Ross, CB, DSO, MC)

4 ARMD BDE (Type A) (Brigadier R. M. P. Carver, CBE, DSO, MC)
    4 RHA (SP 25 pr)
    GREYS (Sherman 75 mm and 17 pr)
    3/4 CLY (Sherman 75 mm and 17 pr)
    44 R Tks (DD) (Sherman 75 mm amphibious)
    2 KRRC (motor battalion)

34 ARMD BDE (Type B) (Brigadier W. S. Clarke, CBE, DSO)
    9 R Tks   (Churchills)
    107 RAC   (Churchills)
    147 RAC   (Churchills)

1 CDO BDE (Brigadier D. Mills-Roberts, DSO, MC)
    3 Cdo
    6 Cdo
    45 (RM) Cdo
    46 (RM) Cdo

115 INF BDE (Brigadier E. L. Luce, DSO, TD)
    1 CHESHIRE
    4 NORTHAMPTONS
    5 R BERKS

3 AGRA ⎫ for details of RA units ⎧ (Brigadier F. L. F. Cleeve, CBE, DSO, MC)
8 AGRA ⎬ see ⎨ (Brigadier A. P. Campbell, DSO, OBE)
9 AGRA ⎭ APPENDIX "A2" ⎩ (Brigadier C. H. M. Brunker, DSO)

11 AGRE for details of RE units see APPENDIX "A3"

85 Cdn Br Coy, RCASC

In support of 12 Corps

31 ARMD BDE (79 Armd Div)   (Brigadier G. S. Knight, DSO)

with under command
W DGNS (30 Armd Bde) (Flails)
7 R Tks (Crocodiles)
49 APC Regt (RHQ and two sqns only) (Kangaroos)
1 Indep Tk Sqn RAC (CDL Tks)
RHQ 42 Aslt Regt, RE ⎫
16 Aslt Sqn, RE ⎪
222 Aslt Sqn, RE ⎬ (1 Aslt Bde, RE)
77 Aslt Sqn, RE (5 Aslt Regt, RE) ⎪
81 Aslt Sqn, RE (6 Aslt Regt, RE) ⎪
82 Aslt Sqn, RE (6 Aslt Regt, RE) ⎭

Note.   31 Armd Bde was also in support of Ninth US Army.
Only units allotted in support of 12 Corps are shown.

100 AA BDE (for details see APPENDIX "A2")   (Brigadier M. B. Turner, DSO)

E RIDING YEO (LVsT) (33 Armd Bde)

11 R Tks (LVsT) (33 Armd Bde)

APPENDIX "A2"

RA ORDER OF BATTLE AND GROUPING

(CCRA—Brigadier G. W. E. HEATH, CBE, DSO, MC)

Note. Grouping is given as at H hour. For subsequent developments see text, Part I, Section VII).

(All Groups under operational command CCRA)

1. **Grouped under CsRA and CsAGRA :**

    (a) *RA 7 Armd Div Group*
    3 RHA
    5 RHA
    65 (NY) A Tk Regt
    One Bty 15 (IOM) LAA Regt
    1 Mtn Regt (52 (L) Div)
    B Flt 653 Air OP Sqn

    (b) *RA 15 (S) Div Group*
    131 Fd Regt
    181 Fd Regt
    190 Fd Regt
    102 (NH) A Tk Regt
    119 LAA Regt
    4 RHA (4 Armd Bde)
    6 Fd Regt (3 AGRA)
    129 SP Bty 86 A Tk Regt
    364/112 LAA Bty (RP)
    C Flt 653 Air OP Sqn

    (c) *RA 52 (L) Div Group*
    79 Fd Regt
    80 Fd Regt
    186 Fd Regt
    54 A Tk Regt
    108 LAA Regt
    63 Med Regt (8 AGRA)
    146 Med Regt (8 AGRA)
    (with under op comd one bty
     108 HAA Regt)

    (d) *RA 53 (W) Div Group*
    81 Fd Regt
    83 Fd Regt
    133 Fd Regt
    71 A Tk Regt
    25 LAA Regt
    77 Med Regt (8 AGRA)
    (with under op comd one bty
     108 HAA Regt)
    A Flt 653 Air OP Sqn

    (e) *3 AGRA Group*
    13 Med Regt
    59 Med Regt (with under op comd
     one bty 108 HAA Regt)
    67 Med Regt
    72 Med Regt
    59 Hy Regt
    A Flt 658 Air OP Sqn

    (f) *8 AGRA Group*
    25 Fd Regt (with under op comd
     one sec C Flt 658 Air OP Sqn)
    61 Med Regt
    53 Hy Regt
    40 US FA Gp (Three bns 155 mm)
    C Flt 658 Air OP Sqn
     (less one sec)

    (g) *9 AGRA Group*
    9 Med Regt
    11 Med Regt
    107 Med Regt
    3 Super Hy Regt
    90 HAA Regt
     (under op comd for ground role)
    C Flt 659 Air OP Sqn

    (h) *100 AA Bde Group*
    86 A Tk Regt (less one SP Bty)
     (reverts to Corps Control on D+2)
    113 LAA Regt
    123 LAA Regt
    90 HAA Regt ⎫ under comd groups shown
    108 HAA Regt ⎭ while in ground role
    151 AAOR
    2 (Indep) LAA/SL Bty
    One Bty 93 LAA Regt (20 mm SP)
    One tp 474 SL Bty
    806 Pnr Smoke Coy R Pnr Corps
    112 LAA Regt (less one bty)
     (with under comd one SP tp 15 IOM
      LAA Regt)
    399/121 LAA Bty

2. **Under direct comd CCRA for all purposes :**

    7 Svy Regt (with under comd B Obs Bty, 10 Svy Regt and two 4 pen dets)
    CBO 12 Corps
    344 (Indep) ML Bty (with under comd 581 (Indep) ML Bty), in sp 15 (S) Div for assault
    653 Air OP Sqn less three flts
    A Tp 100 Radar Bty (one det in sp RA 7 Armd Div and two dets in sp RA 15 (S) Div).

APPENDIX "A3"

RE ORDER OF BATTLE AND GROUPING

(CE—Brigadier F. W. L. McC. PARKER, CBE)

(Note. Grouping is given as at H hour)

Assaulting Formations

15 (S) DIV

under command
11 AGRE

with under command
15 (S) Div RE
52 (L) Div RE (Note 1)
4 & 621 Fd Sqns
   (7 Armd Div RE) (Note 1)
8 Corps Tps RE
   (less Fd Pk Coy) (Note 2)
12 Corps Tps RE (less Fd Pk Coy)
7 Army Tps RE
4 GHQ Tps RE
Two Fd Coys, 7 GHQ Tps RE

15 (K) GHQ Tps RE

C Pl 117 Coy RASC (tippers)
A Pl 486 Coy RASC

53 Coy R Pnr Corps

3 Dog Pl

with in support
RHQ 42 Aslt Regt RE
   16 Aslt Sqn RE
   81 Aslt Sqn RE
   222 Aslt Sqn RE
One fd coy 53 (W) Div RE (Note 1)
6 Mech Eqpt Pl RE
24 Mech Eqpt Pl RE

85 Br Coy RCASC

RN Boom Det
K Sqn Naval Force 'U' RN

4 ARMD BDE

in support
82 Aslt Sqn RE

1 CDO BDE

under command
84 Fd Coy RE (7 GHQ Tps RE)

in support
77 Aslt Sqn RE (LVsT)

Corps Troops

CE 12 CORPS

under command
53 (W) Div RE (less one fd coy) (Note 1)
13 GHQ Tps RE (less one fd coy)
265 Fd Pk Coy RE (12 Corps Tps RE)
129 Forestry Coy RE
16 BD Pl RE
48 BD Pl RE
53 BD Pl RE
58 BD Pl RE

B Pl 486 Coy RASC

73 Coy R Pnr Corps
84 Coy R Pnr Corps
119 Coy R Pnr Corps
191 Coy R Pnr Corps

in support
619 Fd Pk Coy RE (7 GHQ Tps RE)

Notes:—

(1) 52 (L) and 53 (W) Divs RE, 4 and 621 Fd Sqns revert to comd parent fmns, as latter pass over RHINE.

(2) 8 Corps Tps RE pass to under command XVIII US Corps (Airborne) on completion of task (FBE bridge). Fd Pk Coy under command XVIII US Corps (Airborne) from start of operation.

APPENDIX "A4"

ALLIED AIR FORCES

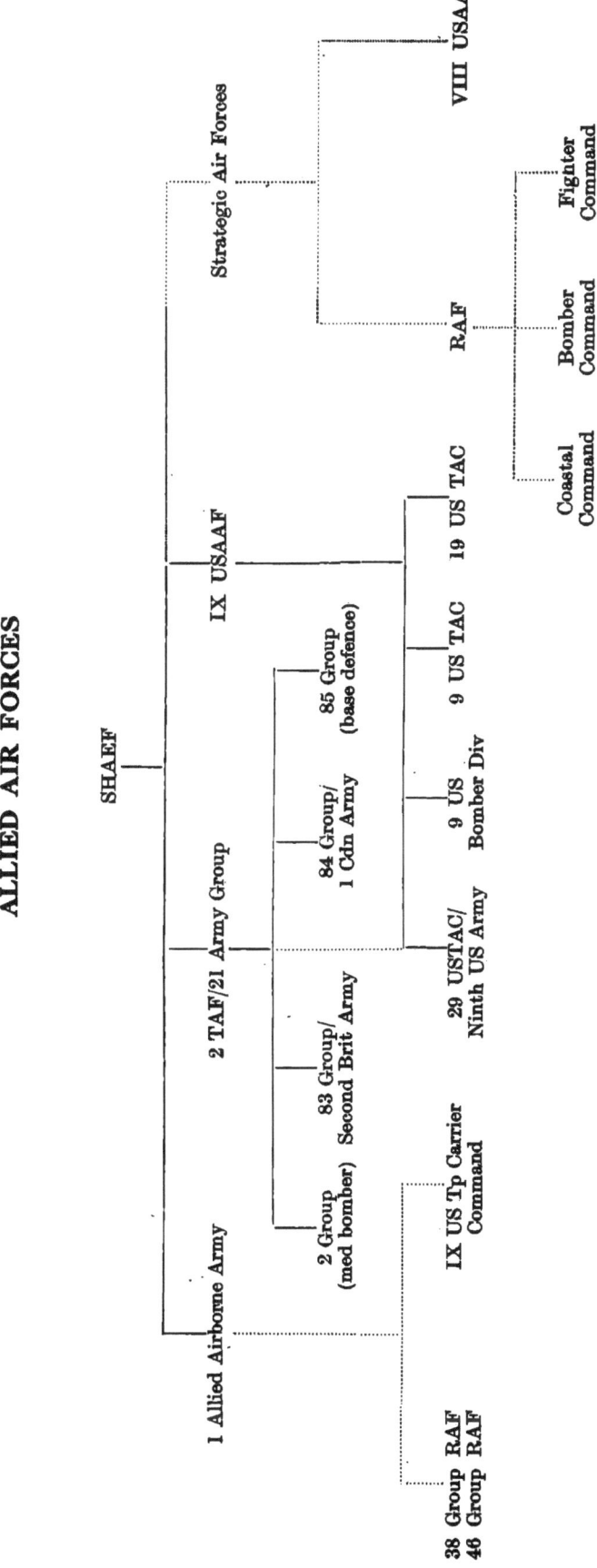

APPENDIX "B"

EQUIPMENT AND ORGANISATION OF FORCES ENGAGED IN OPERATION PLUNDER

PART I—EQUIPMENT WITH BRITISH FORMATIONS

Table 1—Gun Tanks

Country of Origin	Type	Crew	Weight (tons)	Armament	Amn Carried (rds)	Max Speed (mph)	Radius of Action (miles)
USA	Sherman V (75 mm)	5	31.75	1×75 mm 2×.300 Browning MGs	99 6,750	22	125
USA	Sherman Vc (17 pr)	4	34	1×17 pr 1×.300 Browning MG	78 5,000	22	125
GB	Churchill IV	5	38.5	1×6 pr 2×7.92 mm Besa MGs	84 6,975	16.9	123
GB	Churchill V	5	38.5	1×95 mm 2×7.92 mm Besa MGs	47 6,525	16.4	123
GB	Churchill VII	5	39.5	1×75 mm 2×7.92 mm Besa MGs	83 6,525	13.5	142
GB GB	Cromwell IV Cromwell V	5	27.5	1×75 mm 2×7.92 mm Besa MGs	64 4,950	38	165
GB	Cromwell VI	5	27.5	1×95 mm 2×7.92 mm Besa MGs	51 4,950	38	165

Table 2—Special Tanks

AVRE (Assault Vehicle Royal Engineers) (see Plate No. 2 following page 142).

Equipment of Assault Squadrons, R.E. It consisted of a Churchill Tank, with or without a turret. Without turret it was used for carrying equipment such as trackway bridge; with turret, the normal gun was replaced by a "petard" which fired a large explosive charge a short distance for the purpose of demolishing concrete defences etc.

An Assault Squadron RE also had a proportion of Tankdozers (bulldozer blade fitted to a tank), and armoured bridge layers.

CDL Tank

This was a Grant Tank from which the turret armament (37 mm) had been removed and a CDL searchlight substituted. This searchlight was invulnerable to small arms and MG fire and could be switched on and off, or made to flicker, at will.

The tank could use its 75 mm gun in the right hand sponson on targets illuminated by the searchlight.

Length 19 ft. Height 10 ft 10 ins. Width 8 ft 7 ins.

CROCODILES

A Churchill VII Tank, with flame thrower installed in place of the hull MG. It towed a trailer containing 400 gallons of special fuel. Overall length of the tank and trailer was 40 ft 6 ins and weight 47.2 tons. The flame thrower had a maximum range of 110 yards. In other repects the machine had the same performance as a normal Churchill VII and carried 83 rounds 75 mm and 3,600 rounds 7.92 ammunition.

DD Tanks (see Plate No. 1 following page 142)

The Sherman DD Tank was a Sherman V or Sherman III waterproofed and fitted with a canvas screen which increased the height to 13 feet when erected. This canvas screen was held in place by rubber air columns and steel struts. The tank was completely amphibious when the canvas screens were raised and was then propelled by two propellors driven from the main engine. Its speed in the water was 4½ knots and a depth of nine feet was required for flotation. Its performance on land was that of a normal Sherman tank.

Once inflated the canvas was very liable to damage from trees, bushes and shrubs. An Inflation Area, from which a clear run over open country to the river was available, was essential.

FLAILS

A mine clearing device fitted to a normal Sherman V tank. It carried a rotating drum mounted on the front, and fitted with 43 heavy chains. The drum rotated at 180 rpm, the chains beating the ground in front of the tank and so exploding mines. Speed while flailing was reduced to 3 mph.

Dimensions of this tank were:— Length 27 ft 5½ ins. Width 11 ft 6 ins, weight 34 tons. The crew was five and radius of action 120 miles.

Armament was as for a normal Sherman V, but ammunition was reduced to 73 rounds of 75 mm and 4,250 of .300 for the Browning MGs.

Artillery of British Formations

Table 3A—Towed Artillery

Country of Origin	Equipment	Weight of projectile (lbs)	Max range (yards)	Remarks
GB	3.7 in mountain	20	6,924	
GB	25 pr field (towed)	25	13,400	
GB	4.5 in. medium	55	20,500	gun obsolescent
GB	5.5 in. medium	80 / 100	18,100 / 16,200	100 lb shell obsolescent
USA	155 mm heavy	95	25,500	
GB/USA	7.2 in. heavy (How)	200	19,600	on USA carriage
USA	8" super heavy (How)	200	18,500	
GB	240 mm super heavy	360	25,250	
GB	3.7 in. HAA (ground role)	27¾	18,600	
GB	Rocket Projector (land mattress)	29	7,880	See Table 4 & Plate 4

Table 3B—SP Artillery

Country of Origin	Equipment	Projectile (lbs)	Max range (yards)	Crew	Weight (tons)	Max speed (mph)	Radius of action (miles)	Remarks
GB/CANADA	25 pr field (RAM)	25	13,300	6	24	25	125	British piece in RAM (Canadian Sherman) chassis (see Plate 5)
GB	17 pr A Tk (VALENTINE)	17	1,200 (shot) 6,500 (HE)	4	16	20	140	
USA	17 pr A Tk (M10)	17	1,200 (shot) 7,700 (HE)	5	28	30	75	Some M10s were fitted with US 3" guns

Table 4—Special Equipment

APC (Armoured Personnel Carrier)

The "Kangaroo" APC was a normal Sherman Tank (or Canadian RAM) without the turret, and could carry one section of infantry.

BUFFALO See under "LVT."

DUKW

A six-wheeled (6 × 6) amphibious 3 ton lorry of USA origin. In appearance it resembled a pontoon with wheels.

Those available were all very old and weak mechanically, and were therefore reserved for a Q lift.

They needed a good hard on both banks to enable them to get out of the water. Such hards required to be 50 to 60 feet wide reaching down into the water until the latter was about 2 ft 6 ins deep. The width was necessary because of the current, while the extension into the water allowed the front wheels to grip firmly as soon as they grounded.

Very good for evacuating casualties as they gave a much smoother ride than LVsT.

KANGAROO See under "APC".

LVT (Landing vehicle, Tracked) (Plate No. 3)

    (i) *The vehicle*

The "Buffalo" LVT existed in two forms, Mark II and IV.

The LVT II had no door and so could only normally carry personnel. Any stores carried had to be loaded into and unloaded from a deep well. It could, however, carry a 17 pounder on top and some personnel in the well by a modification which could be put in or removed within half an hour in the LVT Collecting Area.

The LVT IV had a door which could be lowered, and could take the following vehicles only:—

    Jeep   Weasel
    Scout Car (Dingo)   Airborne Bulldozer
    Carrier   6 pr A Tk gun

It could not take a Windsor anti tank gun tower.

Both types carried light armour in front only.

They had a very low silhouette in the water but were badly silhouetted on top of the river banks.

About a third of the total number of Buffaloes carried 20 mm Polsten guns. Performance figures were as under:—

    Loading capacity   — 4 tons
    Maximum speed, land — 30 mph
    Maximum speed, water — 5.9 mph
    Maximum gradient   — 29 degrees.

They had a wonderful performance except in deep mud when they stuck owing to the fact that they had only two feet belly clearance. They were devils for picking up wire which wrecks their steering. This needed watching both on their approach track and in the river. Any sort of wire—telephone cable or fence wire—had to be avoided like the plague.

They were very noisy and could only go very short distances indeed on a road or any hard surface owing to their cup shaped tracks which gave them their high performance in water. They cut any road to ribbons and completely wreck the shoulders of narrow roads. Prior to PLUNDER it was estimated that only one in three would be kept running continuously over long periods—that is 90 LVsT were necessary to provide a continuous service by 30 LVsT.

    (ii) *Regimental Organisation*

The LVT Regt was organised into two squadrons each of which lifted an assault battalion.

Two LVsT on Sqn HQ were NOT available for loading, and the remaining thirty-six were in six troops of six. Four troops were all LVsT IV and two troops each consisted of three LVsT II and three LVsT IV. A reserve of 10% "Left out of Battle" had to be withheld but this was done on a regimental basis and did not affect the 36 available for a battalion.

ROCKET PROJECTOR (Land Mattress) (Plate No. 4)

At a range of 7,600 yards it was possible for 12 projectors to neutralise an are aof approximately 68,600 square yards, in about 4 seconds. This required 68 men for projector crews and total weight of projectors and ammunition of 15¼ tons. To obtain the same effect with medium artillery assuming 2 rounds of rapid gun fire could be fired in the same time, would require 4½ medium regiments ; i.e. 612 men in gun crews and a total weight of guns and ammunition of 400 tons.

It fired a 5" projectile of weight 29 pounds or 34.25 pounds, the latter being obsolescent.

WEASEL (M 29 c)

A light amphibious tracked vehicle of USA origin, resembling the British carrier, but lighter. It possessed an excellent cross-country performance in waterlogged ground, but was mechanically delicate ; it could not be relied upon to cross the RHINE under its own power.

Table 5—RE Ferry and Bridge Equipment

Stormboat (Plate No. 6)

A light boat of plywood construction with 22 horsepower outboard motor engine and capable of carrying one section of infantry. The outboard engines were very temperamental and each one had its own individual characteristics. It was essential therefore that the man who was going to work one on D Day had practised on that engine for a week beforehand.

The engine ran on a mixture of petrol and oil, and it was vital to get this mixture right.

The engine alone needed three men to carry it, and the boat fourteen.

Boats needed three feet of water before starting the engine. A common habit was to start them too near the bank so as to be sure that the engines were running before the boat got into the current. The result was a weakened shearpin which broke half way across. It was therefore most desirable to find a lagoon or bit of sheltered water where they could be started without damage.

Class 9 Raft (Plate No. 7)

Class 9 (close support) rafts were constructed of light pontoons and a trackway superstructure, and driven by motor propulsion units.

RE personnel needed considerable training in watermanship in order to obviate the necessity for a hawser across the river on which to run the raft. The rafts would carry up to a D 4 tractor or a 15-cwt armoured personnel carrier or half-track, but were to be used principally for 3-ton or 15-cwt load-carriers.

They had a very slow turn round (about 12 vehicles per hour per rafting site of four rafts in daylight and nine by night), and required about four hours to construct after arrival on site. The equipment could be towed to site on a sledge by a half-track.

Class 50/60 Raft (Plate No. 8)

A heavy raft constructed of special metal pontoons and girder superstructure carrying a trackway. The raft ran on cables stretched across the river and was hauled by balloon winches on the banks. The equipment was carried on special trailers towed behind MATADOR wheeled tractors or on sledges which could be hauled across country by AVsRE. The great size of the pontoon made their movement both on road and across country something of a problem and concealment was practically impossible.

The Aslt Sqns RE employed in PLUNDER specialised in this equipment.

The raft carried one tank or M10 SP A Tk gun at a time or two Kangaroos or 15-cwt armoured half-tracks; smaller vehicles, such as a scout car, could be carried at the same time on the pontoons

The turn round was slow—about nine major vehicles per hour and seven by night per rafting site.

Rafts required about four hours to construct after arrival on site.

Class 9 FBE (folding boat equipment) **Bridge** (see Plate No. 9)

A light bridge composed of canvas and wood folding boats (capable of folding flat for transport purposes) and a trackway superstructure. The equipment was rather delicate and across a river of the size of the RHINE required a lot of nursing; it was expected to be out of action for maintenance for eight hours out of every twenty-four.

Special police or officers were appointed in Vehicle Waiting areas to see that no vehicle got through on to the FBE bridge which was not well within Class 9.

Bailey Pontoon Equipment (Plates Nos 10 and 11)

Consisted of standard Bailey equipment, carried on pontoons, with special landing bay arrangements to carry the bridge from dry land to the floating bays.

It could be constructed in various forms by varying the number of pontoons and the arrangement of Bailey girders, giving a fully decked bridge of any classification from Class 9 to 70 as required.

It could also be adapted to give a high level approach in order to cope with rises of level of the river.

Table 6A

Main Armament of standard British Formations under 12 Corps for Operation PLUNDER

Formation	Unit	Armament	Remarks
7 Armd Div	Armd Regts	Cromwell IV or V Sherman Vc	Three regts (each 61 tanks) (Each tp comprised three Cromwells and one Sherman)
	Armd Recce Regt	Cromwell V and VI	One regt (76 tanks) (Cromwell VI employed as close support tank)
	Field Artillery	24 × 25 pr (SP) 24 × 25 pr (towed)	One RHA regt } (total 48 guns) One RHA regt
	A Tk Artillery	24 × M10's (3" gun SP) 24 × 17 pr (towed)	One A Tk regt (48 guns)
	LAA Artillery	40 mm Bofors (SP)	One LAA regt (54 guns)
4 Armd Bde	Armd regts	Sherman V and Vc	Three regts (44 R Tks equipped with amphibious Sherman Vs (DD)) (each 61 tanks)
	Field Artillery	25 pr (SP)	One RHA regt (24 guns)
34 Armd Bde	Armd regts	Churchill IV and V	Three regts (each 61 tanks)
15 (S) Div	Field Artillery	25 pr (towed)	Three field regiments (each 24 guns)
	A Tk Artillery	24 × 17 pr (towed) 24 × 17 pr Valentine (SP)	One A Tk regiment (48 guns)
	LAA Artillery	40 mm Bofors (towed)	One LAA regiment (54 guns)
	Mortars and MMGs	12 × 4.2" heavy mortars 36 × .303 MMGs (Vickers)	One MG battalion

Note.—52 (L) and 53 (W) Divs were similar to 15 (S) Div, except that 52 (L) Div had also one Mountain Regiment of 24 × 3.7" hows.

Table 6B

Armament of Corps and Army Artillery with 12 Corps for Operation PLUNDER

Type of Unit	Armament	Remarks
Medium Regt	16 × 5.5" guns	One regt had 16 × 4.5"
Heavy Regt	8 × 155 mm guns 8 × 7.2" hows	
Super-heavy Regt	2 × 8" hows 4 × 240 mm guns	
Corps A Tk Regt	24 × M10 (SP) 24 × 17 pr (towed)	One regt per Corps
US Fd Arty Bn	12 × 155 mm guns	Three bns in a Group

PART II

Table 7—German Equipment

Very little German armour was engaged against 12 Corps during the stages of the battle studied. The following table gives details of the two most formidable German tanks.

Type	Crew	Weight (tons)	Armament	Amn carried (rds)	Max Speed (mph)	Radius of action (miles)
PzKw V "PANTHER"	5	45	1×75 mm 2×7.92 mm MGs	79 4500	34	125
PzKw VI "TIGER"	5	56	1×88 mm 2×7.92 mm MGs	87 5700	23	73

PART III—ORGANISATION

A. BRITISH FORCES

Standard organisations of British formations taking part in Operation PLUNDER are shewn in Tables 8 and 9 below.

B. GERMAN FORCES

Standard organisation of the German Infantry Division is shewn at Table 10, and German Parachute Division at Table 11.

TABLE 8 — OUTLINE ORGANISATION OF A

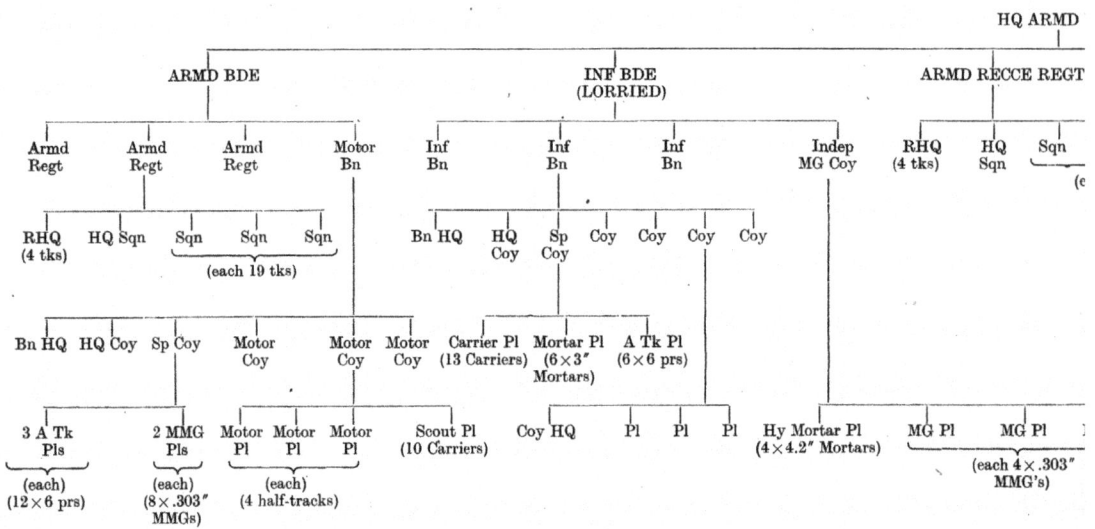

NOTES

1. Approx total strength (WE) of the A
2. Strength of fighting tanks in the Arm
3. 20 TCVs were allotted to each Lorrie

TABLE 9 — OUTLINE ORGANISATION OF A

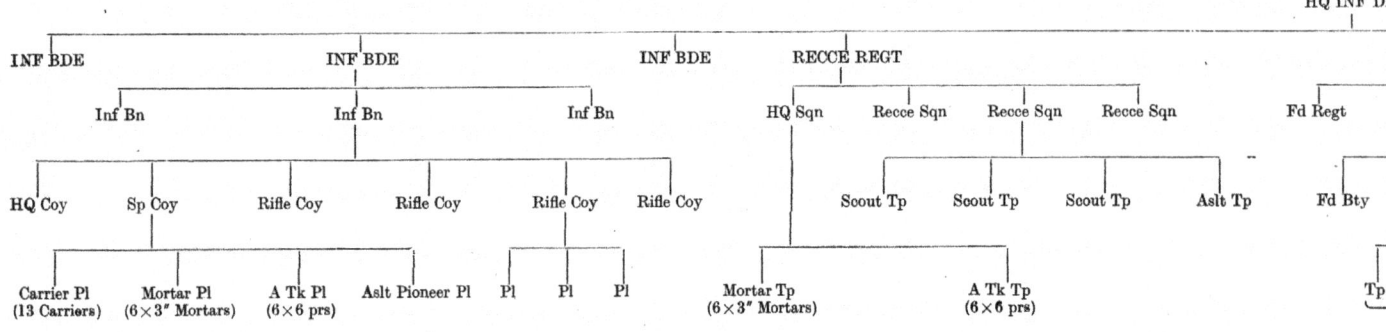

NOTES

1. Total strength of part of Inf Div show
   (i.e. Div less Sigs and Services)
2. No weapon smaller than a MMG is sho

A BRITISH ARMOURED DIVISION (1945)

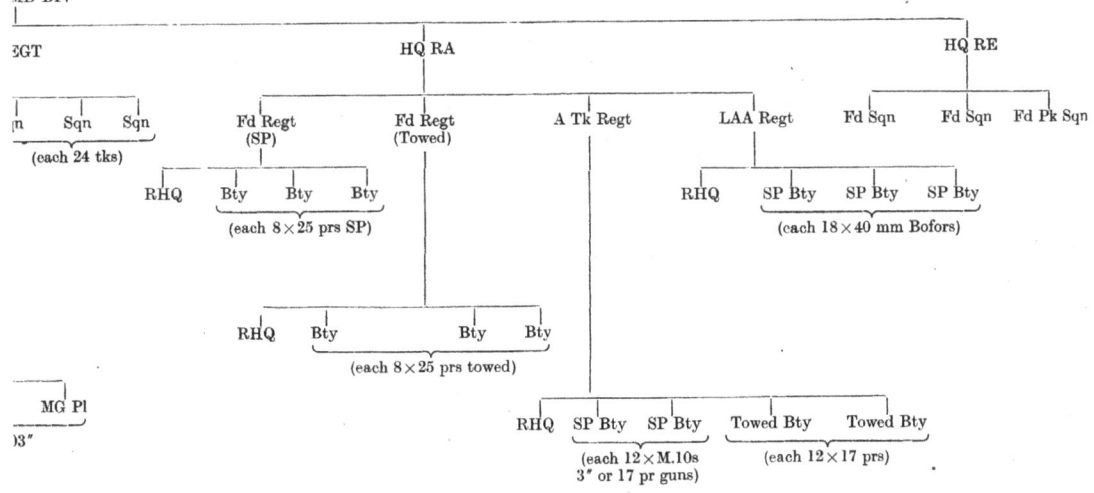

he Armd Div = 13,500 (incl Services)
Armd Div = 259
orried Inf Bn from Div RASC.

OF A BRITISH INFANTRY DIVISION (1945)

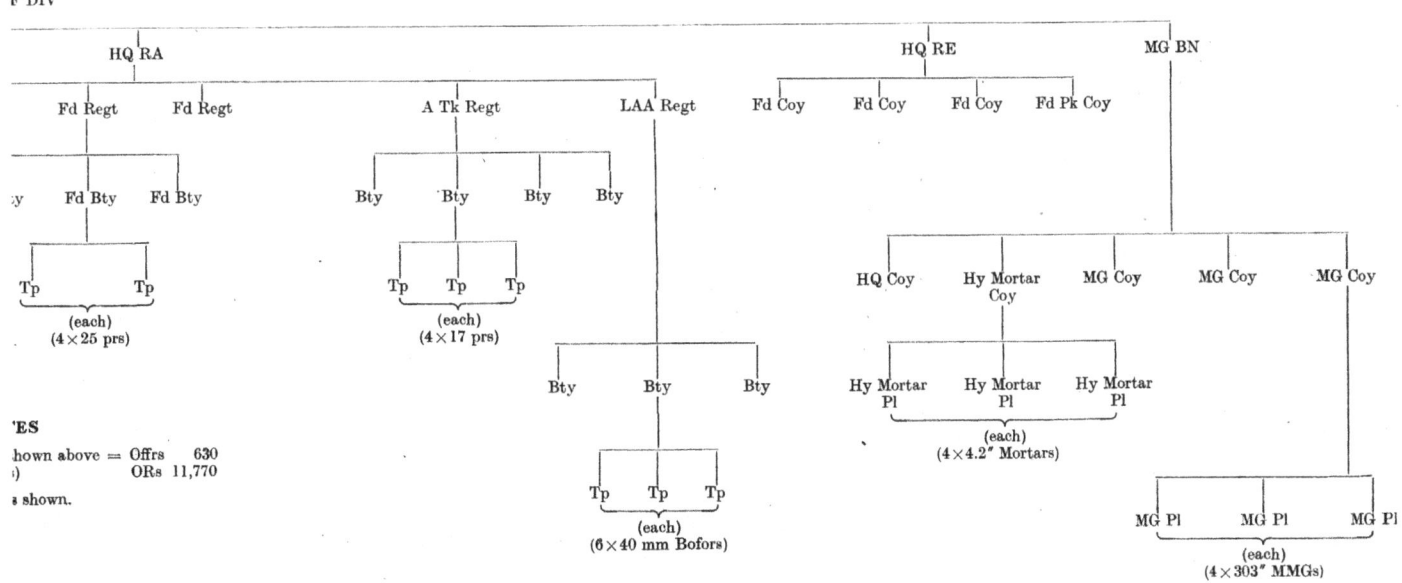

hown above = Offrs 630
                ORs 11,770

s shown.

Table 10 — OUTLINE ORGANISATION OF A GERMAN

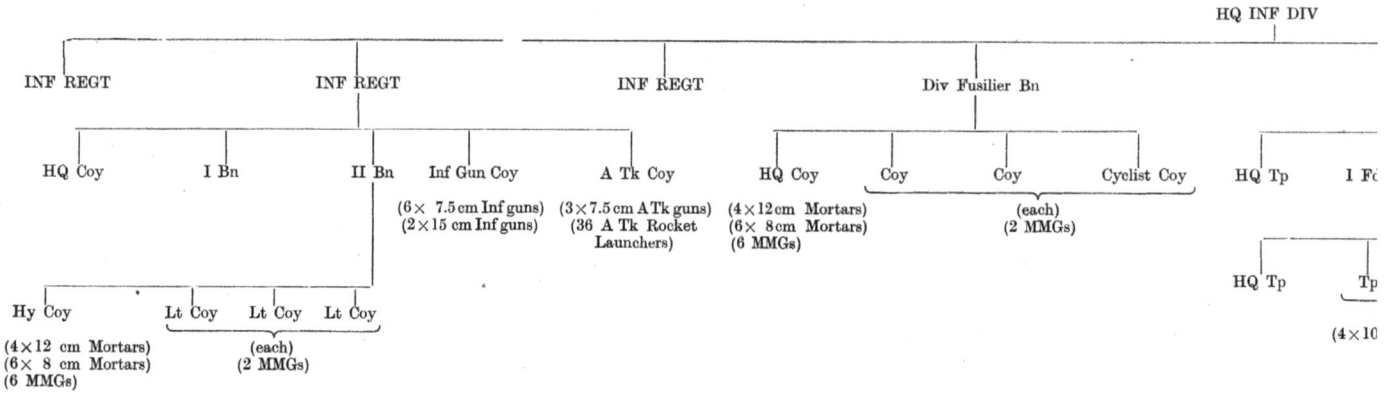

NOT

1. Total strength of part of German Inf I
   (i.e. Div less Sigs and
2. No weapon smaller than a MMG is sho

Table 11 — OUTLINE ORGANISATION

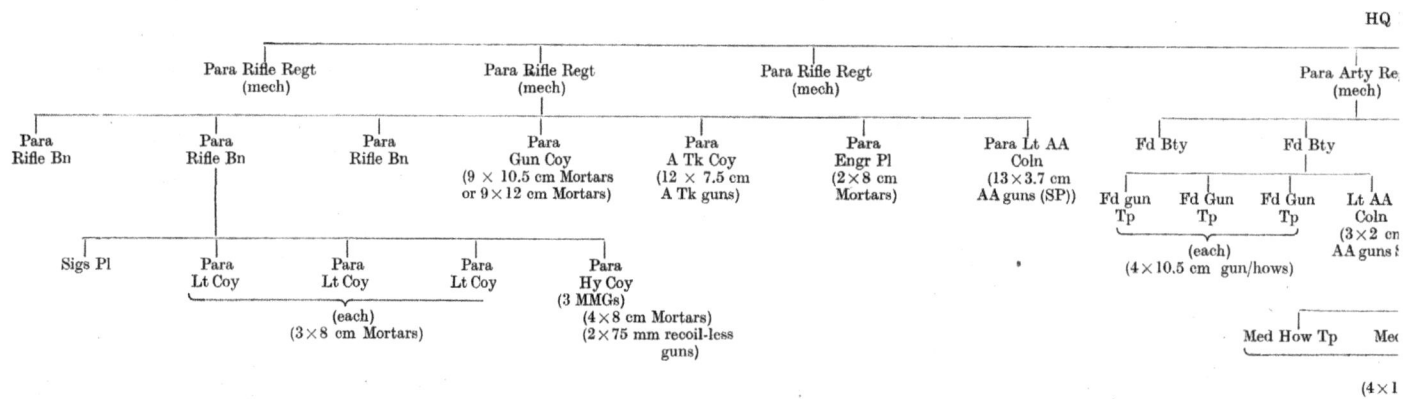

N

1. The German Parachute Division was designed for employment in an airborne role.
2. The division was fully mechanised.
3. It is almost certain that no parachute divisio table, owing to shortage of equipment.
4. The total strength of the parachute division is

INFANTRY DIVISION (1945)

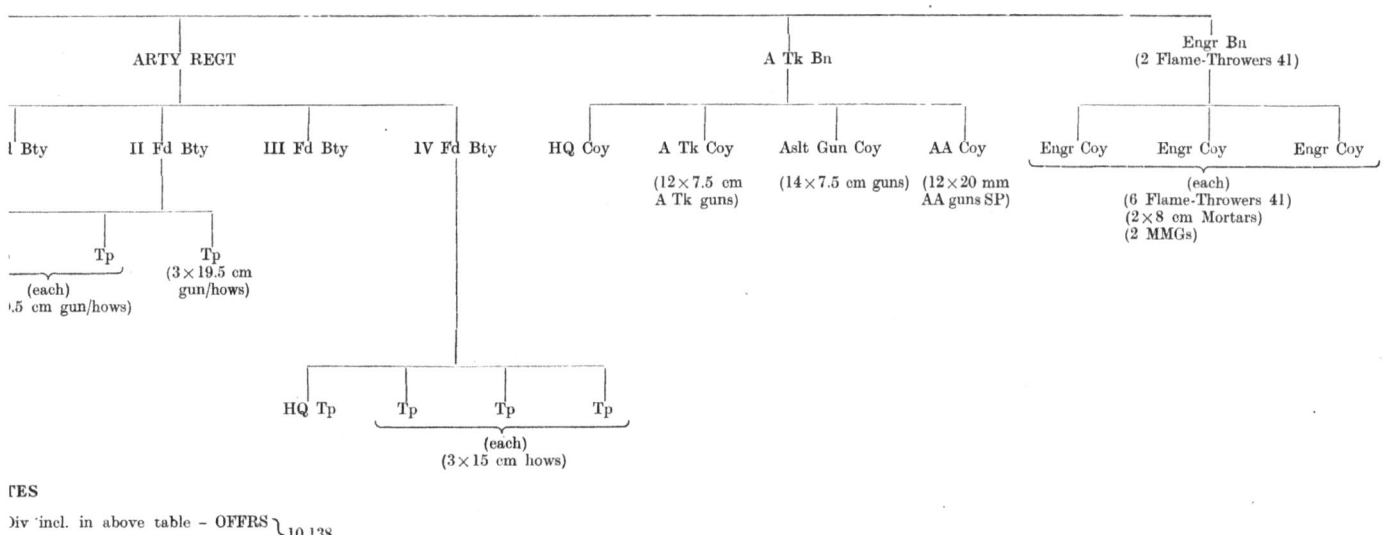

TES

Div incl. in above table – OFFRS
Services)   ORs } 10,138

wn.

OF A GERMAN PARACHUTE DIVISION (1945)

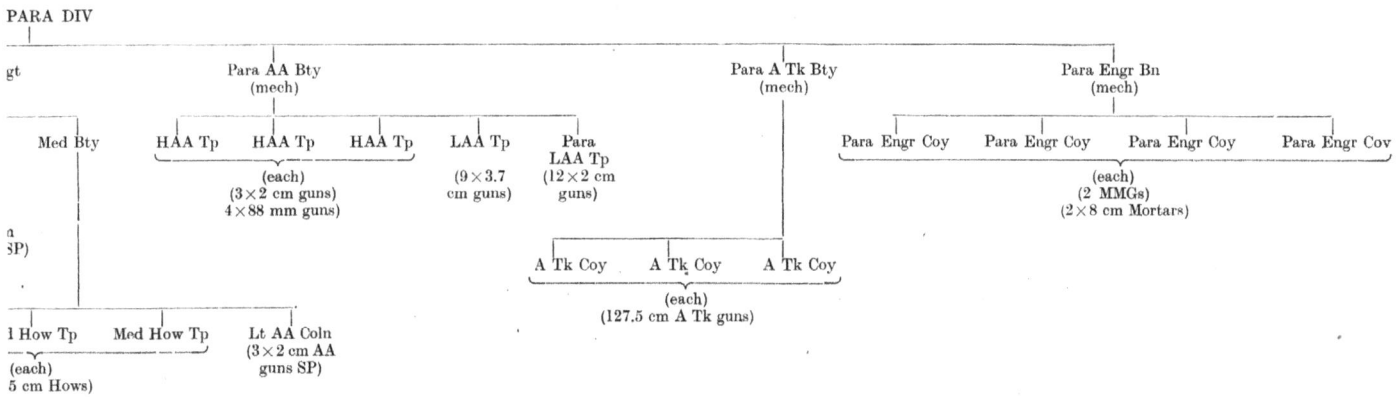

OTES

to fight in an ordinary ground role, and to be readily available

n was ever equipped up to the scale of AA guns shown in this

not known.

APPENDIX "C"

LIST OF REFERENCE MAPS

1 : 250,000   NORTH WEST EUROPE (series GSGS 4042)
                    Sheets 2A/3A, 3

                  GERMANY (series GSGS 4346)
                    Sheets K52, K53

1 : 100,000   CENTRAL EUROPE (series GSGS 4416)
                    Sheets P1, Q1

1 : 50,000   GERMANY (series GSGS 4507)
                    Sheets 6, 7, 16, 17, 36, 37

1 : 25,000   GERMANY (series GSGS 4414)
                  Sheets 4204, 4205, 4206, 4304, 4305, 4306

APPENDIX "D"

12 CORPS PLANNING INSTRUCTION NO. 1

Ref Maps: 1 : 100,000 Sheets P1, Q1

TOP SECRET
5 Feb 45
Copy No.

1. **BACKGROUND**

   (a) Ops are about to start, designed to close up to the R RHINE. 12 Corps has no part in these.

   (b) 21 A Gp's task is to reach the RHINE from incl RHEINBURG 2128 Northward with RIGHT Ninth US Army, LEFT First Cdn Army.

   (c) Generally, First Cdn Army operates on axis NIJMEGEN–CLEVE 8955–XANTEN 1141, while Ninth US Army operates NE from area AACHEN–ROERMOND towards WESEL 2240.

   (d) In conjunction with this, Second Army (8 Corps) is to be prepared to seize the VENLO rd centre and clear the triangular area to the RHINE between the thrusts of the other armies.

   (e) HQ 12 Corps in res for planning Op 'PLUNDER', which is the actual aslt crossing of R RHINE. Until later HQ 12 Corps will not have any specific fmns allotted for the op.

   (f) Should the op develop fast and favourably, then it is possible that the WESEL brs may be seized intact. In this case a modified 'PLUNDER PLAN' will no doubt be adopted, but the instrs that follow do NOT envisage this.

2. **TASKS OF 12 CORPS**

   (a) In conjunction with 79 Armd Div, to evolve a technique suitable for the crossing of a wide river, such as the RHINE, and to carry out practical trg to test this technique.

   (b) To produce a specific plan (PLUNDER) for the aslt crossing of the RHINE within the limitations set out below.

   (c) To be prepared to take over certain fmns, to be detailed later, and to prepare them, *in the shortest possible time*, to carry out 'PLUNDER'.

3. **POLICY**

   (a) All action will be co-ordinated towards achieving the following aims :—

   "The enemy must NOT be allowed to seal off the bridgehead, and it is essential that ops on the far bank should NOT congeal. Speed is therefore of the highest importance."

   (b) This postulates the need :—

   (i) to est first a firm base in the form of a series of shallow brheads, with light recce ahead. These must be joined up to fan out laterally ;

   (ii) next to est as large a balanced force as possible on the far bank, so that strong thrust, with armour, in sp, can be made at the earliest time to seize centres of comns and dominating ground on the enemy side of the obstacle ;

   (iii) the seizing of centres of comns (usually towns on the enemy bank) from the rear.

   (c) Delay to construct rds cannot be accepted, nor can ops be retarded to await constr of brs. Therefore :—

   (i) A high proportion of tracked vehs will be used in order to be independent of rds in the early stages.

   (ii) All resources for ferrying are to be developed to the utmost.

   (d) This op is in many ways akin to an aslt landing on an open beach, and the problem will be tackled from this angle. The proved technique for an opposed landing will, therefore, be modified to suit this wide river problem, and so far as possible the already est and understood nomenclature employed for beach landings will be adopted.

4. **THE TECHNIQUE**

   As little time is likely to be available for the preparation of fmns to undertake this op, the technique evolved must be relatively rigid.

   The following principles will be observed :—

   (a) **The Assault**

   (i) On as broad a front as possible.

   (ii) In certain very favourable conditions of weather and banks, DD tks may lead. But planning will be carried out envisaging inf in LVsT forming the leading waves with DDs, in separate waves, to follow as soon as recce has est, and marked, the most suitable exits for them on the far bank.

(iii) In principle assaulting waves will be organised in coy gps; one tp LVsT to each coy gp.

(iv) Leading waves of inf will proceed *in their LVsT* direct to their pre-determined objectives on the far bank. LVsT will then be returned.

(v) These objectives must inevitably depend on the ground, but their purpose is to prevent the enemy bringing observed small arms fire on to the crossing places. For planning purposes this may be assumed to be some 2,000 yards beyond the far bank.

(vi) Subsequent waves, whether proceeding in LVsT, DUKWs or TERRAPINS will "debus" dryshod on the far bank itself.

(vii) LVsT, etc. will then be returned as early as possible to the LVT, etc. parks and will NOT be retained by units.

(viii) To avoid cluttering up the banks, special arrangements must be made for calling fwd reinforcing gps only as needed.

(b) **"Bank Control"**

(i) Special organisations, comparable to the 'BEACH GPS', will be provided at a scale of one per assaulting div.

(ii) During the aslt phase they will operate under comd of divs, subsequently reverting to Corps control.

(iii) Special 'BANK GP' areas will be laid down by divs in consultation with Corps delimitating the areas of responsibility of 'BANK GPS'.

(iv) Duties of 'BANK GPS' within their areas will incl :—
  (a) Org and layout of *both* banks and the est of their own intercomn between the two.
  (b) Control of all amphibious craft and their allotment to suit div plans.
  (c) Control of all traffic and mov within 'BANK AREAS'.

(c) **"River Control"**

(i) All resources for getting personnel, vehs, stores, etc. down or up the banks and across the water gap will be controlled by assaulting divs through CsAGRE, who will be appointed one to each assaulting div and who will comd all RE allotted to effect the passage over the river.

(ii) The resources incl all brs, rafts, storm boats and amphibians (while on the water).

(iii) 'RIVER CONTROL' will be responsible for the complete org and layout of the water crossing. This incl the selection of sites for all types of brs, rafts, amphibian crossings, together with the constr and maint of the immediate approaches and exits to and from them on both banks.

(iv) Protection against damage to craft, or brs, through certain of our own craft getting out of control in the current is also the responsibility of 'RIVER CONTROL'.

(v) 'RIVER CONTROL' may also be charged with the task of coord def against hostile interference by water from either up or down stream of the crossing site.

(vi) Subsequent to the aslt phase 'RIVER CONTROL' will be transferred from assaulting divs to Corps.

5. **"PLUNDER" PLAN**

Editorial Note :

For the sake of simplicity, certain alternatives based on the possibility of the Left of Ninth US Army extending as far North as XANTEN have been omitted. The decision to allot the XANTEN crossing area exclusively to Second Army was made very shortly after the issue of this instruction.

(a) Aslt crossing will be made on a two div front.

(b) It is desirable for each div to cross on a two bde front; each bde two bns up.

(c) The crossing places likely to be suitable are :—
  (i) *Reach incl XANTEN–excl REES* 0752.
   Sufficient for a frontage of two bdes.
  (ii) *Reach incl REES–excl EMMERICH* 9760.
   Sufficient for a frontage of two bdes.

(d) "PLUNDER" must therefore cater for two divs each on a two bde front, each bde with two bns up crossing vide (c) above.

(e) It can be assumed that a very large scale of air sp will be available if weather conditions permit.
  The plan will NOT be dependent for its staging upon flying conditions being suitable. It must be prepared to take place without air sp.

(f) Airborne ops in conjunction with the aslt crossing will be superimposed. Details later

6. **PREPARATIONS OF FMNS**

(a) **Time Available**

If enemy opposition goes 'soft' it will be necessary to follow up across the RHINE with all possible speed. In this case one week will be the maximum time available to lay on the aslt crossing. On the other hand, should opposition be considerable, a most deliberate op will be needed and time will be available to plan in detail, incl time for rehearsal.

(b) **Planning**

    (i) Corps plan will be issued to divs as soon as it is clear which fmns are to take part.

    (ii) 'BANK GPS' and 'RIVER CONTROL' reps will join divs at this stage.

    (iii) Portable models will be prepared by Corps for :—

        (a) Corps HQ ;

        (b) Issue to divs.

(c) **Trg**

    (i) Trg of fmns who will do the aslt is not possible at present, but trg of 'BANK GPS', 'RIVER CONTROL' and elts of 79 Armd Div will commence at once.

    (ii) When specific fmns are detailed for the op, trg will be undertaken as follows :—

        (a) Individual trg of personnel :—

            (i) Loading of LVsT by a few of these vehs being sent complete with trg teams to units.

            (ii) Practice of drivers in driving their vehs on to rafts, etc. will be done dryshod by use of "Mockups" to be constr within unit areas.

        (b) Collective trg and rehearsals will not be possible on a large scale, but skeleton exercises may be possible to test out the comns and to illustrate the technique that has been evolved.

            To this end it is important to wed up early personnel who will be grouped together in the aslt so that they live in close proximity to each other and can practise "dryshod".

Lieutenant-General,
Commander,
12 Corps.

BLA

APPENDIX "E"

GLOSSARY OF TERMS USED IN THE ASSAULT CROSSING OF THE RHINE

ARMOUR WAITING AREA

An area just off the tank track and handy to the Cl 50/60 Ferry site into which armd vehs are fed from the Concentration or Marshalling Areas. Its purpose is to provide a small 'cushion' of vehs which prevents the ferry from ever having to wait for a load and which also enables the maximum number of vehs to be held back out of the congested fwd zone in comparative security.

ASSAULT PHASE

This comprises the passage of the Aslt Wave (personnel and some vehs of the aslt bns) and the Ferry Wave (remaining personnel and essential vehs of the Aslt Bde). It begins when all aslt bdes are poised for attack in Marshalling Areas and before the earliest to move is due to leave. This should be about H — 1 hour.

It ends when the last essential veh of the res bns of the aslt bdes has crossed the river. This should be about H + 4 hours (H hour is taken to be when the leading wave of the aslt enters the river from the near bank).

ASSAULT WAVE

This is the pre-stowed LVT lift of personnel, vehs and anti-tk guns which leads the aslt. It is divided into two flights each of three tps of LVsT. The first flight carries three coys (pl 28 strong) and some mortars and the second the fourth coy, anti-tk guns, MGs and more mortars. Both flights incl an FOO party. Some variation in this stock allotment and fmn is possible, incl division into three flights instead of two, but LVT organisation must be maintained.

BANK CONTROL

See also under Bank Unit below, and Diagram 1 in the Text (Part I, Section V, G).

The org from which all RE and Transit work and arrangements on the near bank are controlled.

It is est with Tac Div HQ of the assaulting div and comprises :—
- The CAGRE and his staff.
- The CO of the Bank Unit with additional Q (M) Staff.
- Rep 79 Armd Div (advisor on special equipment).

Directly under it there is a 'Crossing Control' per assaulting bde established with the Tac HQ of the latter and containing a CRE (Assault), a Coy Comd of the Bank Unit, and an LVT Regimental Comd.

BANK UNIT

An armd C regt or an inf bn with additional signals, CMP and Q (M) staff whose task is to help the comd of the assaulting div in the mov, policing, assembly and dispersal of all his personnel and vehs through the transit area which comprises the river itself and a strip of country on both of its banks. It provides for the following :—

	FORWARD CONTROL	
FAR BANK	DISPERSAL CONTROL	DISPERSAL CONTROL

RIVER

NEAR BANK	CROSSING CONTROL	CROSSING CONTROL
	BANK CONTROL	

BRIDGE MARSHALLING HARBOUR

A small area near a br site where a small 'cushion' of RE vehs can be held so as to ensure that br stores are available when required.

BRIDGE VEHICLE MARSHALLING AREA

An area where vehs carrying br stores are received from the main RE dump and despatched to the br site as required.

BUILD-UP

This phase, as in Combined Ops, comes immediately after the Follow-Up Phase and comprises the passage across the river of the bulk of the guns of the assaulting divs and AGsRA followed by res divs.

BUND

A steep-sided flood bank.

CAGRE (Assault)

Comd Army Gp RE. A Colonel, with appropriate RE HQ staff, whose tasks are to command all RE units placed under command of the assaulting div, to advise its Comd on all RE matters and to be responsible for all RE work within that fmn's boundaries.

CROSSING CONTROL

See Bank Control above.

Working directly under Bank Control, it is responsible for all RE and Transit work and arrangements on the near bank on the front of an assaulting bde less any special RE tasks, like the building of a br, allotted by the CAGRE (Assault) to another CRE. Established with the HQ of the assaulting brigade it contains a CRE (Assault), a Coy Comd of the Bank Unit, and an LVT Regimental Comd.

DD INFLATION AREAS

Fwd areas in which DD tks can halt and inflate their special eqpt and from which access is available across open country to the river.

(Passage through woods, hedges, bushes, etc., ruins the eqpt once it has been inflated).

DISPERSAL CONTROL

See Bank Unit.

The counterpart of Crossing Control on the far bank of the river. Established by a Coy Comd of the Bank Unit, it controls all transit arrangements, within its bde bdys on the far bank. Works directly under Fwd Control which is the counterpart of Bank Control on the far bank.

At Crossing Control there will also be a rep from the CRE responsible for all RE work on the far bank.

DUKW COLLECTING AREA

Established in the early stages on the near bank to control returning DUKWs and prevent them from jamming narrow approach rds which may be full of 'fwd' tfc. Dispensed with as soon as a one-way return route has been org. Sited as near to the DUKW ferry exit as suitable cover can be found.

FERRY RESERVE

Takes the place of the familiar Floating Res of Combined Ops.

It is, in fact, the res bn of each assaulting bde and starts to cross in Stormboat and LVT ferries as soon as possible after the assaulting bns have crossed.

FERRY WAVE

Follows the Aslt Wave and is the second wave of the Aslt Phase. It comprises :—

(a) The remaining essential vehs and eqpt of assaulting bns which have not been able to accompany the Aslt Wave.
(b) The personnel and essential vehs and eqpt of the res bn.

It is carried in the newly established Stormboat and LVT ferries.

FLIGHT

A part of a Wave, e.g. the Aslt Wave, has two 'flights'. It comprises a definite unit or sub-unit of craft, e.g. each flight of the Aslt Wave is composed of three tps of LVsT while the first flight of the Ferry Wave might well be the first three or four tps of LVsT to be collected and reorganised.

FOLLOW-UP

This phase, as in Combined Ops, comes immediately after the Aslt Phase and immediately before the Build-Up Phase. Actually it will probably overlap the end of the Aslt Phase as the Class 50/60 ferry may well be operating early taking over armd vehs of the Follow-Up before the Ferry Wave has ended on the Storm-boat and LVT ferries.

This phase is, broadly speaking, the crossing of the Res Bde and Armour with the Div Mobile Striking Force in high priority.

FORWARD ASSEMBLY AREA

An area, or, if the going is bad, a point on the far bank where all vehs are collected, reorg and sent fwd. Ideally it will be a 'park' clear of the rd, but, if none is available, it may well have to be a rd junc or some other convenient point.

All vehs (except those carried in LVsT of the Assault Wave to objectives inland) will report to the Fwd Assembly Area where reps from each fmn or unit concerned will be present to org them into small formed bodies and send them fwd to conc areas under an offr or NCO.

Initially each bn will have a Fwd Assembly Area. Later one of these will close down and the other will become the Bde Fwd Assembly Area. And, as soon as the Bank Unit can take control, the permanent Fwd Assembly Area will be est based on the Bde Assembly Area.

FORWARD CONTROL

The counterpart of the Bank Control on the far bank from which all transit arrangements of the assaulting div on the far bank are controlled.

One Dispersal Control per assaulting bde works directly under it; it is established on the far side of the river and it contains the CO or 2 IC of the Bank Unit and the CRE responsible for all RE work on the far bank.

H HOUR

For this river crossing operation is the time at which the leading LVsT of the aslt waves of all assaulting bns enter the river from the near bank.

INFLATION AREA

See 'DD Inflation Area' above.

LVT START LINE

The LVsT carrying each assaulting bn leave their Marshalling Areas by their own prepared track at a time calculated to bring them to the near bank of the river at H Hour. Once they have started, their aim is to check as little as possible but they need a point fairly close to the river where they can fan out from Line Ahead and also check their timing.

LVT COLLECTING AREA

This is the area on the near bank where returning LVsT are collected, maint, rapidly reorg and made ready for the next trip.

It is org by the LVT Regt and must be sited far enough back from the river and with enough cover to make maint and reorg possible. Within the above limits the closer it is to the LVT Ferry exit point on the near bank the better and the route between the two must be easy to find on the darkest night.

LVT LOADING AREA

An area on the near bank close to the LVT Collecting Area, with good access to the LVT Ferry entrance and with a metalled rd access where vehs are loaded into LVsT for the next ferry trip after having been called fwd as required from the Veh Waiting Area further back.

It should be chosen so that the LVT turn round on the near bank is as short as possible and interferes with other tfc as little as possible.

LVT UNLOADING POINT

A point on the far bank and as near to the river and an exit rd as possible where LVsT unload vehs before returning across the river. As LVsT are carried downstream while crossing, this unloading point should be upstream of their ferry exit. It should, also, of course, be sited so as to give the vehs a good firm getaway.

MARSHALLING AREAS

Large areas with good cover and metalled rd access and far enough back to be out of enemy observation and def fire, in which are assembled initially all tps and vehs which are due to cross the river before H + 12 hours; and through which subsequently all tps and vehs crossing the river will pass. (An exception to this is those units—e.g. Fd Arty—of the assaulting div deployed in front of these areas on D Day). They are the link in the chain between Staging Areas to the rear and Waiting Areas near the river.

MOVEMENT LIGHT

The provision of illumination of the battlefield and approaches by night by the use of searchlights to the extent which makes mov easy without giving enough lt for the use of sights (fighting light).

PRE-STOWED

To differentiate between the load in a veh and the pre-loading of the veh itself in an LVT: the term 'pre-stowed' will be used for the latter op.

The term 'pre-loaded veh' will denote that the load has been placed in the veh beforehand while 'pre-stowed vehs' will mean that the vehs themselves have been loaded in LVsT already.

SQUATTER'S RIGHTS

The right to remain in a specified area within the bdys of another fmn or unit. Granted to units which cannot move at once and clear the area, e.g. FDS holding serious cases or units of the div holding the line after the assaulting div has taken over the area.

STAGING AREA

The link in the chain between Rear Accn Areas behind and Marshalling Areas fwd. Large areas with good cover within fairly easy reach of the latter.

TABBY

For the purpose of the operation, a "Tabby" Light is one that is invisible to the unaided human eye but which can be clearly seen by using "Tabby" spectacles. There is only one colour available (green) but a simple device is being produced for switching the light off and on to form distinctive alternating signals.

UNIT LANDING OFFICER

A Regtl Offr detailed to assist and direct craft during the initial stages of the assault, until the Bank Unit organisation is operating.

VEH WAITING AREA

An area just clear of the approach rd—or a point on it if the going is very bad—and handy to the class 9 and LVT ferry sites into which vehs are fed from the Marshalling Area. Its purpose is to provide a 'cushion' of vehs which prevents any ferry from ever having to wait for a load and which also enables the maximum number of vehs to be held back out of the congested fwd zone in the comparative security of the Marshalling Area.

APPENDIX "F"

SOME PROBLEMS IN THE TECHNIQUE OF AN OPPOSED CROSSING OF A MAJOR RIVER OBSTACLE

(a) **Allotment** of Craft, infantry and supporting arms to each wave.

(b) **Assembly**
  (i) Areas for assault wave, ferry wave, follow-up and build-up troops, Q dumps, RE dumps, gun positions.
  (ii) Responsibility of fmns.
  (iii) Passing through, relief of, tps on the ground.
  (iv) Accumulation of stores and amn dumping.
  (v) Inf in LVsT off roads, bridging vehicles on roads.

(c) **Marshalling**
  (i) Where LVsT leave transporters.
  (ii) Responsibility of Bank Gps.
  (iii) Routes for LVsT and vehicles and marking of these.
  (iv) FUPs, Transit Areas, or Fwd Assembly Areas.
  (v) Preparation of maps of Lay-out.

(d) **Bank Groups**
  (i) Limits of responsibility.
  (ii) When to pass to Corps control.
  (iii) Relationship with River Control.
  (iv) Relationship with Comd Aslt Div and Bdes.
  (v) Position of HQs.
  (vi) When to start (NOT during Assault Phase).
  (vii) Returning of empty craft, near and far banks.
  (viii) Collecting, sorting and re-allotment of returned craft.
  (ix) Means for calling fwd echs as required.
  (x) Means for controlling priorities.
  (xi) Responsibility for defence against attack from ground, air and water.

(e) **River Control**
  (i) Limits of responsibility.
  (ii) When to pass to Corps Control.
  (iii) Comd and composition.
  (iv) Relationship to RE work on river, approaches and exits.
  (v) Relationship to Bank Group.
  (vi) Relationship to Comd Aslt Div and Bdes.
  (vii) Position of HQ.
  (viii) Recovery of loose craft.
  (ix) Protection against damage by loose craft.
  (x) When to start (NOT during Assault Phase).
  (xi) Crossing sites for various craft—selection, allotment, marking.

(f) **Assault Phase**
  (i) Responsibility of fmn.
  (ii) Beginning and end of phase and approximate timings.
  (iii) Recce of near bank, far bank, river itself.
  (iv) Preparation of near and far banks and approcahes. (Marking of separate sites for LVsT, Rafts, DD Tanks, etc.).
  (v) Tactical formations.
  (vi) Release of craft.

(g) **Ferry Phase**

    (i) Beginning and end of Phase and approximate timings.
    (ii) Amount of bank control possible.
    (iii) Time rafting of vehicles can start.
    (iv) Collecting and re-allotment of craft.
    (v) Starting-up of stormboats.
    (vi) Vehicle control on far bank.
    (vii) Smoke screens.
    (viii) Evacuation of wounded.

(h) **Follow-Up Phase**

    (i) Beginning and end of phase and approximate timings.
    (ii) Bank Control.
    (iii) River Control.
    (iv) Smoke screens.
    (v) Rafting.
    (vi) Evacuation of wounded.

(i) **Build-Up Phase**

    (i) Beginning of Phase.
    (ii) Time bridges might be completed.
    (iii) Technique for passing Reserve Divs through.

APPENDIX "G"

15 (S) DIV OPERATION ORDER FOR "TORCHLIGHT"

Note:—For the sake of brevity, paragraphs 1 to 6 (INFORMATION) have been omitted, as their subject matter is fully dealt with elsewhere in the book.

No appendices are reproduced, but Trace P, mentioned in paragraph 21, is reproduced elsewhere as Map 6.

TOP SECRET
Copy No. ....
20 March 45

OPERATION TORCHLIGHT

15 (S) INF DIV OO No. 9

Ref maps : 1 : 25,000 Sheets 4204, 4205, 4304, 4305

INTENTION

7. 15 (S) Inf Div will force the passage of River RHINE between incl BISLICH 1342 and VYNEN 0845 and capture the area CLASENHO 1491–MEHRHOO 1549–SCHUTTWICK 1544–LOH 1542–BISLICH–MEHR 1348–HAFFEN 1149, preparatory to securing the area WISSMANN 1855–br 203530 and relieving 6 Brit Airborne Div in area HAMMINKELN and brs over River ISSEL there.

METHOD

8. The Div will assault with two Bdes up.

   (a) *Right*—Codeword "POKER".

   44 (L) Inf Bde sp by 11 R Tks will capture and hold area SCHUTTWICK–LOH–BISLICH.

   (b) *Left*—Codeword "NAP".

   227 (H) Inf Bde with in sp E RIDING YEO will capture and hold area HAFFEN–MEHR.

   (c) The clearance of the area between 44 (L) and 227 (H) Inf Bdes objectives will be carried out by them, dividing line being incl 44 (L) Inf Bde rd from rd junc 1546–rd and track junc 142464–track to rd junc 136453–cross tracks 130453–thence track to river at 125453.

   (d) *Res*—Codeword "WHIST".

   46 (H) Inf Bde with in sp 44 R Tks will capture and hold the area CLASENHO–MEHRHOO. They will firmly est themselves on the high ground 1452–1351 and will ensure clearance of woods 1252–1352 overlooking HALDERN 1153.

   They will cross one bn through 44 (L) Bde LVT and SB ferries to assemble with 44 R Tks in area North of VISSEL 1345. The remaining bns will cross through 227 (H) Inf Bde and assemble in area OVERKAMP 1247 and SANDENHOF 1047. The initial adv will be carried out by a bn carried on 44 R Tks but should blown brs or going preclude use of tks the bde will carry out a normal adv through posns held by 227 (H) Inf Bde.

   (e) A mob striking force consisting of :—

   One Armd Regt (carrying Motor Bn),
   One SP Regt RA,
   One SP A Tk Bty RA,
   One Inf Bn in Kangaroos,
   One Sqn AVsRE,

   will cross with high priority on Cl 50/60 Rafts and should be available for ops on the far bank by 1700 hrs D+1. It will initially be used to seize area WISSMANN–br 203530.

9. **Subsequent Developments**

   (a) 44 (L) *Bde*

   Once Airborne tps are firm on their objectives and have cleared Westward up to Div bdy, 44 (L) Inf Bde will come into Div res and be available for seizing WISSMANN and br 203530. This will be carried out in conjunction with the mob striking force of 4 Armd Bde. It is not likely that this can take place before 1700 hrs D+1.

   Should opposition be very light, 44 (L) Inf Bde may be ordered to seize this objective under mov light Night D/D+1 without assistance of Armd Bde.

   (b) 227 (H) *Bde*

   Will later relieve 6 Brit Airborne Div.

   (c) 46 (H) *Bde and 4 Armd Bde*

   Will come into res.

10. **Junc Pts**
    (a) *With 17 US Airborne Div on Right*
        44 (L) Bde at rd junc 175437 and track junc 155453.
    (b) *With 6 Brit Airborne Div on Right*
        46 (H) Inf Bde at corner of wood 155477.
    (c) *With 51 (H) Div on Left*
        (i) 227 (H) Inf Bde at crossrds 104513.
        (ii) 46 (H) Inf Bde at rly 123529.

11. **Grouping for Crossing**

Under Comd :	44 (L) Inf Bde "B" MG Coy 1 MX Det 194 Fd Amb One Sec Pro	Under Comd :	227 (H) Inf Bde "C" Coy 1 MX Det 153 Fd Amb One Sec Pro
In Sp :	11 R Tks	In Sp :	E RIDING YEO
Under Comd :	46 (H) Inf Bde "A" Coy 1 MX Det 193 Fd Amb Half Sec Pro		
In Sp :	44 R Tks (DD)		

12. **RA**
    (a) *Outline Fire Plan—Op "TORCHLIGHT"*
        (i) CB H—5 to H—1 hr.
        (ii) Softening H—3½ hrs to H—1½ hrs.
        (iii) Bombardment or covering fire H—1 hr to H+3½ hrs.
        (iv) Thereafter pre-arranged conc at call.
        (v) Smoke on Right front to deny visibility from high woods in that area.
    (b) *Outline Fire Plan—Op "VARSITY"*
        (i) CB and softening bombardment P—2 to P—1 hrs.
        (ii) Anti-flak bombardment P—½ hr to P hr.
    (c) *Arty Allotment*
        (i) Until P—2 hrs in sp 227 (H) Inf Bde :—
            Six Fd Regts
            Five Med Regts
            Two Hy AA Btys
            One 7.2 Bty
            One Super Hy Bty
        (ii) Until P—2 hrs in sp 44 (L) Inf Bde :—
            Six Fd Regts
            Four Med Regts
            One Hy AA Bty
            Two 7.2 Btys
        (iii) From P—2 hrs in sp 227 (H) Inf Bde :—
            Four Fd Regts
            One Med Regt
            One Hy AA Bty
        (iv) From P—2 hrs in sp 44 (L) Inf Bde :—
            One Fd Regt
            One Med Regt
    (d) *Pepperpot*
        A pepperpot sited in three gps, Left, Right and Central will pepper from H—60 mins to H hr.
    (e) *Navigational Aids*
        Main axes of LVT crossings will be marked by :—
        (i) Bofors tracer fired every 100 secs from H—5 mins to H+15 mins.
        (ii) Marker shell will be fired as directed by Aslt Bde Comds.

13. **AA**

    Comd 100 AA Bde will be responsible for AA def of brs and ferries on both sides of River RHINE w.e.f. first light D Day.

14. **A Tk**

    Apart from bn 6 prs and tks of 44 R Tks earliest arrival of 17 prs will be 99/102 (NH) A Tk Regt (SP) about 1500 hrs D Day.

15. **4.2" Mortars**

   Are phased to cross over at 1230 hrs D+1 day, but may be called fwd earlier if urgently needed. Under comd 46 (H) Bde on conclusion of Pepperpot.

16. **RE**

   (a) The following brs and ferries will be constructed and operated at the earliest possible moment under orders CAGRE :—

	Approx Map Ref
Two LVT Ferries	131418 and 116456
Two Stormboat Ferries	127428 and 104462
Four Cl 9 Raft Ferries sites at	126429 and 113459
Two Cl 50/60 Raft Ferries	123447 and 120452
One DUKW Ferry	135414
One Cl 9 FBE Br	117456
One Cl 12 Bailey pontoon	087467
One Cl 40 Br	132415

   (b) The following Cl 40 route will be developed across the RHINE :—
   From Cl 40 Br 132415 via BISLICH–BERGEN 1346–rd junc 157470–cross rds 146495–rd and rly junc 158498.

   (c) Two Cl 9 routes will be est from Cl 9 brs to line of rly WESEL to HALDERN within Div bdys.

   (d) One Cl 9 lateral will be est from DIERSFORDT 1744 via BISLICH–VISSEL–OVERKAMP–HAFFEN and also a Cl 40 lateral on main rd WESEL–HALDERN within Div bdys.

   (e) The primary task of Div RE is to develop routes on the far side of the RHINE. Fd Coys are not under comd or in sp of Bdes, but in the event of Comds requiring RE assistance not connected with clearing these routes, application will be made to Div.

   (f) Assault Bdes will be responsible for prevention of sabotage assaults on brs and ferries from East side of RHINE.

17. **Mines**

   No A per mines or A Tk mines will be laid. Hawkins necklaces should be ready to impede enemy SP guns and vehs on rds.

18. **Demolitions**

   Any brs secured, especially over River ISSEL, will be prepared for demolition. They will not be blown unless capture by enemy is imminent. Bde Comds are responsible for executive order to blow.

19. **Air Sp**

   Armd Recce will be preventing arrival of enemy rfts. Normal close air sp by Typhoons on call through Div HQ or tcls where allotted.

20. **Timings**

   (a) H hr for Op "TURNSCREW" 2100 hrs D—1, Op "WIDGEON" 2200 hrs D—1.

   (b) P hr for Op "VARSITY" 6 Airborne Div 1000 hrs D Day,
   17 Airborne Div 1100 hrs D Day.
   If weather conditions are unsuitable in morning, P hr will be at 1400 hrs D Day.

   (c) H hr for Op "TORCHLICHT" 0200 hrs D Day.
   D Day to be notified later.

   Note.—In the event of Airborne Ops having to be postponed due to weather conditions, D Day will also be postponed up to 48 hrs. After this period, if conditions still unfavourable for "VARSITY", Op "TORCHLIGHT" will take place without sp of XVIII Airborne Corps and H hr for Op "TORCHLIGHT" will probably be at 2300 hrs. In this event Op "WIDGEON" will take place at 2200 hrs D+1.

21. Div layout in fwd assembly areas is shown on Trace P. (See Map 6 in text, Part I).

ADM

22. To be issued separately.

INTERCOMN

23. **Location of HQ**

15 (S) Inf Div	Tac	091428
	Main	070387
	Rear	060362

24. **Wireless Silence**

Will be observed in fwd conc area until H—3 hrs. This does not apply to certain RA nets.

25. **Allotment of Tcls**

   (a) One tcl at Div HQ.

   (b) One tcl with 46 (H) Inf Bde. This tcl will be carried in a DD Tk provided by 4 Armd Bde and duplicated by two jeeps in case the DD tk fails to cross.

   (c) One tcl with Mob Striking Force in jeep, later to be replaced by normal tcl.

   (d) One jeep tcl with 227 (H) Inf Bde, later to be replaced by normal tcl.

26. **Recognition sigs for comn with Airborne Tps**

   (a) By waving YELLOW celanese triangles. These will be carried by all ranks of Bde Gps who cross on D Day.

   (b) By use of pre-arranged passwords. Passwords for period D—1 to D+3 as under :—

From 1200–1200 hrs	*Challenge*	*Answer*
D—1 to D Day	LIGHTNING	THUNDER
D Day to D+1	HITHER	THITHER
D+1 to D+2	HUNDREDS	THOUSANDS
D+2 to D+3	PLEASE	THANKS

   (c) By using Contact Channel No. 33 for which no special call signs or codes will be used. Further details through Sig Channels.

   (d) RED berets may be worn by Airborne tps after initial drop as an aid to recognition.

   (e) Ground to air—fluorescent panels.

27. **LOs**

227 (H) Inf Bde will send one LO to 153 Bde (51 (H) Div)
46 (H) Inf Bde will send one LO to 152 Bde (51 (H) Div) } 15 (S) Recce to provide.

28. **ACK**

Lt Col,
GS,
15 (S) Inf Div.

EH

Time of Signature .... hrs

Time issued to Sigs .... hrs

Method of issue.

APPENDIX "H"

12 CORPS SEVEN DAY SYLLABUS OF TRG
FOR AN ASLT BDE GROUP

Serial No. (a)	Period (b)	Subject (c)	Area (d)	Remarks (e)
1	FIRST DAY	(a) Explanation on cloth model of op (incl marshalling, assembly and functions of BANK CONTROL)	Billets	ACTUAL PLACE NAMES WILL NOT BE USED
		(b) Demonstrations by LVT Regts to units of leading LVsT with :— (i) 6 pr (ii) Carrier (iii) Jeep (iv) Pl load with actual numbers	LVT Harbours	(b) This can be done whilst offrs and certain NCOs are at the briefing
2	SECOND DAY	(a) Practice of dvrs in driving vehs on and off LVsT Cl 9 and Cl 50/60 rafts	Billets	This will be done dryshod on mock-ups in billets
		(b) Inf loading and dismounting from LVsT (Mk II and IV) and Stormboats both in and out of the water	Nearby canal or river	
		(c) Loading 17 prs on modified LVsT II		
3	THIRD DAY	(a) Practice of dvrs in driving vehs on and off LVsT and on to Cl 9 and Cl 50/60 Rafts in the water	Nearby canal or river	
		(b) Starting of Stormboats		
		(c) Recces to be carried out for first rehearsal on THIRD and FOURTH DAYS as if they were being done for Op. This is to incl recces for :— (i) Marshalling Area (ii) Routes fwd from Marshalling Area (iii) Veh Waiting Area (iv) LVT Loading Area	River Rehearsal Area	
4	FOURTH DAY	(a) Explanation and practice in use of following special eqpts :— Wireless Set 46 Wireless Set 68 TABBY INDICATOR LOOPS LIFEJACKETS	Billets	
		(b) Waterproofing of wrls sets and other signal eqpt		
		(c) See Serial 3 coln (c) sub para (c)	River	
		(d) Revision of any subject which requires further practice		

Serial No. (a)	Period (b)	Subject (c)	Area (d)	Remarks (e)
5	FIFTH DAY	First Full-Scale Rehearsal	River Rehearsal Area	(a) Appropriate Bank Unit will take part (b) Special attention will be paid to comns and CSO 12 Corps will assist by laying any line and providing any additional wrls sets that may be required (c) This rehearsal to be carried out by day
6	SIXTH DAY	(a) Conference and discussions on the first rehearsal (b) Further trg in weak points		
7	SEVENTH DAY	Second Full-Scale rehearsal followed by final conference	River Rehearsal Area	As against Serial 5 above, *except that rehearsal will begin after dark*

Note.—Following additional staff available :—

One GSO 2 and one GSO 3 per div

Photographs

Plate 1. *DD Tank*

Plate 2. *AVRE carrying Assault Bridge, and CENTAUR tankdozer*

Plate 3 (A): LVT IV (BUFFALO)

Plate 3 (B): LVT IV entering RHINE
(Note low silhouette of LVT already in water)

Plate 4: Rocket Projector

Plate 5: 25 pr SP gun (RAM)

Plate 6: Stormboat bringing back Prisoners

Plate 7: Class 9 (close-support) Raft carrying 15-cwt Armd Personnel Truck (WHITE scout car)

Plate 8: Class 50/60 Raft carrying M 10 SP ATk Gun
(Note scout car loaded on pontoons direct)

Plate 9: Class 9 FBE Bridge (30 Corps Sector)

Plate 10: Class 40 (Tactical) Bailey Pontoon Bridge (BISLICH)

Plate 11: Class 40 (high-level) Bailey Pontoon Bridge
(Note class 40 tactical bridge and village of BISLICH in background)

www.ingramcontent.com/pod-product-compliance
Lightning Source LLC
Chambersburg PA
CBHW061542010526
44113CB00023B/2775